REGIONAL SECURITY IN THE MIDDLE EAST

Of Related Interest

Military Power: Land Power in Theory and Practice
edited by Brian Holden Reid

The Transformation of Security in the Asia/Pacific Region
edited by Desmond Ball

Airpower: Theory and Practice
edited by John Gooch

Seapower: Theory and Practice
edited by Geoffrey Till

Security Challenges in the Mediterranean Region
edited by Roberto Aliboni, George Joffé and Tim Niblock

The National Security of Small States in a Changing World
edited by Efraim Inbar and Gabriel Sheffer

U.S.–Israeli Relations at the Crossroads
edited by Gabriel Sheffer

From Rabin to Netanyahu – Israel's Troubled Agenda
edited by Efraim Karsh

Population Dilemmas in the Middle East
by Gad G. Gilbar

Israeli Strategy after Desert Storm – Lessons of the Second Gulf War
by Aharon Levran

Between War and Peace – Dilemmas of Israeli Security
edited by Efraim Karsh

Religious Radicalism in the Greater Middle East
edited by Bruce Maddy-Weitzman and Efraim Inbar

REGIONAL SECURITY IN THE MIDDLE EAST

Past Present and Future

Edited by

Zeev Maoz

(Head of the Jaffee Center for Strategic Studies, Israel)

FRANK CASS
LONDON • PORTLAND, OR

First published 1997 in Great Britain by
FRANK CASS & COMPANY LTD
Newbury House, 900 Eastern Avenue, London IG2 7HH

and in the United States of America by
FRANK CASS
c/o ISBS
5804 N.E. Hassalo Street, Portland, Oregon 97213-3644

Copyright © 1997 Frank Cass & Co. Ltd.

British Library Cataloguing in Publication Data:

A catalogue record for this book is available from the British Library

Regional security in the Middle East: past, present and future. - (A journal of strategic studies special issue)
1. Security, International 2. Jewish-Arab relations – 1949–
3. Israel-Arab conflicts – Middle East 4. Middle East – Politics and government – 1945–
I. Maoz, Zeev
956.9'4'05
    ISBN 0 7146 4808 6 (cloth)
    ISBN 0 7146 4375 0 (paper)

Library of Congress Cataloging-in-Publication Data:

A catalog record for this book is available from the Library of Congress.

Regional security in the Middle East : past, present, and future /
  edited by Zeev Maoz.
    p. cm.
  Special issue of the Journal of strategic studies.
  Includes bibliographical references and index.
  ISBN 0-7146-4808-6 (cloth). -- ISBN 0-7146-4375-0 (pbk.)
  1. Security, International. 2. Middle East--Foreign relations.
I. Maoiz, Zeev. II. Journal of strategic studies.
JZ6009.M628R44 1997
327.56--cd21   97-22900
                                                                           CIP

This group of studies first appeared in a Special Issue on Regional Security in the Middle East: Past, Present, and Future in *Journal of Strategic Studies*, Vol.20, No.1 (March 1997)

All rights reserved. No part of this publication may be reproduced, stored in a retrieval system, or transmitted in any form, or by any means, electronic, mechanical, photocopying, recording or otherwise without the prior permission of Frank Cass and Company Limited.

Typeset by Frank Cass & Company Limited
Printed in Great Britain by Antony Rowe Ltd., Chippenham, Wilts.

Contents

Editor's Introduction Zeev Maoz vii

Regional Security in the Middle East: Past Trends, Present Realities, and Future Challenges Zeev Maoz 1

Patrons, Clients, and Allies in the Arab–Israeli Conflict Gerard L. Sorokin 46

War and Peace as Rational Choice in the Middle East Martin Sherman and Gideon Doron 72

Great Powers and Regional Peacekeeping: Patterns in the Middle East and Beyond Benjamin Miller 103

Confidence and Security Building Measures in the Middle East Ariel E. Levite and Emily B. Landau 143

The Middle East Peace Process and Regional Security Ben D. Mor 172

About the Contributors 203

Index 205

Editor's Introduction

The international politics of the Middle East in the 1990s have been characterized by great changes in some of the more enduring rivalries in the region. The Arab–Israeli peace process, with its ups and downs, has captured the attention of many observers inside and outside the region. Because of the perceived centrality of this conflict to regional security in the past, the possible shift towards its peaceful resolution has led some observers and participants to suggest that the region may have reached an historical turning point. Some have gone so far to suggest that we may be at the dawn of a new era and at the dawn of a 'New Middle East'.

Whether or not this is the case is questionable, as some of the articles in this volume argue. Yet, one of the by-products of the Arab-Israeli peace process is that the states in the Middle East, as well as major actors from outside the region have started a serious dialog on regional problems as part of the multilateral agenda of the Madrid conference. Problems of regional security and arms control have been one of the major items on the multilateral agenda. Along with the thinking and action on regional security issues in the policy-making communities, a growing interest has emerged among scholars regarding aspects of regional security in the Middle East. The present volume reflects some of the theoretical and practical dilemmas involved in thinking about regional security in a Middle Eastern context. The various articles discuss, as the subtitle of the volume suggests, past trends and future dilemmas of regional security in the region.

The first study, by Zeev Maoz, examines the principal characteristics of regional security in the region in the past. It focuses on patterns of international conflict in the Middle East over the last 50 years, on patterns of human and material allocation in military capability, and on institutional and collective security patterns among regional actors. It then examines the relations among these patterns and discusses some of the most pertinent problems that may affect regional security in the future. It concludes that the region faces grave risks, some of which stem from strategic trends, but others stem from economic and demographic processes. Whether or not these risks would materialize in the mid and long-term future depends to a large extent on what states would do in the near future.

The second study by Gerald Sorokin focuses on patron-client relations and their effects on Israeli–Syrian strategic interactions. It proposes that semi-institutional arrangements between patrons and clients seem to have served the interests of such states as Israel as preferable to formal alliance relations. As Israel and the United States are contemplating their strategic relations, such an observation may be of significance.

The third article, by Martin Sherman and Gideon Doron, presents a theoretical framework for the analysis of war and peace in the Middle East. In the center of their analysis is the juxtaposition of *realpolitik* foreign policy calculations of states and their regime types. They argue that democracies have a fundamentally different preference structure than non-democracies and these differences have major implications for how different states behave in a regional context. They discuss the implications of this framework for regional security, and point out the significance of democratization in regional stability.

The fourth article, by Benjamin Miller, looks at factors that have affected superpower conflict management and conflict resolution policies in the Cold War and how these factors may have changed following the Cold War. His model is also based on a combination of systemic and national factors. He argues that an analysis of such patterns must focus on two aspects of conflict management: The preference for a unilateral or multilateral approach, and the (coercive or benign) attitude towards regional actors. Miller argues that both realist factors and liberal factors (regime type of the great powers) account for their choice of approach. Miller argues that the values that these factors assume in the post-Cold War era will determine future peacekeeping efforts in the Middle East.

The fifth article in this volume, by Ariel Levite and Emily Landau, examines the potential use of Confidence and Security Building Measures (CSBMs) in the Arms Control and Regional Security (ACRS) process. They explore the extent to which past experiences of application of CSBMs in the US–Soviet and European context are transferable to the Middle East. They assess the utility and prospects of CSBMs in the region and argue that, though CSBMs operate within a broader political context and cannot be seen as a substitute for a more structured security regime, they do serve some very important functions in the process.

The article by Ben Mor discusses the relationship between the Arab–Israeli peace process and regional security. It employs a social choice framework to examine the extent to which recent developments in the peace process may lead to greater stability or to renewed conflict. His overall assessment is quite pessimistic. Analyzing the preferences of the parties, most specifically from the election of Benjamin Netanyahu to the post of Prime Minister in Israel on 29 May 1996, and the strategies available to them, he concludes that the likelihood of violence is on the rise, and that such violence would have severe implications for the prospects of regional stability in the Middle East.

These studies provide a scholarly glimpse into the risks and opportunities that lay ahead in a region that has had its share of problems, and may face new kinds of problems. They also provide some practical ideas on how these risks could be minimized and on how these opportunities could be seized. The fluidity of regional politics, domestic and international, suggests that the issues discussed in this volume are significant, timely, and deserve serious consideration by scholars and practitioners in and outside the region.

ND
Regional Security in the Middle East: Past Trends, Present Realities and Future Challenges

ZEEV MAOZ

The revolution in world politics in the last decade requires reassessment of global security issues.[1] The bipolar structure of global politics which has defined the basic rules of conduct of both major powers and of minor states is no longer present. Nor is contemporary world politics characterised by the seeming stability induced by the strategic imperatives of mutually-assured (nuclear) destruction, which defined superpower relations with one another, as well as their relations with local clients.[2] In the last half-decade we have been faced with a fluid evolution of the international system that has yet to settle down into a well-defined alternative structure. Consequently, there is considerable uncertainty regarding rules of conduct in such a system and such uncertainty is seen by some scholars as a source of instability.

> In parallel with or perhaps as a result of the changes in the global balance of power, significant changes are taking place in the geopolitical structure of various regions. These changes are sometimes as general, multi-layered, and far-reaching as changes in the structure of the global system. Such changes are taking place principally in two types of region; first and foremost, in Eastern Europe which has been part of the Soviet sphere of influence during the cold war; and second, in 'gray' regions such as the Middle East which have been a principal arena of superpower competition through local proxies.

Such changes and fluidity offer both new risks and new opportunities for the indigenous states in such regions. An analysis of security issues in global politics must be based on an assessment of these risks and opportunities. The present study attempts such an assessment which is based on an analysis of basic patterns of regional security in the Middle East.

The study is designed as follows: I start with a discussion of the concept of regional security in Section 2. Following the definition of this concept, Section 3 traces patterns of regional security in the Middle East in three areas: internal and international conflict, alliance formation, and military allocations. These are the key areas that reflect degrees of security or insecurity in the region. Section 4 discusses the relations among these dimensions in an effort to examine various factors which affect the future of the regional system. Section 5 examines potential threats to regional security in the future, both in terms of extrapolation from past and present patterns and in terms of the emergence of new threats to regional stability. Section 6 concludes this study by examining policy implications for the states in the region and for regional institutions.

What is Regional Security?

The last couple of years have seen a resurgence in the literature on regional security. Yet, the renewed focus on this subject was not theoretically informed and lacks empirical rigor. One of the characteristics of this literature is that most studies generally gloss over the concept without providing a clear definition. In fact, the term which is used in many titles, and which is part of the major subject of many books, is often left undefined. What is more, in many of these recent books on the subject, the subtitles are more telling of the content of the book than is the title that consists of the term regional security. The typical subjects of such books involve either security concerns of certain national actors in a given region, or a specific aspect of security problems of a region such as proliferation of weapons of mass destruction, ethnic conflict, and so forth.[3]

The conceptual ambiguity is understandable because the concept is a slippery one. Yet, discussing regional security while not clarifying what we mean by the term is even more problematic. Some examples provide a sense of the problem. The only theoretical article in a recently published volume on regional security in the Middle East[4] discusses security regimes, providing examples of such regimes from the Concert of Europe in the early nineteenth century and the American-Soviet relationship during the Cold War.[5] Yet, security regimes are typically taken to characterise a set of formal or informal arrangements among a group of states that stipulate some norms or rules of behaviour in the security realm. As such, security regimes presuppose an underlying set of common interests or shared norms that causes members of the regime to deviate – under some circumstances –

from the strict notions of 'self-help' that are assumed to characterise strategic behaviour in an anarchic environment.[6]

In a regional incarnation, security regimes may represent one form of solution to the problem of regional security, but they certainly do not *describe* the problem. Nor does the concept of security regimes provide an adequate synonym of the regional security concept. Regional security encompasses a state of affairs that includes both self-help behaviour under anarchical conditions as well as some collective arrangements that deviate from such a mode. Students of security problems in Third World regions suggest that security problems encompass both issues of international interaction and management, and of domestic order, economic, and political development. International security problems include traditional issues of war and peace, of alliance formation and dissolution, and of arms races. Yet, international security may also include problems of economics, resources, political stability within states, and human rights.[7] Given such a theoretical void, it is important to start a study of regional security by offering a definition of the term.

We may want to consider the concept of regional security as a marriage of two terms: region and security. Both concepts are very complex and no commonly accepted definition exists on each.[8] Under such circumstances, perhaps the most instructive way of approaching this subject is through an analogy. Consider a residential neighborhood.[9] Here the residents have major stakes in what is going on because events in the neighborhood have an immediate and direct effect on their lives and their well-being. But there are also outsiders – for example owners of businesses in the neighborhood – who reside in other regions, and who are affected by events and processes in the neighborhood. Neighborhood life is affected both by the interrelations among members of the community and by their interaction with others who are involved in various aspects of the community's life.

Security in any community is determined by the extent to which members of the community feel safe, or by the extent to which outsiders feel safe when entering the neighbourhood. If we wish to assess levels of safety in various communities, we must examine several issues. First, we must analyze crime rates. High crime rates in the community – whether they are due to inside crime or to crime committed by outsiders – indicate security problems. If a given community experiences a significant rise in crime rates, we can conclude that it experiences increasing security problems. But crime rates may be too general an indicator of security in residential communities. Different communities which exhibit similar rates of crime may be considered very different in terms of relative safety. If one community exhibits relatively high rates of violent crimes and the other exhibits relatively high rates of non-violent property crime, the former community may be considered less safe than the latter. The source of crime also matters. Crime committed mostly by outsiders against members of the community represents a different kind of risk than crime committed by members of the community against each other or within families in the community.

Just as crime rates are a principal indicator of the extent and nature of safety and security in a residential and social context, we can see rates of conflict as a principal indicator of the extent and nature of security problems in an international regional context. A region with numerous conflicts has more security problems than a region with few conflicts. A shift in the locus of conflict from one region to the other indicates a shift in the degree of security problems in various regions. For example, studies of global patterns of international conflict in the 1816–1986 period,[10] found that in the post World War II era, conflict has shifted from Europe and Latin America to the 'new' regions of the globe (e.g. the Middle East, Asia, Africa). Europe which was the more dangerous place to live in during the nineteenth and first half of the twentieth century, became a relatively 'safe' region during the nuclear era. It was also shown that if the focus is on conflicts which involve the actual use of military force, this conclusion is even more pronounced.[11]

While the extent and nature of crime is an indicator of the extent and nature of security problems in various communities, the relative absence of crime is not necessarily an indicator of 'safe' communities. The reason for that is that there is a fundamental difference between communities which are inherently safe, in that there is simply little or no incentive to commit crime against their members, and those communities which buy or establish security by various crime-prevention measures. For example, crime rates in rural areas are typically lower than crime rates in urban areas – even on a per capita basis – because there are fewer incentives for members of the community to commit crimes against each other and because there are few incentives for outsiders to commit crimes against members of the community. In towns, however, there are dramatic differences among communities in terms of safety. But in some communities safety is bought with money. This is the case in high-income neighborhoods where members buy security by investing in preventive and deterrent measures that bring about reduction in crime rates. In some communities, safety is established simply because each family invests individually in the safety of its residence, and thus crime rates are low because it is difficult to penetrate such security measures.

Because wealth is typically a good predictor of low crime rates among indigenous members of a given community, the principal source of crime in affluent communities is from the outside. Thus, members of such communities typically insure themselves against crime by adopting collective measures such as a neighbourhood watch. These collective security measures may also have the important spin-off effects of reducing tensions and increasing coordination and cooperation among members of the community on matters other than guarding against outside intruders. At any rate, the kind of security problems that a given community has may be reflected not only by the crime rates it experiences, but also by the kind of visible measures that are adopted by members of the community – individually or collectively – to guard themselves against various risks.

Again, the analogy to international politics in a regional context is telling. Certain regions may experience a low level of violence not because the causes or incentives for such violence have disappeared either within the region or from outside sources. Rather, visible levels of violence in the region may have diminished because the members of the region have employed ways of deterring others from attacking them. These measures may be *individual,* such as changes in resource allocation for national defence, *bilateral* or *multilateral,* such as alliance structures, or *collective,* such as the formation and maintenance of a regional security organization that works above the nation state.

In considering the measures that members of the community adopt in their pursuit of security, we typically consider two types of things. The set of measures adopted by each household individually, and the set of measures adopted by collectives within the community. Installing a burglar alarm in a house, setting up a fence around the house, and bringing in a watchdog represent individual protection devices. Setting up neighbourhood watches, or hiring a company from the outside that patrols the area and is paid by all members of the community, represent collective devices.[12]

In an international context, we can assess the extent to which members of a region are insecure by the measures they take to protect themselves. Individual measures in an international context consist of military allocations in personnel, budget, and military technology. Those who spend more on such devices do so not because such resources are useful, but because they are needed more than for those who spend less.

The extent to which states are concerned with their security is reflected not only in terms of their violent military activity, or in the amount of money they spend on defense, but also in the kind of diplomacy they conduct. The product of security-related diplomacy is typically formation of bilateral or multilateral alliances. Thus, alliance structures among members of a region represent the nature of security challenges to such states, because alliances have targets against which they are designed to defend. Even in the absence of overt conflict, the presence of a significant network of alliances reflects the kind of security concerns of members of a given region. The actors which are included in an alliance network and those that are not included are quite valid indicators of the nature of security problems that characterize the region.

What then is regional security? Can we develop a bird's eye definition of the concept that goes above and beyond the definition of security concerns of individual states? One may argue that such a term cannot be defined for several reasons. First, each state in a given geographical expanse has a different view of its security problems. The list of threats for one state in a given region may be fundamentally different from the list of threats for another state. Consider, for example, a comparison of the threats of a state such as Turkey as opposed to the threats of a state such as Israel. Turkey's major concerns during the Cold War era were with the Soviet Union and – to a lesser extent – with Greece, both of which are situated outside the region. On the other hand, Israel's security concerns were principally those emanating from states that are part and parcel of the Middle East.

Second, while the meaning of security is difficult to pin down, a perception of insecurity may leave more visible traces. A state that feels secure does not differ markedly from a state that feels insecure in terms of what both states do on a regular basis. However, states that feel secure differ from states that feel insecure in terms of what they do not do. States that feel secure do not spend as many resources on defence as states that feel insecure. States concerned with security still trade with other states, maintain and develop cultural exchanges, and participate in film or song festivals, but they also take part in alliances, engage in conflicts, and collect intelligence about other states. This point implies that regional security is best understood in terms of levels of *insecurity*.

Third, as was pointed out by students of national security, the concept of security operates on various levels, and each level of analysis adds an important layer to the overall concept.[13] This has implications for the definition of the concept of regional security because, by its very emphasis on the regional level, it may overshadow aspects of security and insecurity that operate on the individual state level or international systemic level.

With these difficulties in mind, it is possible to offer a tentative definition of regional security that builds on the ideas reviewed herein. This definition is:

> Regional Security is the sum total of perceptions of national safety (or perception of freedom of external threats) which members of a regional system feel at a given point in time. This perception is inversely correlated with the sum total of – individual or collective – measures that states in a region employ at a given point in time to ensure their independence and deal with external and internal threats.

Regional security or insecurity can thus be inferred from aggregate regional levels of conflict, military allocations, and collective institutions, or alliances.

Regional security is seen as a variable that can assume various values across regions and over time. The extent or level of regional security at any given point in time (or over any given time span) is determined by three principal attributes: (1) The severity and magnitude of internal and international conflicts involving members of the region;[14] (2) The extent of human and material resources to military and security affairs allocated by members of the region; and (3) The extent of formal security alliances and other collective security institutions involving members of the region. The *higher* the values of any of these variables at a given point in time, the *lower* the level of regional security during this time.[15]

It is instructive to discuss the elements of this definition. First, it is important to note that – as in our residential neighborhood metaphor – regional security is seen as a perceptual variable. A region can be said to be relatively 'safe' if members of the region feel – and therefore act as if – they are not subject to any major threats. This may or may not correspond to an 'objective' level of threat facing these states.

Second, this perception of freedom from threat has observable implications. States that feel free from threats do not resort to the national security items on the foreign policy menu; they do not invest heavily in national defense, they do not form security alliances, and they do not start international conflicts. Thus, we can assess regional security levels as the inverse of those specific actions of regional actors. The more insecure states feel, the more resources – human and material – they invest in national defence. The less secure members of a regional system feel, the more alliances and other security-related organizations are formed that involve members of the region. Finally, the more insecure states feel, the more likely they are to confront these threats by fighting them.

Third, this definition conceives of regional security as a variable. Thus we can use this concept to compare regions in terms of their level of security. We can also conduct within-region comparisons of various time-periods. Moreover, this definition – while still incomplete in some respects – provides at least some operational clues as to the contents of the term. It tells us that if we want to assess levels of regional security we need to look at levels of conflict, at military allocations, and at formal arrangements among members of the region to develop collective security mechanisms (neighborhood watches of sorts).

Fourth, as noted above, regional security, like other commodities in international politics, such as power, prestige, wealth, and influence, is a relative term. Like these terms, it has no absolute upper bound. Again, as in the case of other central concepts in international conflict such as deterrence, we cannot really tell when a region is secure, but we can discern levels of regional insecurity.

A key problem with this definition is that it does not tell us what a region is. I avoid this issue for two principal reasons. First, there is little consensus among scholars regarding the specific characteristics of regions, in terms of a theoretical conception of the term. There is also little evidence that conforms to one of these definitions.[16] Second, and more importantly, when it comes down to identifying regions, there seems to be considerable agreement among scholars about: (a) the specific division of the globe into regional systems, and (b) on the composition of these regions in terms of state-actors. Third, since our discussion is the Middle East regional system, we need to concern ourselves mostly with the boundaries and contents of this region. In this case, the agreement among scholars is generally very high.[17] Thus, from a practical point of view, a definition of a region is not essential at this point. The consensus view on the Middle East includes in this region all states from Morocco to Iran. This includes all the Northern African states bordering the Mediterranean, as well as Sudan. The Asian Middle East includes all the states bordering the Mediterranean (excluding Cyprus but including Turkey), Jordan, Yemen, and the states bordering the Persian Gulf.[18]

This definition of regional security is closely linked with Buzan's concept of 'Security Complex'.[19] As seen in the definition, the idea is that each state is faced with an external environment which, by its structure, poses a set of potential – if not actual – threats to the focal state. A set of states with an overlapping, though clearly not identical, set of concerns forms a 'security complex' which sometimes organizes in some collective fashion against common threats, but for the most part, is engaged in guarding themselves against each other.

Patterns in Middle East Regional Security

Several methodological comments are in order before we begin the survey of regional security in the Middle East. First, in what follows, I present various data on aspects of regional security. The data, their sources, and the operational definitions and measurement of various concepts are all discussed in the appendix. In this section, I confine myself to brief expositions of the substantive issues.

Second, it is important to emphasise at the outset that regional security issues entail as much domestic political processes as they concern international interactions. Traditional treatments of regional security issues –

principally those that are embedded in realist conceptions of world politics – deal principally with international relations within regions. Yet, more recent approaches – principally those that emanate from studies of Third World security problems, emphasize the need to merge internal with external security issues.[20] Because the aspects of regional security entailed in the definition consist of both conflicts and military allocations, it is clear that both of these indicators concern internal processes as well as external ones. States in the Third World decide on the form and extent of military allocations on the basis of internal as well as external threat perception. Much state activity in the Third World is based on dealing with internal instability. Since it was shown that internal instability, especially regime change, is both influenced by, and influences the rate of conflict involvement of a state,[21] it is necessary to consider domestic as well as international aspects.

In this section I discuss the major trends in the three aspects of regional security contained in the definition: conflict activity, military allocations, and regional security-related cooperation.

TRENDS IN REGIONAL CONFLICTS

In discussing the past trends in regional security, we must concentrate on two types of threats to security: external threats and internal security threats with international implications. External threats emanate from conflicts that states in the region had with one another, and conflicts that states in the region had with states outside the region, but which took place inside the Middle East. Internal threats emanate from domestic conflicts with international implications. The severity of conflicts in the region can be evaluated in terms of the number of fatalities in conflicts involving regional members. Figure 1 (p.10) shows trends in the severity of regional conflicts in terms of overall numbers of fatalities and in terms of the number of military fatalities.

As can be clearly seen from the figure, there is an upward trend in the severity of regional conflicts, with the year 1980 being the turning point to the worse. This upward trend is reflected both in terms of a significant increase in the number of military fatalities, and in the number of civilian fatalities. The Iran–Iraq War and the Gulf War of 1991 were responsible for much of this increase, but this is only part of the story. Since 1992, there are several civil wars in the region which exact a large number of – mostly civilian – fatalities, including the Algerian Civil War, the continued massacre of Kurds by Iraq (and since 1995 by Turkey), the continued pursuit of Mujahedin by Iran, the renewal of the Yemen Civil War in 1993, and the continued civil war in the Sudan.

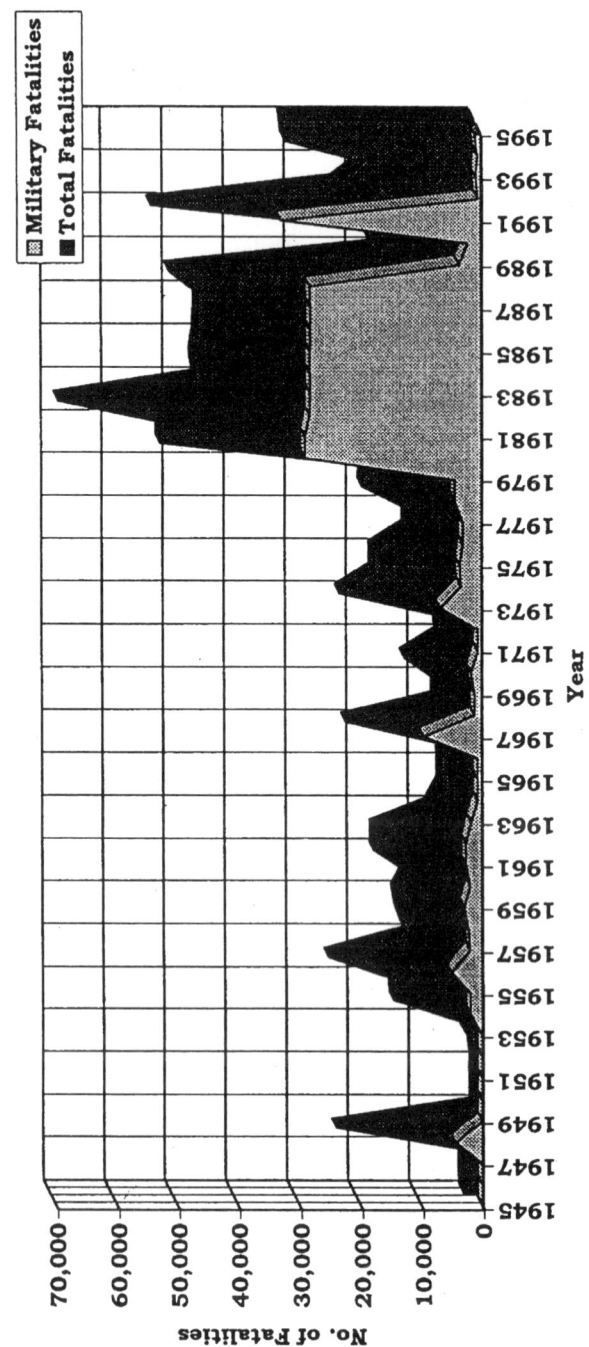

FIGURE 1
NUMBER OF FATALITIES IN INTERNAL AND INTERNATIONAL
CONFLICTS IN THE MIDDLE EAST, 1945–1995

TABLE 1
FATALITIES IN POLITICAL VIOLENCE IN THE MIDDLE EAST, 1945–1995

Period	Military Fatalities Arab–Israel Number*	Military Fatalities Arab–Israel Pct.**	Military Fatalities Other Conflicts Number*	Military Fatalities Other Conflicts Pct.**	Civilian Fatalities Arab–Israel Number	Civilian Fatalities Arab–Israel Pct.	Civilian Fatalities Other Conflicts Number	Civilian Fatalities Other Conflicts Pct.
1945–1970	53,660	67.29%	26,083	32.71%	13,873	9.00%	140,214	91.00%
1971–1980	16,868	24.34%	52,433	75.66%	562	0.52%	107.754	99.48%
1981–1990	3,226	1.38%	230,359	98.26%	2,690	1.35%	194,399	98.63%
1991–1995	150	0.42%	35,700	99.58%	758	0.63%	118,828	99.37%
Total	73,904	17.66%	344,575	82.34%	17,883	3.09%	561,195	96.91%

* Number refers to the overall number of fatalities across all participants in political violence.
** Per cent of military (or civilian) fatalities.

Since most of the literature on Middle East international politics featured the Arab–Israeli conflict as the most severe and dangerous one in the region, it is interesting to examine to what extent it accounted for regional security problems. This is given in Table 1 which traces not only the impact of the Arab–Israeli conflict on the overall severity level of regional conflicts, but also the evolution of these conflicts in terms of severity over time.

This table reveals what may appear to many observers an amazing fact: The Arab–Israeli conflict accounted for a small proportion of the regional security problems, as measured in terms of the severity of conflicts in the region. In fact, the overall number of fatalities – military and civilian – accounted for by the Arab–Israeli conflict is slightly over nine per cent of the total number of fatalities in violent conflict in the region. Even in military terms, the Arab–Israeli conflict accounted for less than 18 per cent of all fatalities.

If we look at the trends in the severity of regional conflict over time, we can see two important facts. First, the severity of the military dimension of the Arab-Israeli conflict is in decline since the first period. In the 1945–70 period, the number of military fatalities in this conflict averaged 2,064 military fatalities per annum. In the 1971–80 period, the number of military fatalities per year went down to 1,687. From 1981 to 1990 this number went down further to a level of 323 military fatalities per year, and further down to an average of 10 fatalities per year in the 1990s. This is a clear indication that the Arab–Israeli conflict has been declining in terms of international violence over time. To a large extent, this holds also true with regard to the civilian death toll of this conflict. The height of the Palestinian–Israeli Civil War of 1945–1948, and the Fidayeen incursions of the 1950s, accounted for an average of 533 civilian deaths per year in the 1945–1970 period. By contrast, in the 1990s, the civil conflict between Arabs and Jews – mostly between Palestinians and Israelis – exacted on average of less than 151 deaths per annum.

As suggested by Figure 2 (opposite), the trend with regard to non Arab-Israeli conflicts in the Middle East is the opposite of the Arab–Israeli conflict. Both the military dimension of this problem and the domestic dimension of the problem suggest a growing degree of regional instability over time. In 1945–70, the region averaged 1,004 military fatalities per year. The 1971–80 period averaged 5,244 deaths per year. The 1981–90 witnessed a sharp increase in the number of military deaths to a high of 23,036 dead per annum. This high was accounted for mostly by the Iran–Iraq War that raged throughout most of the 1980s. In the 1990s, levels of military fatalities dropped down again to an average of 7,140 per year, still higher than any other period save the 1980s.

TRENDS, REALITIES, AND CHALLENGES 13

FIGURE 2
NUMBER OF DISPUTING DYADS IN THE MIDDLE EAST, 1945–1995

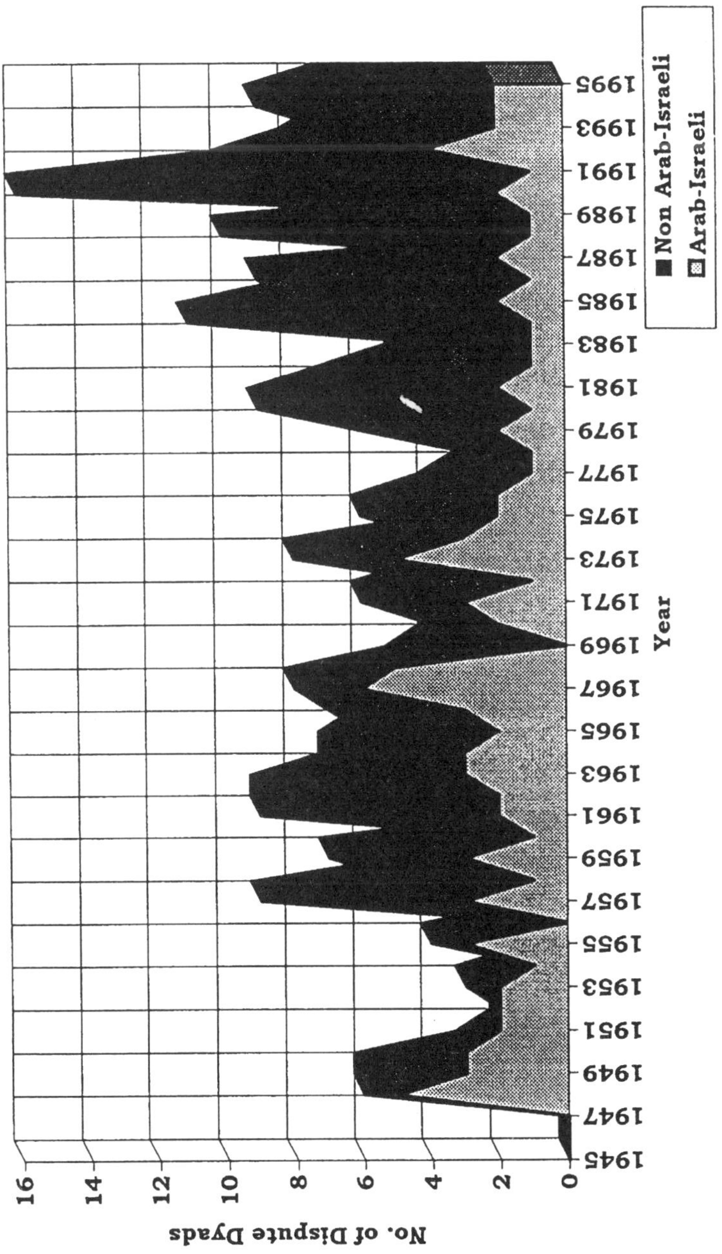

With civilian fatalities we get much of the same story. Civilian deaths in non Arab–Israeli conflicts averaged 5,394 for 1945–70, 10,775 for 1971–80, 19,440 for 1981–90, and 23,766 for 1991–95. The picture emanating from a review of the death tolls in internal and international conflict in the Middle East suggests that the region as a whole is becoming increasingly insecure over time. At the same time – some of the seemingly most threatening conflicts in the region seem to be winding down.

A similar picture of growing regional insecurity emerges when we examine the number of dyads engaged in militarised disputes over time. There is a trend of growing insecurity with more dyads engaged in militarized disputes involving the threat to use force, display of force, or actual use of force over time. Also, as in the case of the severity of conflict, the Arab–Israeli dyads which accounted for many disputes in 1945–80 seem no longer to dominate the Middle East conflict arena. Instead, a growing number of conflicts between Arab states, internal conflict within various Arab states, and conflicts between Arab and other Muslim states (e.g. Iran–Iraq) is beginning to dominate regional conflicts.

The key insights obtained from these figures are the following. First, the nature of security-related problems in the Middle East may be changing, but the region as a whole is certainly not more secure than in the past. On the contrary. The region is emerging as a danger zone on a global scale, with more and more states becoming embroiled in highly violent conflicts. Some of these conflicts are internal and some of these conflicts are international. But these conflicts are becoming increasingly severe and violent over time. Second, an analysis of the types of conflict and their related fatalities reveals that, just as in other regions in the world, civil conflicts become increasingly violent, thus posing a grave regional concern over time. In contrast to other regions, the risk of international war in the Middle East does not seem to have diminished. Three of the five international wars that raged throughout the globe since 1980 took place in the Middle East (Iran–Iraq, Lebanon, and the Gulf War), and the fourth (the Afghanistan War) was on the fringes of the region. Yet, the 1980s and 1990s have witnessed the spread of civil wars throughout the Middle East, and these wars caused substantially more human suffering than the civil wars that have captured the attention of the international community in former Yugoslavia and the former Soviet Union (Azerbaijan, Georgia, Armenia, Chechnya). Certainly, judging from the death toll of such conflicts as Algeria, Iran, Iraq, and the less-known figures from Yemen and Sudan, the number of fatalities is considerably larger than in these other areas.

If the number of conflicts is taken to be equivalent to crime rates in a neighbourhood context, and if the number of fatalities in such conflicts is taken to be equivalent to violent crime victims in our metaphorical context, then the Middle East, which was always seen as a risky region, is becoming even riskier over time. The sources of such risks may have changed, but the overall risk factors in terms of regional security are increasing over time.

MILITARY ALLOCATIONS

How have the various actors in the region worked to maintain security under these circumstances? Have the patterns of dealing with internal and external threats to national security paralleled the changing types of security threats? Human and material allocations to military purposes have been the oldest and most prevalent device that governments have employed to cope with security threats. Thus, it is instructive to examine how trends in military allocations have evolved over time in the Middle East. Figure 3 (p.16) shows trends in the defense burden of Middle Eastern states (defined as regional military expenditures as proportion of regional GDP).

These figures show very clearly an upward trend in the material defence burden of the Middle East. This trend is statistically significant and exhibits an average increase of about 0.1 per cent per annum. Clearly, Middle Eastern states have responded to the security challenges posed by internal and international conflicts by increasing their defense burdens quite significantly. This trend is just the opposite of what has happened over the last half-decade within the states that form Israel's strategic reference group (Egypt, Iran, Iraq, Israel, Jordan, and Syria), where it was found that defence burdens dropped by as much as 50 per cent over the decade from 1986–1995.[22] The explanation of this seeming discrepancy is twofold. First, it is evident that the rapid rise in the defense burdens during the 1980s was due to the fact that both Iraq and Iran had dramatically increased their defence burdens during the Iran–Iraq War, and – for Iraq – this trend continued up to 1991. Since then, the drop of the GDP of these two states was very sharp, and so were their defense expenditures. However the decline in the regional GDP was more substantial than the drop of their defence expenditures, leaving their defense efforts relatively high. Second, other states, such as Saudi Arabia and the 1991 Gulf States have increased their defense burden dramatically since the Gulf War. Still other states, such as Algeria, have increased their defense spending due to their internal security problems.

The military allocation aspect of regional security has a human dimension as well. The size of the armed forces of the states in the region is also a meaningful indicator of the extent to which they are concerned about their security. Since many of the challenges to national security are internal in nature, military forces have at least two important functions besides facing enemies from the outside. First, they are an important instrument of internal political order and must face challenges both from contenders to

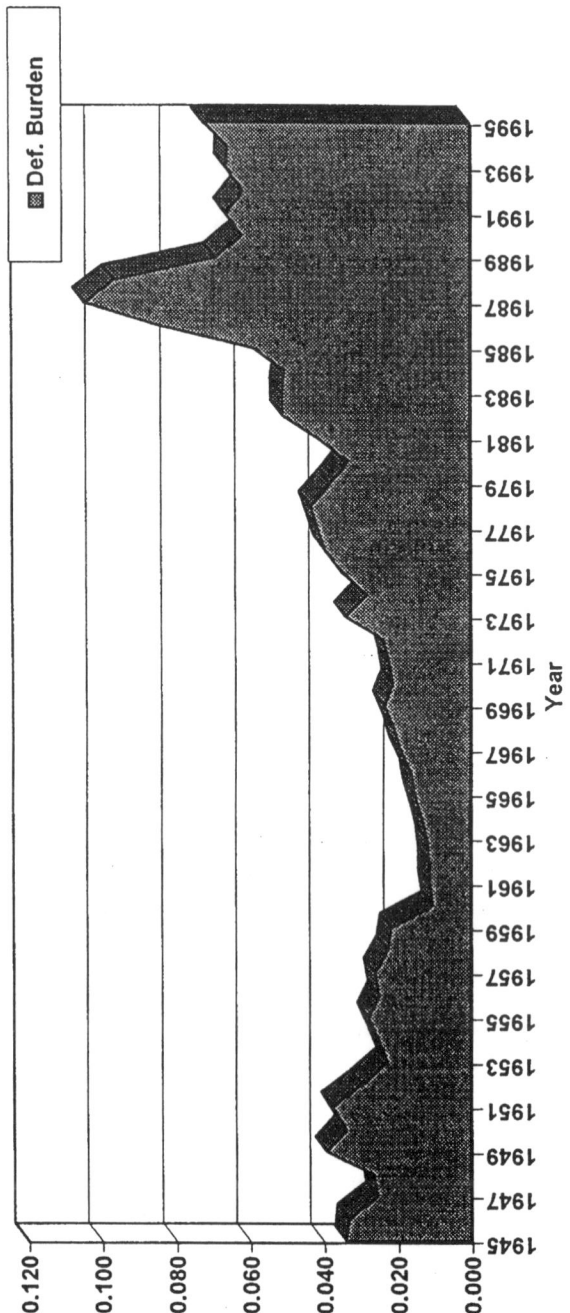

FIGURE 3
DEFENCE BURDEN IN THE MIDDLE EAST, 1945–1995

TRENDS, REALITIES, AND CHALLENGES

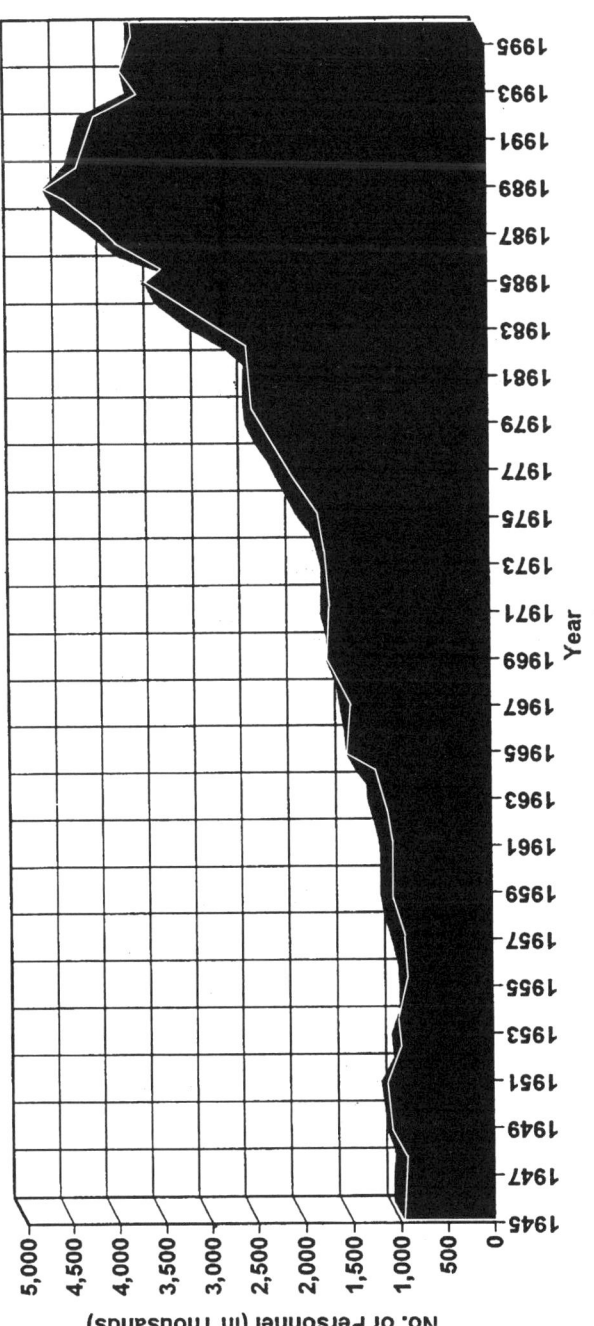

FIGURE 4
TOTAL MILITARY PERSONNEL IN THE MIDDLE EAST, 1945–1995

political power from within the state and from minority ethnic or other groups seeking some form of separation or secession. Second, military forces serve as an important instrument of political legitimacy in many Middle Eastern states. In such military regimes, the future of the regime as well as the persistence and survival of political leaders rests almost exclusively on the loyalty and cooperation of the armed forces. Many political leaders in the region come from the armed forces. Even in a democratic state such as Israel, ex-military officers have held and continue to hold high-ranking political offices, and are often perceived as attractive candidates to various civilian positions on both the national and municipal level.[23] Figure 4 shows the evolution of the military forces in the region.

As can be seen from this figure, the trend of the growth of military forces in the Middle East largely parallels that of the monetary defense burden. There is a fairly constant rise in the size of military forces in the region, with a sharp acceleration in the rate of growth in the 1980s – again largely affected by the Iran–Iraq War. However, in contrast to the monetary aspect of military allocations which has continued to grow following the immediate drop after the Gulf War, the human defence burden shows some degree of decline in the early 1990s and some stability toward 1994–95. At any event, the rate of military mobilization in the 1990s is almost twice the rate of the early 1980s.[24]

The story of military allocations could be broken down into additional components. For example, an examination of arms sales to the region, and an inspection of quantities of key military equipment such as combat aircraft, tanks, ballistic missile launchers, and suspected programmes of weapons of mass destruction would reveal the same story. The region is becoming increasingly armed with increasingly sophisticated weapons and with increasingly destructive technology.

One aspect that has posed growing concern in the region concerns surface-to-surface missiles. In contrast to many other elements of the regional military balance which display relative stability over time, the Middle East surface-to-surface missile race has intensified considerably since the 1991 Gulf War. The key players in this game consist of Israel, Syria, Saudi Arabia, and Iran. Iraq, under UN sanctions and supervision, has lost most of its ability to launch missiles, but it has the technological know-how, the political will, and the operational capacity to return to the pre-war levels of missile launchers, some of which have been proven to be capable of carrying chemical warheads.[25] The fact that this has been the only region where chemical weapons were used twice since World War I and that it has also been the only region where ballistic missiles were fired since World War II suggests that these capabilities – once in place and operational – may not be confined to deterrence purposes alone.

COLLECTIVE SECURITY STRUCTURES

Were there any changes over time in the patterns of collective security arrangements among members of the region, and between members of the region and outside powers? The answer to this question requires inspection of various institutions and security arrangements that have functioned in the region. It also necessitates an assessment of their effectiveness over time. Two types of collective security arrangements are examined herein. The first is the Arab League, which was designed as an institution which manages and resolves conflicts between or among Arab states, and a mechanism for regulating political, economic, and cultural cooperation among its members. It was also designed to serve as an instrument of coordination of inter-Arab activity *vis-à-vis* common threats, such as Israel. The second type of institution is that of formal alliances. Formal alliances serve as a collective security mechanism which allows states to: (a) create a common pool of resources designed to deter outside threats, or to help confront them, and/or (b) prevent the transfer of resources of certain states to opposing alliances by binding these states by formal commitment to the goals of the alliance.[26] In a world of egoists operating under anarchy, both types of institutions pose states with a tradeoff between autonomy, on the one hand, and *a chance* of better security, on the other.[27] By becoming members of regional institutions or alliances, states give up a certain measure of autonomy of decision in order to perhaps gain power, security, and cooperation.

Other than the Arab League, no strictly indigenous security-related institutions existed in the Middle East. Members of the region participated as individual states in other collective security arrangements. Turkey was and still is a full-fledged member of NATO. Iraq, Turkey, and Jordan formed, together with the United Kingdom, the Baghdad Pact in 1954. Egypt was a founding member of the non-aligned movement, and all of the African members of the Middle East are members of the OAU.

It is difficult to make an overall assessment of the performance of the Arab League as a security organization. However, it is clear that it failed to perform in any of the key tests of conflict management and conflict resolution among Arab states. Starting with the 1948 meeting on Palestine, going through the conflicts between radical and conservative Arab regimes in the 1950s and 1960s, dealing with the civil wars in Yemen (1962–67, and again in 1994), Jordan (September 1970, July 1971), and Lebanon (1974–present), dealing with the split in the Arab world during the Iran–Iraq war, and finally, dealing with the Iraqi invasion of Kuwait in 1990. In none of these cases was there any sign of effective management of the conflicts, let alone any type of resolution.

The Arab League also failed in most cases to provide a measure of coordination in negotiations between its members and Israel. It was partly effective in devising a common formula of rejection of negotiations in the Khartoum summit of 1967, and in blocking a separate Jordanian-Israeli negotiation over the West Bank during the Rabat summit of 1974. However, it failed in stopping the Egyptian-Israeli peace process starting in 1975 and culminating in the 1979 peace treaty. It also failed to organize a common front of Arab states in the negotiations that started in Madrid in 1991. The Arab League is seen by its own leading members as a 'dead horse.'

It remains therefore to be seen whether alliances formed any guarantee of security in the region. To examine that, let us first look at the evolution of alliance commitments of Middle East states over time. Obviously, two issues matter when we consider alliance commitments: the nature of alliance and the nature of the allies. The accepted formulation of alliances in world politics consists of three security-related types of alliances: defense pacts, non-aggression pacts, and ententes. Defense pacts commit states to defend any of the alliance members which is attacked by an outside party as if they defended their own territory and national integrity against external attack. These alliances entail the greatest degree of autonomy loss due to the demanding nature of the alliance commitment, but they are supposed to provide the greatest degree of security. Non-aggression pacts commit members not to attack each other. Non-aggression pacts enable some level of enhanced security because the partners to such a treaty can presumably count each other out as enemies with some probability which is higher than without such a pact. Here the loss of autonomy is lower than in defence pacts, but so is the gain in security. Finally entente treaties entail coordination and exchange of information on security affairs. The members to an entente treaty lose little in terms of decision making autonomy but gain little in terms of security compared to a situation of non-alliance.[28]

The extent of gain or loss on both decisional autonomy and security depends of course on who are one's allies. Signing an alliance with a major power carries more weight than signing an alliance with a minor power. A major power can bring more capabilities to bear in the event of a conflict, thus considerably enhancing the security-related benefits of minor allies. A major power is typically taken to be a more reliable alliance partner than a minor power, due to its international status, the extended scope of its commitments, and the greater need to preserve its reputation. Thus alliances with major powers count more than alliances with minor powers.

Figure 5 (opposite) shows changes in weighted alliance commitments of Middle Eastern states over the 1945–1995 period.

The magnitude of alliance commitments seem to have taken a slow decline over time. If the 1950s and 1960s exhibited significant levels of

TRENDS, REALITIES, AND CHALLENGES

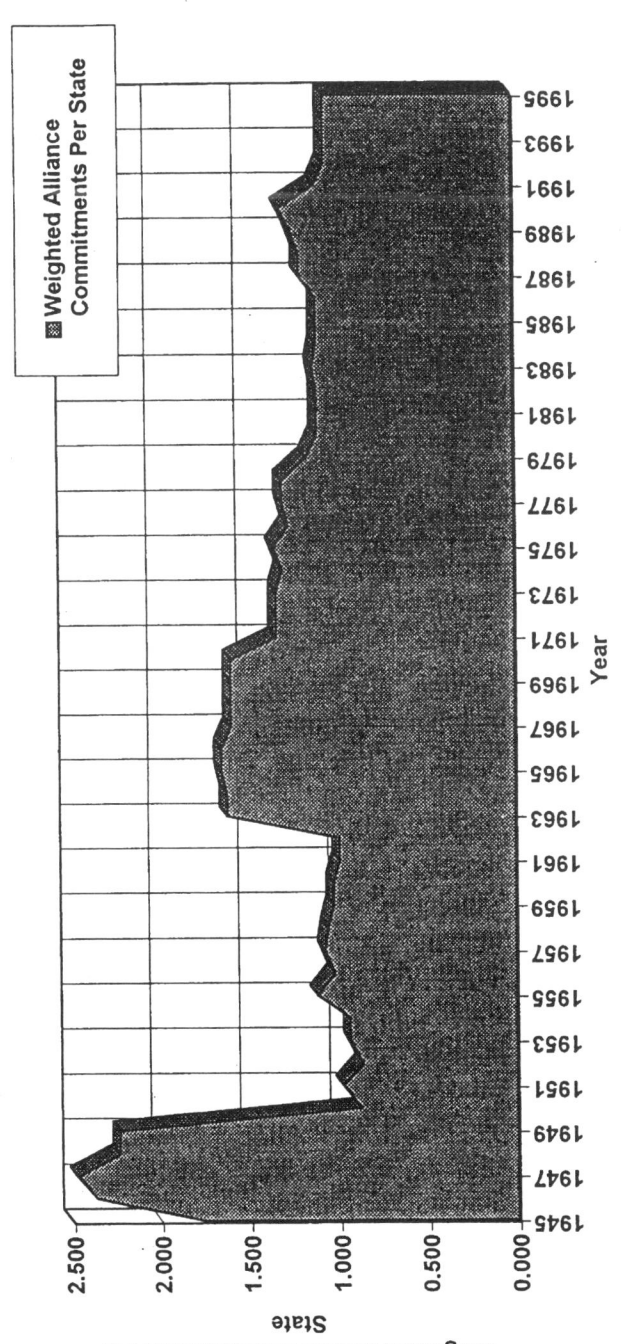

FIGURE 5
WEIGHTED NUMBER OF ALLIANCE COMMITMENTS IN THE MIDDLE EAST, 1945–1995

commitments, the 1970s, 1980s and 1990s exhibit a greater reluctance of states to get entangled in strategic commitments to each other. This is in line with the increased nationalistic politics of most Arab states which have abandoned notions of solidarity and Pan-Arabisim in favor of more national inward-looking policies. We can add to this the two major causes of political splits in the Arab world during these periods: the peace process with Israel (starting from the aftermath of the 1973 War), and the political polarization of the Arab world in the context of the Iran–Iraq war. In the late 1980s and 1990s we see additional forms of realignment, typically from the non strictly binding form (ententes of various sorts), among various states, mostly with some relevance to the Persian Gulf.

It must be noted, however, that these figures represent shifts only in *strategic* alignments, not in other types of political, economic, or cultural exchanges in the Middle East. In addition, the fact that the analysis is limited only to *formal* alliance commitments may also distort the picture somewhat, as the decline in the scope and types of formal alliance commitments over time may represent a parallel increase in the scope and extent of *informal* security arrangements between or among states in the region. For example, there is an increase in joint strategic activity in the region that involves non-regional actors – especially the United States – but which is not grounded in formal alliance terms, such as joint maneuvers with Egypt, Saudi Arabia, and Israel, prepositioning of American air and naval forces in various states in the region (including most recently in Jordan), and so forth. Yet, one may argue that this growing level of direct American military presence in the region which is grounded in a series of bilateral understandings and *ad hoc* agreements is a source for the reduced need in indigenous security arrangements – just as increased police presence in a residential neighbourhood reduces the need to institute patrols by the local residents themselves.

In sum, looking at patterns of conflict, of military allocations, and alliance commitment in the Middle East, the general picture is quite bleak. Although some of the conflicts in the region seem to be in a process of winding down, both international and internal conflicts continue to rage in the region, and the cost of these conflicts is growing constantly larger. International conflicts are fewer but – in many respect – more severe than in the past. Internal conflicts increase in frequency and in severity at an alarming rate. This point is intuitively internalised by most states in the region, and expresses itself very clearly in terms of their self-help response to such patterns. States have increased their military allocations dramatically over time. Levels of defense expenditures and sizes of armed forces have been growing steadily. Although these patterns have slowed down somewhat in the early 1990s, the level of military spending and sizes of armed forces is significantly higher than in the early 1980s. The same can be said with respect to certain aspects of military hardware – mostly surface-to-surface missiles – that may make future international wars in the region more dangerous and more severe than those experienced in the past.

The Arab–Israeli peace process creates a false impression that regional security in the Middle East may well be improving. If the Arab–Israeli conflict is examined separately from other regional security complexes, then the impression is that the recent past and the present hold good prospects for a safer future.[29] Yet, as we have seen in the case of the 1991 Gulf War, the Arab–Israeli conflict may not lend itself to attempts to isolate it from other regional conflicts. Thus, the individual aspects of levels of regional security suggest growing levels of violence, growing levels of investments in human and material capabilities in the region, and a slow decline in formal structures for strategic cooperation.

Relations Among Dimensions of Regional Security

In order to examine the present state of Middle East regional security, and – more importantly – to identify future challenges to regional security, it is necessary to examine the relations among various dimensions of security and to identify some factors that have an effect on levels of security-related patterns. Due to the regional focus of this study, I explore only aggregate regional-level relationships among the three dimensions of regional security.[30]

Without going in detail into the vast and diverse literature on the sources of internal and international conflict,[31] it seems that most observers of international security mention three groups of factors affecting national strategic behavior of states: external strategic factors, domestic political factors, and economic factors. External factors refer to events and processes in the external environment of states which have implications for their strategic considerations and calculations. These include the balance of capabilities between a state and its strategic reference group, the balance of alliances in the state's strategic environment, and the level of conflict in its environment.

At an individual state level there is a general consensus on how military balances and diplomatic-strategic balances affect state behavior.[32] However, at an aggregate level, the relevant literature is marred by disagreements regarding the effects of military capability and of alliances on conflict levels. On the one hand, there is a body of research which asserts that high level military preparedness in a dyadic (or regional) context is indicative of an arms race which contributes to the level of suspicion and mistrust that characterises states' perceptions under international anarchy. On the other hand, military preparedness is said to foster stable mutual deterrence, thus leading to lower levels of conflict in the system.[33]

The same applies to the hypothesized effects of alliances on levels of conflict. If states form 'balancing' alliances, then alliances may well produce mutual deterrence and thus stability. However, if states form 'bandwagoning' alliances, then increased alliance commitments produce higher levels of conflict.[34]

Political factors include levels of democratization and of political stability. Again, at the individual state level, there is a general consensus that regime type is not a good predictor of national behavior. Yet, it is an important factor that accounts for the probability of dyadic conflict. Finally, at a systemic level, there is no consistent relationship between the number or proportion of democratic states in a given domain and the level of conflict in that system.[35] There is, however, a consistent body of findings that connects political instability to levels of conflict. This generalization applies both to the level of individual state behavior and to the systemic level.[36]

Economic factors are often mentioned as individual and regional-level determinants of domestic and international conflict. However, there is no consensus on just how these factors are related to conflict. Some suggest that economic growth fosters national as well as regional stability because conflict is detrimental to economic prosperity. Others claim that economic growth increases domestic discontent and raises expectations for shared welfare. When this is not the case, domestic as well as international instability follows.[37] On a regional level, economic growth is also seen as a cause of stability as more states become economically content with the status quo and thus wish to preserve it.

The sources of military preparedness and alliance formation are generally seen to be similar to the sources of conflict. Here too strategic, economic, and political factors are expected to be chiefly responsible because the sources of security and insecurity that prompt states to get involved in conflict also prompt them to build up their defences and enter into strategic alliances.

Examining the relationships among the various determinants of regional security also enables us to see just to what extent the patterns that we discussed in the previous section can be used as a basis for assessing the future of the region in terms of security. The analysis on regional patterns is performed in the methodological appendix (Tables A.2–A.5 pp.34 and 38–41). The results are quite revealing. In the interest of space, these results could be summarized by the following points.

1. *There is a significant relationship between regime stability and regional security in the Middle East.* On an individual state basis, revolutionary political change in states affects their conflict behavior. Political instability on a regional level also increases the likelihood of conflict in the region.

2. *There is a significant relationship between alliance commitments and regional security.* This relationship is not consistent across levels of analysis, probably due to the fact that our measure does not distinguish between alliance as collective security mechanisms and alliances as offensive devices. But on the whole the relationship between alliance and conflict, and the fact that alliances themselves are affected by levels of human and material burdens is quite meaningful. It suggests that alliances can both increase and decrease regional security. The relationship between the number of alliances in the region and war suggests that, as in the literature on alliances and war in general, we see that strategic deals among states in the region do not have a pacifying effect. On the contrary, higher levels of alliance commitments in the region may be a source of instability.[38] It is important to note, therefore, that not all strategic cooperation agreements between states are necessarily peaceful. Thus, the architects of regional security systems must be aware of this fact.

3. *Military efforts of Middle Eastern states have, by and large, a significant but mixed effect on the frequency of conflict in the region.* On an individual state level, military capability ratios between a state and its strategic reference group have a positive effect on the level of conflict. However, levels of human military burdens and of material defense burdens have a dampening effect on regional conflict. On the other side of the regional security equation, levels of regional conflict have a strong and positive effect on military allocations – both human and material – and on the level of alliance commitments.

4. Generally speaking, *economic development* (measured as per capita GDP) does not appear to have a marked effect on individual state-level conflict behavior, at least not in an immediate sense. On a regional level, however, economic growth appears to be positively related to both lower level conflict and war, contrary to what one may expect. Economic growth also positively affects levels of human and material military allocations in the region.

All in all, these findings indicate that the various dimensions of regional security that were discussed in the previous sections appear to be related to each other and tend mutually to affect one another. It is thus important to realize that these relationships, however complex, must be considered in any future design of a regional security system in the Middle East. In light of these relationships, we may now turn to a discussion of present and future trends in regional security.

Present and Future Trends

The previous analyses of past trends leave us with a bleak image of the state of regional security in the Middle East. In terms of the residential neighborhood analogy, we can say that the Middle East is a high-crime neighborhood wherein there are frequent and fairly violent clashes within individual households, among residents, and between residents and people from outside the neighbourhood. These clashes have become increasingly frequent and increasingly violent over time. While some of the structural enmities of the region appear to be on their way to resolution, other enmities – perhaps less visible, but certainly as dangerous – are as viable as ever.

Members of the neighborhood have also spent considerable resources on means of self-defense as well as attack weapons. However, such an investment did not appear to make the neighborhood safer than in the past. On the contrary. The accumulation of weapons of all sorts has made the Middle East a more dangerous place. The massive use of surface-to-surface missiles during the Iran–Iraq War and during the Gulf War, as well as the use of chemical weapons during the Yemen Civil War in the 1960s and the Iran–Iraq War in the 1980s, suggests that in the Middle East – perhaps unlike in other regions – once a weapon system is in place, it may actually be used.

At the same time, no effective regional institution was established to manage, let alone resolve, indigenous conflicts through peaceful means. Nor was an effective system of collective security instituted in the region. Hence both individual-national and collective-regional measures of enhancing security did not appear to have a marked effect on internal or international conflicts in the region.

With this set of facts in mind, we can turn to an assessment of the future outlook of regional security. It is important to note that what follows is not an exercise in point prediction, but rather, as in geological research, we can identify certain structural conditions and seismic trends that allow a general mapping of regional security risks. When, where, how, and whether or not these risks would materialize is something that is clearly beyond the capabilities of such an analysis.

Moreover, any assessment of future regional security risks must consider some of the non-military factors that may affect regional security problems in the future. I will focus here only on three such factors: population growth, economic development, and regime stability.[39]

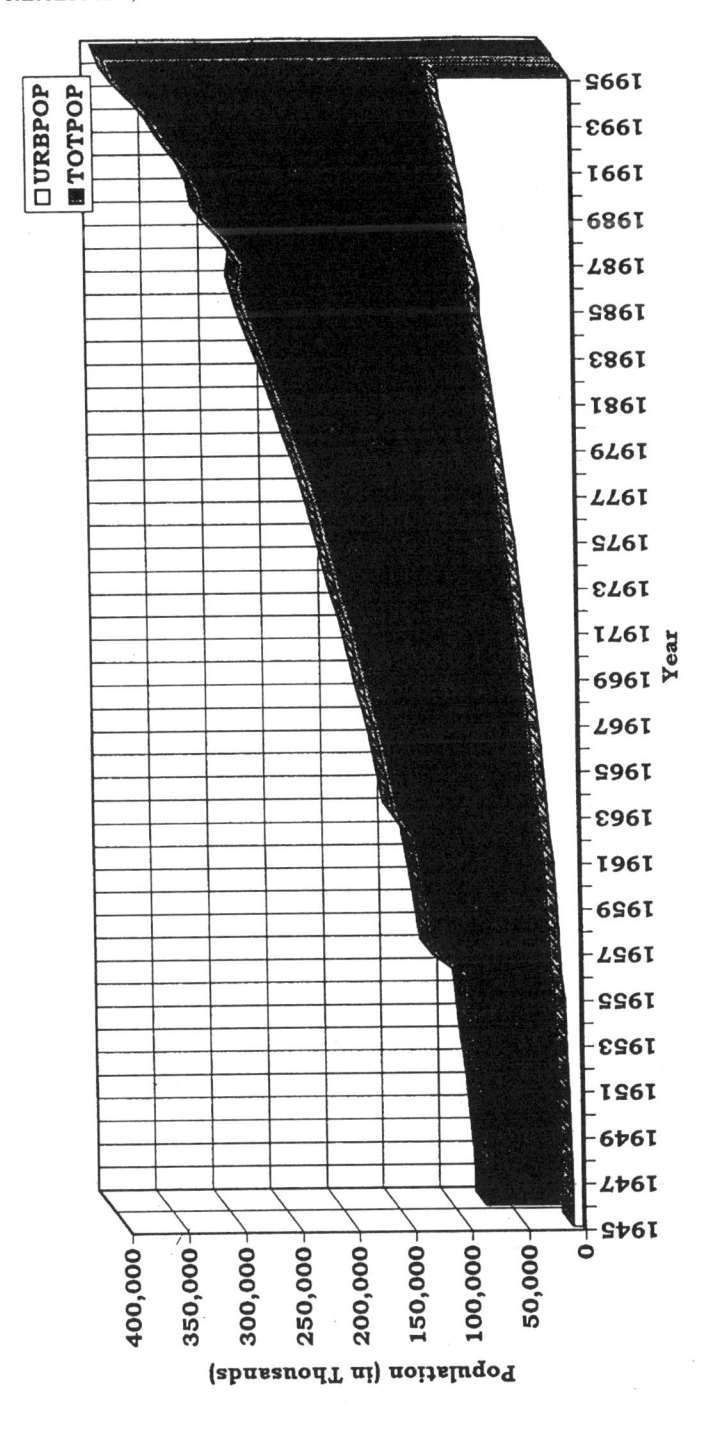

FIGURE 6
TOTAL AND URBAN POPULATION IN THE MIDDLE EAST, 1945–1995

FIGURE 7
PER CAPITA GDP IN THE MIDDLE EAST, 1945–1995

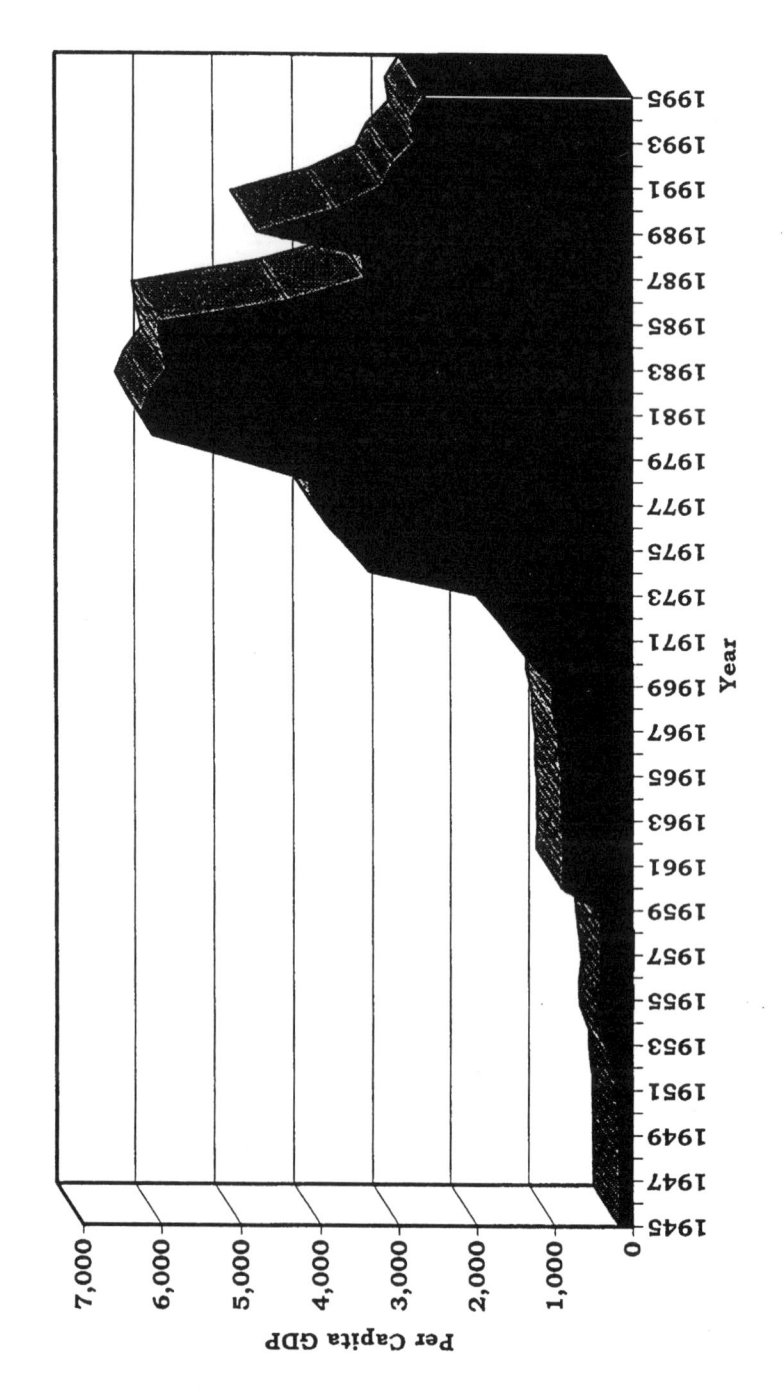

POPULATION GROWTH

Regional patterns of population growth show this to be one of the chief concerns of the future, with major implications for security. Figure 6 provides a sense of the regional trends in population growth in total and urban population over time.

This figure suggests that the rate of population growth in the region has picked up considerably and so has the rate of urban population growth. It is evident that, out of a regional population of close to 400 million people in 1995, 180 to 190 million people (or between 45 and 47 per cent) belong to three states: Egypt, Iran, and Turkey. The average population growth rate in the region over the last decade was 2.8 per cent per annum, which suggests that – all things being equal – the population of the Middle East will double itself in less than 50 years. Efforts by Egypt, Turkey, and Iran at slowing down population growth rates are the key to the solution, because no matter how much effort is invested by other Middle East states to curb growth rates, the three giants are going to determine the future of the Middle East in terms of population.

The urban population growth rates are slower but are also increasing at a faster rate than the logistical foundations of Middle East cities. Cairo, with a population of about 13 million, Istanbul with 10 million, Tehran with 10 million people all represent urban quagmires of major proportions, the physical infrastructure of which is lagging decades behind their populations. These may well become centers of social discontent and social unrest in the future.

ECONOMIC DEVELOPMENT

It is difficult to put a single number on the issue of economic development, yet clearly economic development is related to the overall resources available domestically to the states in the region. Figure 7 provides a sense of the patterns of economic development in the region as measured in terms of regional per capita GDP.

As can be seen from this figure, the region's economies have been mostly stagnant or declining. Since the rapid rise in the region's GDP in the 1970s and early 1980s, the region's economies – for most part – have been on the decline. Obviously these figures represent regional averages, and these regional averages are greatly affected by oil-related revenues of several principal economic actors in the region, including the Gulf states and some north-African states. Other states in the region – such as Israel – have experienced relatively high levels of real growth over the last decade.[40] The economic slowdown of the 1990s is due to the reduced oil-related revenues and the limitations on oil sales of such states as Iraq, Libya, and

Iran. However, this is not the key source for the drop in regional per capita GDP. The two principal sources of economic stagnation in the region consist of population growth and lack of basic transformation in the economies of the key members of the region.

The high population growth rates are the killer of any meaningful economic development in the region. For a state such as Egypt to exhibit real growth in terms of per capita GDP, it has to grow at a rate faster than 3.3 per cent per annum, which is its population growth rate. Such a growth rate is difficult to accomplish anywhere in the world, let alone in the Middle East. Any real growth in the Egyptian GDP that is smaller than its population growth rate actually translates into negative growth. The same applies to other states in the region.

The last decade did not show a marked structural change in the key economies in the region. What is more, regional defense burdens were kept high, and therefore prevented major transformation in the allocation of budget to the civilian sectors. Structural problems of regional – mostly labor-intensive – economies (low level of industrialization, lack of infrastructure for technological and industrial development, high security-related risks which limit foreign investment), have prevented real economic development in the region. If this trend persists, the people of the region are likely to become even poorer than they are at present. More importantly, even if a major shift takes place, such as a major turnaround in the prices and demand for oil in the future, the benefits will accrue only to few of those people, while the burden of poverty and underdevelopment threatens to become more severe to most others.[41]

REGIME STABILITY

The picture here may be bleak or promising depending on one's outlook. On the bright side, it is noteworthy that only two regime changes have taken place in the Middle East in the last 20 years: Iran and Sudan.[42] This is a stark contrast to the frequent changes in various regimes in the region in the preceding three decades. Even more importantly, many of the principal regimes in the region have survived major political shocks, including defeats in major wars (the Arab states in 1967), assassinations of political leaders (Sadat in 1981, Rabin in 1995), and even civil wars of major magnitudes which were aimed at toppling a given regime (the Yemen Civil War, the September 1970 Civil War in Jordan). This may suggest that, despite the economic and social problems of many Middle Eastern regimes, the political institutions and state machinery have emerged as viable structures. with good shock absorbers.

But regime stability is not an issue that lends itself to trend prediction. As was the case in Iran in 1978–79, regimes that had been considered stable were overthrown quite unexpectedly. Rather, on a regional level, it is important to consider the states in terms of their regime-related risks. First, several states in the region are under considerable and imminent internal threat. Chief among those are states such as Algeria, Lebanon, and Sudan, and Yemen that recently have been or currently are embroiled in civil wars. Thus, they are subject to severe social and political problems that may well translate into widespread social unrest and regime change. Second, the increased activity and popularity of Islamic movements in states such as Egypt, Turkey, and Jordan, as well as inside the Palestinian authority, puts these regimes under potential threat, if not in the immediate future, certainly in the longer run. Third, states that have over a long time failed to meet basic social and economic needs of the population, such as Iran and Iraq, must be considered regimes at risk, although it is difficult to pinpoint an organised and effective opposition force.[43]

In short, all existing trends of the visible aspects of regional security – namely, severity and frequency of internal and international conflicts, military allocations, and alliance commitments – suggest that the future state of regional security is likely to become much worse before it gets any better. This conclusion is corroborated by the trends in non-military factors that may affect regional security, that is, unchecked population growth, economic stagnation, and regime instability. Unless dramatic shifts take place in regional politics, strategic affairs, demographics, and economics, this region is likely to experience growing problems of regional security in the future. Given that major security-related shocks in the region have had an important impact on international politics, the risks that the region poses to global stability should not be taken lightly by actors and institutions outside the region that are interested in stability and order.

Conclusion and Policy Implications

The overall picture emerging from this analysis of past trends and present issues in Middle East regional security is quite gloomy. This picture is in stark contrast to images of a 'New Middle East', that are invoked by politicians engaged in the Arab–Israeli peace process. In fact, the focus of many analysts, commentators and political leaders in and outside the region on Arab–Israeli issues may be quite misleading, because it may create an impression that the resolution of the Arab–Israeli conflict may bring cure to many of the problems that have plagued the Middle East in the past. This view is quite misleading not because the Arab–Israeli peace process is unreal or unimportant. It is because the impact of the Arab–Israeli conflict on overall problems of regional security in the Middle East has always been limited, and – since the mid-1980s – this impact has been marginal at best.

Clearly, the continuation or escalation of the Arab–Israeli conflict may create severe security threats in the region. These problems may pose grave risks to actors both within and outside the region. However, the opposite does not necessarily follow. In other words, political resolution of the Arab–Israeli conflict will not, and cannot solve the key problems of regional security in and of itself. If the resolution of the Arab–Israeli conflict would amount only to a series of bilateral agreements exchanging land for peace and security, its impact on stabilizing the region is likely to be marginal. More importantly, the structural problems of the Middle East will have a detrimental effect on the stability of the Arab–Israeli agreements more than the Arab–Israeli agreements would positively affect the ability to resolve the structural problems of the region.

Can something be done to reduce these risks? Paradoxically, while the Arab-Israeli peace process deceptively paints in rosy paints the more general picture of regional security risks, it also offers the key to a regional strategy that may enable treatment of most of these problems. Perhaps the key promise that the Arab–Israeli peace process offers with respect to increased regional security is the multilateral aspect of this process. Bilateral agreements may stabilise relations between Israel and its neighbours. As such they will offer a new dimension of stability to one part of the region. However, future problems are likely to go beyond bilateral crises. Future security threats are increasingly likely to emerge from non-military problems, and from problems that are not caused by a single state or a single coalition of states. Rather, they are likely to reflect spillover effects of problems that start with one state or one part of the region and diffuse to other states or other parts of the region. In order to deal with these problems, the states of the region as a whole must devise collective strategies for coping with them. It is unlikely that any of the key problems would be resolved by a single state.

The multilateral talks launched as part of the Madrid process were designed to deal with just this logic. Unfortunately, thus far progress on most working groups has been modest at best, and on some issues (e.g. arms control and regional security – ACRS), talks have been stalled for quite a while.

The fact that some of the principal regional players (e.g. Syria, Iran, Iraq) have not joined the multilateral talks, has also not helped. The prospects of success of the multilateral process depend on how general it is in terms of participation, how comprehensive it is in terms of issue-coverage, and how integrative it is in terms of confronting the various issues involved. Success of the multilateral process depends on the ability of regional actors to recognize the interdependence between multilateral and bilateral issues, on the one hand, and between non-military aspects and strategic aspects of regional security, on the other. It also depends on the ability to devise regional strategies, agreements, and institutions that effectively could manage these problems.

In terms of policy, this implies three principles that must guide the multilateral process. First, the principle of general inclusion. States must seek to include all the regional actors, whether or not they maintain normal relations with each other. Currently Iran and Iraq are out of the multilateral loop not only because they oppose the Arab-Israeli peace process, but also because most other participants in the multilateral talks do not want to include them as long as the current regimes in these states are in power. It is unlikely that effective institutions and strategies will be devised that do not include Iraq and Iran.

Second, the principle of independent progress: It is not constructive to make one aspect of the multilateral process the hostage of another aspect. For example, stalling confidence building measures and agreements on conventional arms control due to the inability to make progress on nonconventional matters does not help resolve any of the problems. Likewise, the voluntary self-exclusion of Syria from the multilateral talks as long as the Israeli-Syrian negotiations have not produced an agreement seems to be counter-productive both for the Israeli-Syrian peace process and for the multilateral talks. The severity and urgency of the problems to be tackled in the multilaterals suggests that delay tactics are likely to backfire in the hands of those who use them. Thus moving along one track of the multilateral process should and could be made independent of moving along another track of this process.

Third, the principle of integration. Ultimately, independent movement along various aspects of regional security would have to be coordinated and integrated into an overall concept of regional security which includes both strategic and military factors and non-military ones. The institutions that are formed and the strategies adopted by the actors inside and outside the region must be based on the notion of interdependence among issues and actors, and on the mutual impact of military security and economic and social security.

In addition to those processes, which are ultimately in the hands of the indigenous states, the international community could be instrumental in helping the Middle East help itself. It should do it not because of altruistic motives, but because the problems of the Middle East are likely to become the problems of the international community, and thus preventive treatment may be less costly and more effective than crisis management or than coping with disasters.

Whether or not the risks identified in this study would intensify in the future is not only a function of whether the assessments made herein are correct. It is also first and foremost a consequence of what regional and non-regional actors would do about these problems. The multilateral talks have created an opportunity for the community to face its problems, whether or not it is capable of coming up with solutions is a matter of policy, not of prediction.

Methodological Appendix

This appendix outlines the research design used in the present study.

Empirical Domain

The study covers the period of 1945-1995 for most analyses. In some cases where data cover only part of the period, or form some of the states, temporal domains may be more limited. For each dataset, the domain covered is noted. As noted in the text, the Middle East includes the following states with their period of independence.

TABLE A.1
STATES AND PERIOD COVERED IN THE STUDY

State Name	State No.	Period Covered	Comments
Morocco	600	1956–1995	Under French Protectorate, 1911–55
Algeria	615	1962–1995	
Tunisia	616	1956–1995	
Libya	620	1952–1995	
Sudan	625	1956–1995	
Iran	630	1945–1995	
Turkey	640	1945–1995	Also part of Europe
Iraq	645	1945–1995	
Egypt	651	1945–1995	
Syria	652	1946–1995	
Lebanon	660	1946–1995	
Jordan	663	1946–1995	
Israel	666	1948–1995	
Saudi Arabia	670	1945–1995	
North Yemen	678	1945–1995	
South Yemen	680	1967–1990	Separation following Civil War in 1967; Union with North Yemen, 1990
Kuwait	690	1961–1995	Occupation by Iraq, Aug. 1990–Feb. 1991
Bahrain	692	1971–1995	
Qatar	694	1971–1995	
UAE	696	1971–1995	
Oman	698	1971–1995	

The selection of 1945 as the start year for our examination is that it is the year in which a system of states began forming in the region, outside of the colonial domain of the major powers. The disputes and relationships that began forming since this year mark – to a large extent – the problems of regional security at present as well.

Key Variables and Sources

The major variables used in this study include the following.

1. *Conflict and Conflict Attributes.* Two types of conflict are examined: internal conflict and international conflict. The definition for these variables are as follows: *internal conflict* is a set of violent clashes between or among segments of the same state involving at least ten fatalities per clash. Definitions and data for internal conflicts are taken from: Margareta Sollenberg and Peter Wallensteen, 'Major Armed Conflicts', in *SIPRI Yearbook 1995* (NY: OUP 1995), p.21, Peter Wallensten and Karin Axell 'Armed Conflict at the End of The Cold War,' *Journal of Peace Research*, 30/3 (Sept. 1993) pp.331–46, and A.J. Jongman with A.P. Schmidt, 'Contemporary Conflicts: A Global Survey of High- and Lower-Intensity Conflicts and Serious Disputes', *PIOOM Newsletter and Report*, 7/1 (Winter 1995) pp.14–23. Additional data were collected from Anthony H. Cordesman. *After the Storm: The Changing Military Balance in the Middle East* (Boulder, CO: Westview Press 1993).

International conflict, is defined in terms of militarized interstate disputes, and follows the definition of Gochman and Maoz (note 10) p.595: 'A set of incidents between or among states, involving the threat to use force, the display of force, and the use of military force in short temporal intervals. In order to be included, these incidents must be overt, non-accidental, government-sanctioned, and government-directed.' The sources of data for militarised interstate disputes are taken from the New Militarized Interstate Dispute dataset, which follows the definitions and measures of Gochman and Maoz and is available at the Inter-University Consortium for Political and Social Research at the University of Michigan, as well as through the internet on the Peace Science Society (International) home page at: http://www.polsci.binghamton.edu/peacesci.htm.

Fatality data was collected from these sources as well as from Melvin Small and J. David Singer. *Resort to Arms: Civil and International Wars* (Beverly Hills, CA: Sage 1982). An updated version of the Singer-Small dataset is available at the Correlates of War Project, the University of Michigan.

2. *Military Fatalities* are defined as members of the armed forces of a given state that are reported dead as a result of armed struggle with another

state or during a violent internal conflict. *Civilian Fatalities* are non-military fatalities incurred during an internal or international conflict as a result of organized violence.

3. *Regime Scores and Regime Change*: Sources for these scores for individuals states are derived from the Polity III Dataset. See Keith Jaggers and Ted Robert Gurr, 'Tracking Democracy's Third Wave with the Polity III Data', *Journal of Peace Research* 32/4 (Nov. 1995) pp.453–68. I am indebted to Prof. Gurr for making the Polity III dataset available to me. The precise coding of regime scores (ranging from −100 for highly authoritarian to +100 for highly democratic) are discussed by Maoz and Russett, 'Normative and Structural Causes', and Maoz, *Domestic Sources* (note 22), Ch.2 (Appendix). Generally speaking, a regime score of a state reflects its institutional and behavioural level of regime openness and the regulation of political participation and institutionalisation.[44] *Average Regime Score* is the average level of regime scores over all states in the region. *Regime change* is defined as a shift from one regime structure to another. The number of regime changes is the number of states that have undergone a regime change at a given year.

4. *Alliances*. Sources for alliances are given by the Correlates of War Formal Alliances dataset. The dataset consists of all formal alliances of states over the 1816–1980 period. These data were updated by Oren, op. cit (appendix), and adapted by Maoz and Russett to cover the 1946–86 period. The same sources and coding rules were used to update the alliances in the region through 1995.

5. *National Capability Data*. Data on defence expenditures and military personnel, as well as on total and urban population were collected from several sources. These include (1) The Correlates of War Project's military capability dataset. (Also available through the ICPSR at the University of Michigan.) (2) *The Middle East Military Balance* (Jerusalem and Boulder: Jerusalem Post and Westview Press), various volumes, (3) International Institute for Strategic Studies, *Military Balance* (London IISS) various volumes. Military expenditure data were collected in current prices and so were Gross Domestic Product (GDP) figures for calculation of defence burdens. Since defence burdens are defined by military expenditures as proportion of GDP, controls for inflation are not necessary. Human Military burden is defined as proportion of the population in the armed forces.

6. *Bipolarity Score*. In accordance with studies of superpower involvement in the Middle East, a bipolarity index was formed in the following manner. First, the years of 1945–54 were defined as years of zero bipolarity given the almost monopolistic influence of the Western Powers in the region. The period of 1955–75 are designated as years of high bipolarity in the region. The period of 1976–91 are described as years of low

bipolarity. Finally, the 1992–95 period is again a period of zero bipolarity.[45]

7. *Economic Data.* Gross Domestic Product data for per-capita GDP figures were employed from the Penn World Table dataset (Version 5.6a).[46] Version 5.6a contains updates of data through 1992. Figures for 1993–95 were updated from the *Middle East Military Balance*, for the years 1993–96, where series comparison adjustments were used in order to preserve consistency with the Penn World Trade Table.

8. *Demographic Data,* Population data were derived from the same sources as the other military capability data. Urban population is defined as the population residing in cities of 100,000 and over. Per cent urban population is the proportion of total population residing in such cities.

Research Methods

In order to examine the relationship among the various dimensions of regional security, I attempted to regress each of the dimensions on the lagged values of the previous dimensions. However, as explained in the text, such an analysis requires us to control for other dimensions of security that may affect this relationship. Hence the addition of economic and political factors to the analyses.

Two levels of analysis were used in the study. The first is the individual nation-level. Each nation was studied for all of the years it existed as a sovereign entity (see Table A.1 above). The analyses for individual states were performed through pooled time-series analysis that allows both distinction between behavioural patterns that may be unique to each state and those that are common to all of them, but vary over time. These analyses are reported in Table A.2 for conflict and war-related measures, and in Table A.4 for the analysis of the military preparedness and alliance formation dimensions of strategic national behavior.[47] The second level of analysis is the aggregate regional level. Here we aggregated the various measures over all states in the region. Each observation in this type of analysis concerns the value of a given variable (level of conflict, regional per capita GDP, total number of alliances in the region, and so forth) at a given year.

The nature of the data require some variability in the estimation methods. Since both the number of conflict dyads and the number of war dyads are event counts, I have used Poisson event-count regression analysis to estimate these variables.[48] This method does not have a time-series version that allows to prevent violations of the serial correlation assumption. In order to minimize autocorrelation, lagged values of the dependent variables were employed. For estimation of all other dependent variables (military and civilian fatalities, defence and human military burden and weighted alliance commitments) time-series regression was used with Cochrane-Orcutt correction for serial correlation.

TABLE A.2
NATIONAL-LEVEL ANALYSIS OF FACTORS AFFECTING LEVELS OF REGIONAL SECURITY: A POOLED TIME-SERIES ANALYSIS

Independent Variable	No. Dyadic Conflict Involvements	No. Dyadic War Involvements	No. Military Fatalities	No. Civilians Fatalities
No. States in PRIE	0.077**	−0.015	63.144	281.887**
	(0.029)	(0.012)	(104.042)	(112.222)
Avg. Regime Score in PRIE	−0.000	−0.003	63.161**	−101.909**
	(0.006)	(0.002)	(22.717)	(23.959)
Regime Score	0.004*	0.0003	−14.756*	22.685**
	(0.002)	(0.0008)	(6.644)	(8.061)
Relative Nat. Capabilities	38.230**	6.741	293602**	4201.667*
	(15.807)	5.612	(58598)	(1918.41)[a]
Alliance Commitments	−0.031	0.017	−285.749+	
	(0.058)	(0.025)	(173.801)	
Lag Target	0.255**	0.119**	1139.08**	563.726**
	(0.056)	(0.024)	(132.285)	(103.555)
Lagged Per Capita GDP	−0.00001	−6.20e–06	0.008	0.027
	(0.0000)	(5.12e–06)	(0.048)	(0.068)
Alliance Commitments in PRIE	−0.013**	−0.0005	13.081	
	(0.004)	(0.001)	(16.835)	
No. Disputes in PRIE	0.017*	−0.008*	17.278	
	(0.009)	(0.003)	(25.355)	
Rev. Political Change	0.617**	0.238**	1733.31**	1624.68**
	(0.168)	(0.071)	(539.252)	(470.884)
Lagged Human Burden[1]	2.406**	12.709**	43140.1+	−174926**
	(5.460)	(2.299)	(24401.2)	(73091.4)
Lagged Pct. Urban Population	0.865*	0.484**	1385.3	1099.141
	(0.409)	(0.166)	(1524.3)	(1496.333)
Adjusted R^2	0.302	0.228	0.242	0.204
No. of Observations	397	397	397	303
No. of States	19	19	19	18

* ≤ 0.05;
** ≤ 0.01;
\+ ≤ 0.10;
a Variable used is lag defence burden.

TABLE A.3
FACTORS AFFECTING REGIONAL VIOLENCE, 1945–95

Independent Variable	No. of Conflict Dyads[1]	No. of War Dyads[1]	No. of Military Fatalities	No. of Civilian Fatalities
No. Regime Changes	0.127*	1.214**	915.170	−173.370
	(0.065)	(0.333)	(1527.848)	(1040.84)
Lagged No. of Weighted Alliances	0.021	0.137**	−290.128	−258.596
	(0.015)	(0.053)	(285.79)	(209.867)
Lagged Human Military Burden	79.230	849.670**	1711675	−2589428**
	(53.397)	(338.386)	(1081367)	(790009.1)
Lagged Defence Burden	−22.141**	−142.296*	16370.42	178674.6+
	(6.832)	(61.748)	(134091.9)	(98265.7)
Lagged Pct. Urban Population	3.262	27.132	−62112.97	52631.5
	(3.174)	20.159	(63067.04)	(48075.3)
Lagged Per Capita GDP	0.0003**	8.10e-06	5.688**	2.455*
	(0.0001)	(0.0003)	(1.380)	(1.107)
Lagged Dependent Variable	0.001	−0.197*	–	–
	(0.007)	(0.111)		
Bipolarity Score	0.531**	0.946	4475.80*	−649.995
	(0.099)	(0.606)	(1873.14)	(1455.043)
Avg. Regime Score	0.028**	0.126*	−67.167	233.285
	(0.011)	(0.065)	(215.012)	(159.428)
Adjusted R^2	0.351	0.394	0.676	0.637
F (Log-Likelihood)	−148.227**	−45.141**	12.52**	11.54**
No. of Years	50	50	49	49

Notes:
1. Poisson Event-Count Regression. Adjusted R2 is pseudo R-squared measure. See *Stata Reference Manual*, Vol.3 (College Station, TX: Stata Press 1995), pp.69–78. Lagged dependent variable is introduced to minimize serial correlation.
2. Time-Series analysis with Cochran-Orcutt Correction for autocorrelation. See *Stata Reference Manual* (note 1) Vol.2, pp.257–60.
+ $p < 0.10$
* $p < 0.05$
** $p < 0.01$

TABLE A.4
FACTORS AFFECTING MILITARY ALLOCATIONS AND ALLIANCE
COMMITMENTS OF MIDDLE EAST STATES, 1945–95

Independent Variable	Defence Burden	Human Burden	Alliance Commitments
No of States in PRIE	0.006*	0.0005**	0.084**
	0.002	(0.0001)	(0.028)
Avg. Regime Score in PRIE	–0.0013**	0.00003	–0.010·
	(0.0004)	(0.0006)	(0.006
Regime Score	–0.0006**	–0.00004**	–0.008**
	(0.0001)	(0.00001)	(0.002)
Revolutionary Change in PRIE	–0.016·	–0.0003	0.013
	(0.009)	(0.0005)	(0.080)
Lagged Capability Ratio	13.854**	0.870**	16.789
	(0.889)	(0.140)	(17.266)
Lagged Alliance Commitments	–0.017**	–0.001**	
	(0.004)	(0.0003)	
Lag Target	0.033**	0.003**	0.0003**
	(0.008)	(0.001)	(0.0001)
Per Capita GDP	1.53e-07**	2.38e-07·	1.06e-06
	(6.02E-08)	(1.32E-07)	(0.00001)
Alliance Commitments in PRIE	0.000	–0.0002*	0.038**
	(0.000)	(0.0000)	(0.000)
No. Disputes in PRIE	–0.0001	–0.0001	–0.015**
	(0.006)	(0.0002)	(0.005)
Rev. Political Change	–0.029*	–0.004**	–0.725**
	(0.013)	(0.001)	(0.106)
Adjusted R^2	0.595	0.256	0.529
No. of Observations	292	393	397
No. of States	18	18	18

TABLE A.5
FACTORS AFFECTING REGIONAL MILITARY ALLOCATIONS
AND ALLIANCE COMMITMENTS, 1945–95

Independent Variable	Defence Burden	Human Military Burden	Weighted Alliance Commitments
No. Regime Changes	0.0003	−0.0002	−0.428
	(0.002)	(0.0001)	(0.451)
Lagged No. of Weighted Alliances	−0.0001	0.0001**	
	(0.0004)	(0.000)	
Lagged Human Military Burden	2.408*		96.273
	(1.206)		(496.270)
Lagged Defence Burden		0.086**	−124.264*
		(0.015)	(63.156)
Lagged Pct. Urban Population	0.351**	−0.038**	103.972*
	(0.087)	(0.011)	(45.971)
Bipolarity Score	−0.001	0.0001	0.678
	(0.003)	(0.0003)	(1.078)
Lagged Per Capita GDP	−1.47e-06	1.04e-06**	−0.0011
	(2.21e-06)	(2.24e-07)	(0.0009)
Avg. Regime Score	0.0005	0.0003	−0.136
	(0.0003)	(0.0002)	(0.095)
Lagged Total Fatalities	1.78e-07⁺	2.00e-08*	−0.0007⁺
	(1.04e-07)	(9.50e-09)	(0.0003)
Adjusted R^2	0.491	0.483	0.170
F (Log-Likelihood)	6.78**	6.60**	2.23*
No. of Years	50	50	49

NOTES

1. This study was supported by a grant from the Foreign Ministry of Japan to the Jaffee Center for Strategic Studies. I wish to thank Gerald Sorokin for his comments. The views and analyses presented in this study are those of the author alone. Neither the Government of Japan, nor the Jaffee Center for Strategic Studies is responsible for any views or arguments made herein.
2. John D. Mearsheimer 'Back to the Future: Instability in Europe After the Cold War', *Int. Security* 15/2 (Spring 1990) pp.5–56.
3. An on-line search of the major university library catalogues in the USA and Great Britain (including Harvard, Berkeley, Stanford, Princeton, Michigan, Illinois, Chicago, Cambridge, and Oxford), as well as the *Social Science Citation Index* of the last five years reveals an amazing fact. There is a total of less than half a dozen books and articles with a title that suggests a theoretical treatment of the subject. All of the book and article titles that contain the term 'regional security' have subtitles which address specific regions, states, and a few of them deal with specific issues such as energy, arms control, etc. A recent exception is David A. Lake and Patrick Morgan (eds.) *Regional Orders: Building Security in a New World* (Harrisburg, PA: Penn State UP, forthcoming 1997).
4. Ephraim Inbar (ed.) *Regional Security Regimes: Israel and Its Neighbors* (Albany: State U of NY Press 1995).
5. Charles Lipson 'Are Security Regimes Possible? Lessons from Historical Cases and Modern Issues', in ibid. pp.3–32.
6. The definition of regimes in various issue areas is discussed at length by various contributors to Stephen D. Krasner (ed.) *International Regimes* (Ithaca, NY: Cornell UP 1983). Most importantly, see Robert Jervis, 'Security Regimes', in ibid. pp.173–94. See also Stephen Haggard and Beth Simmons, 'Theories of International Regimes', *Int. Organization* (Summer 1987) pp.491–517, as well as Patrick Morgan (note 3).
7. The most cogent statement on the need to re-define security is given by Barry Buzan, *People, States, and Fear: The National Security Problem in International Relations* (Chapel Hill: U. of N. Carolina Press 1983) esp. pp.3–13, 245–58. See also the various contributions in Edward A. Azar and Chung-in Moon (eds.) *National Security in the Third World: The Management of Internal and External Threats* (Aldershot, Hants: Edward Elgar 1988). For a more recent debate on the scope of security studies see: Stephen Walt, 'The Renaissance of Security Studies,' *Int. Studies Qtly* 35/2 (June 1991) pp.211–40; Edward A. Kologziej, 'Renaissance in Security Studies? Caveat Lector!' *Int. Studies Qtly* 36/2 (June 1992) pp.421–38; David A. Baldwin, Security Studies and the end of the Cold War,' *World Politics* 71/1 (Oct. 1995) pp.117–41, as well as the books reviewed in this article.
8. See Buzan (note 7) as well as the other sources in the previous note for a discussion of the state of knowledge on definitions of security. On definitions of regional systems, see – among others – Bruce Russett, *International Regions and the International System: A Study in Political Ecology* (Chicago: Rand McNally 1967). Louis J. Cantori and Steven L. Spiegel, 'The International Relations of Regions', *Polity* 2/4 (Dec. 1970) pp.397–425. Michael Brecher, 'The Middle East Subordinate System and Its Impact on Israel's Foreign Policy,' *Int. Studies Qtly* 13/1 (March 1969). For a recent review of this issue see David A. Lake, 'Regional Relations: A Systems Approach', in Lake and Morgan (note 3). Lake also offers a new conceptualization of regions based on 'externalities,' that is, costs or benefits accrued to states as a result of action by other states. This is a useful step toward the conception presented below.
9. A hint to the usefulness of this analogy is given by Lynn E. Miller, 'The Prospect for Order through Regional Security', in Richard A. Falk and Saul H. Mendlowvitz (eds), *Regional Politics and World Order* (San Francisco: W. H. Freeman 1973) pp.61–5.
10. Charles S. Gochman and Zeev Maoz, 'Militarize Interstate Disputes, 1816–1976: Procedures, Patterns, Insights', *Jnl of Conflict Resolution* 28/4 (Dec. 1984) pp.585–615. See also Charles S. Gochman, 'The Escalation of Militarized Disputes', *Int. Interactions* 19/2–3 (June–Sept. 1993), Zeev Maoz, 'The Onset and Initiation of Militarized Interstate Disputes in the Modern Era', ibid. 19/2–3 (June–Sept. 1993) pp.117–41.

11. On the move towards increased regionalism in world politics, mostly in international security problems, see also Oran R. Young, 'Political Discontinuities in the International System', *World Politics* 20/3 (June 1968) pp.369–92; and Miller (note 9) pp.51–3.
12. Members of a community may organize not only against crime committed by people who come from the outside. One neighbourhood within a community may collectively organize against crime emanating from within the community, and they may adopt the same individual or collective measures to defend themselves against intruders, be they from the outside or the inside.
13. Buzan (note 7) pp.13–15.
14. Whether or not these conflicts are against other members of the region or against non-regional actors.
15. One may object to the contention that regional institutionalization is an indicator of *insecurity* rather than of security. The literature on the impact of international institutions on the conduct of international relations, in general, and on international security, in particular, is too large to be considered here. It is important to note, however, that this question is the focus of yet another debate between neorealist and liberal perspectives of international politics. See John D. Mearsheimer, 'The False Promise of International Institutions', *Int. Security* 19/3 (Winter 1994/95) pp.5–48, and responses by Robert Keohane and Lisa L Martin, 'The Promise of Institutional Theory', ibid. 20/1 (Summer 1995) pp.39–51, and Charles A. Kupchan and Clifford A. Kupchan, 'The Promise of Collective Security', ibid. pp.52–61. See Mearsheimer's response, 'A Realist Reply', ibid. pp.82–93. My own position is that this is an empirical question that has yet to be resolved. The fact that security-related institutionalization suggests security problems is a reflection of the fact that both alliances and collective security institutions emerge when members share threat perceptions and a need for collective efforts to thwart common threats.
16. See Russet, *International Regions* (note 8); Miller, Cantori and Spiegel (note 8) and Kay Boals, 'The Concept of Subordinate International System: A Critique', in Richard A. Falk and Saul H. Mendlovitz (eds.) *Regional Politics and World Order* (San Francisco: W.H. Freeman 1973) pp.399–410.
17. See Russett, Cantori and Spiegel, Brecher (note 8), Leonard Binder, 'The Middle East Subordinate International System', *World Politics* 10/3 (April 1958) pp.408–29; Gochman and Maoz (note 10). The empirical analysis of international conflict and crises also exhibits considerable agreement on the composition of the Middle East. See Michael Brecher, *Crises in World Politics: Theory and Reality* (NY: Pergamon Press 1993) esp. pp.70–3. J. David Singer and Melvin Small, *Resort to Arms Civil and International War, 1815-1980* (Beverly Hills, CA: Sage 1982).
18. The Correlates of War list of Interstate System Members (see Singer and Small, *supra*) defines as states belonging to the Middle East all states with nation numbers ranging from 600 to 699. This is the most widely accepted formulation of international system membership – as well as the most widely accepted breakdown to regional systems – in the empirical analysis of international politics. See the appendix for the list of these states.
19. Buzan (note 7) pp.105–6. A security complex is defined as: 'a group of states whose primary security concerns link together sufficiently closely that their national securities cannot realistically be considered apart from one another.' Using a different concept, Politically Relevant International Environment (PRIE), I have defined the strategic reference group of states as made up of all states contiguous to the focal state and all major powers and regional powers. From this perspective a region is composed of states with substantially overlapping PRIEs, that seem to share the same security concerns from a fundamentally-similar environment. See Zeev Maoz, *Domestic Sources of Global Change* (Ann Arbor: U. of Michigan Press 1996) pp.136–42.
20. See Azar and Moon (note 7) pp.25–7 for a discussion of the differences between realist and Third World approaches to regional security. Also Mohamed Ayoob, *The Third World Security Predicament: State Making, Regional Conflict and the International System* (Boulder, CO: Lynne Rienner 1995).
21. Maoz, *Domestic Source* (note 19) Chs.4, 6.

22. See Zeev Maoz, 'The Evolution of the Middle East Military Balance, 1980–1995', in Ephraim Kam and Zeev Eytan (eds.) *The Middle East Military Balance, 1994–95* (Jerusalem/Boulder, CO: Jerusalem Post and Westview Press 1996).
23. On military regimes in the Third World see Samuel Finer, *The Man on Horseback* (London: Pall Mall Press 1962); Amos Perlmutter, *The Military and Politics in Modern Times: On Professionals, Praetorians and Revolutionary Soldiers* (New Haven, CL: Yale UP 1977). On military and politics in Israel see Yoram Peri *Between Battles and Ballots: The Military and Politics in Israel* (Cambridge: CUP 1983), Yehuda Ben-Meir, *Civil-Military Relations in Israel* (NY: Columbia UP 1995).
24. In per-capita terms the Middle East armed forces have slowly declined since the early 1990s.
25. See Maoz, 'Evolution' (note 22), Yiftah Shafir, 'Ballistic Missiles in the Middle East', in Kam and Eytan (note 22), and Shai Feldman, *Nuclear Proliferation and Arms Control in the Middle East* (Cambridge, MA: MIT Press 1996).
26. The theoretical and empirical literature on alliances in world politics is too vast to be considered here. However, the reader is referred to several good sources which summarize the issues of alliances, see: Ole Holsti, Randolph Siverson, and Alexander George, *Change in the International System* (Boulder, CO: Westview Press 1980); Michael Don Ward, *Research Gaps in Alliance Dynamics* (Denver, CO: Denver Monograph Series in World Affairs 1982), and especially Steven Walt, *The Origins of Alliance* (Ithaca, NY: Cornell UP 1987) which deals with alliances in the Middle East.
27. I emphasise the word *a chance* because the questions of whether institutions or alliances actually promote security is an open one. For alliances, there is a serious questions of reliability, that is, the likelihood that alliance members would actually fulfill their treaty obligations when push comes to shove. On this issue see Harvey Starr, *The Reliability of Alliances* (Lexington, MA.: D.C. Heath 1974), and idem and Randolph Siverson *The Diffusion of War: A Study of Opportunity and Willingness* (Ann Arbor: U. Michigan Press 1991). Also, both institutions and alliances may implicate their members in unwanted conflicts and other dilemmas. See Glenn D. Snyder, 'The Alliance Dilemma in World Politics', *World Politics*, (1984), and Zeev Maoz, *Paradoxes of War: On the Art of National Self-Entrapment* (Boston, MA: Unwin Hyman 1990) Ch.7.
28. See Michael Altfeld and Bruce Bueno de Mesquita, 'Choosing Sides in War', *Int. Studies Qtly* 23/1 (March 1979) pp.87–112. Michael Altfeld, 'The Decision to Ally', ibid. 27/4 (Dec. 1984) pp.523–44; Maoz, *Paradoxes of War* (note 27) pp.193–215.
29. For an analysis of changes in the Military Balance in the Arab-Israeli context see Maoz, 'Evolution' (note 22). This analysis which suggests that the Arab-Israeli military confrontation may be winding down, nevertheless does warn of the so-called missile race which even at this level is very disconcerting.
30. For a more general analysis of factors affecting national strategic behaviour see Maoz, 'The Strategic Behaviour of Nations, 1816–1990', Mimeographed, Jaffee Center for Strategic Studies 1996, and Maoz, *Domestic Sources* (note 22) Ch.5. These two sources contain a more elaborate discussions of national-level security models.
31. For broad surveys of the literature on these subjects see Ted Robert Gurr (ed.) *Handbook of Social Conflict* (NY: Free Press 1980), and, more recently, a special issue of *Int. Interactions* 19/2–3 (Sept. 1993).
32. See Maoz, 'Strategic Behaviour (note 30), and Maoz, *Domestic Sources* (note 19) Ch.5.
33. See Michael D. Wallace, 'Arms Races and Escalation: Some New Evidence', *Jnl of Conflict Resolution* 23/1 (March 1979) pp.3–16, and Paul F. Diehl, 'Arms Races and Escalation: A Closer Look', *Jnl of Peace Research* 20/3. (Oct. 1983) pp.205–12.
34. See Walt, *Origins of Alliance* (note 26). Also, Ido Oren 'The War Proneness of Alliances', *Jnl of Conflict Resolution* 34/2 (June 1990) pp.208–33.
35. See James Lee Ray, *Democracy and International Conflict* (Columbia: U. of S. Carolina Press 1995) for a review of the literature. Also, Zeev Maoz. 'The Renewed Controversy Over the Democratic Peace Result: Rearguard Action or Cracks in the Wall?' *Int. Security* 23/1 (July 1997).
36. Stephen Walt, *Revolution and War* (Ithaca, NY: Cornell UP 1996); Edward D. Mansfield and Jack Snyder, 'The Effects of Democratization on War', *Int. Security* 21/4 (Winter 1996);

idem, 'Democratization and the Danger of War,' ibid. 20/1 (Summer 1995) pp.5–38; Zeev Maoz, 'Joining the Club of Nations: Political Development and International Conflict', *Int. Studies Qtly* 33/2 (June 1989) pp.199–231.
37. See Zeev Maoz and Bruce Russett, 'Normative and Structural Causes of Democratic Peace', *American Political Science Review* 87/3 (Sept. 1993) pp.624–38; John Oneal, Frances Oneal, Zeev Maoz ,and Bruce Russett, 'The Liberal Peace: Economic Interdependence, Democracy, and International Conflict', *Jnl of Peace Research* 33/1 (Feb. 1996) pp.11–28.
38. It must be noted that alliance commitments have a marginally insignificant positive effect on the severity of conflicts in terms of military fatalities, but tend to reduce the extent of civilian fatalities in the region.
39. Other factors include depletion of natural resources, such as water, fundamentalism, and general – non material – quality of life issues.
40. For data and additional details on these issues, see Maoz, 'Evolution' (note 22), S. Even, 'Middle East Economic Patterns', in Mark A. Heller (ed.) *The Middle East Military Balance, 1995–1996* (NY: Columbia UP forthcoming 1997).
41. These problems represent only a fraction of the problems of Middle East economies. For a cogent analysis of these broader issues see Alan Richards and John Waterbury, *A Political Economy of the Middle East* (Boulder, CO: Westview Press 1990), and Alan Richards, 'Economic Imperatives and Political Systems', *Middle East Jnl* 47/2 (Spring 1993) pp.217–27.
42. A regime change is defined as a basic shift in the structure of authority and in the relations between political institutions and society in a given state. See Maoz, *Domestic Sources* (note 22) Ch.6.
43. For an important analysis of the relationship between economic processes and political instability in the Middle East see Alan Richards, 'Economic Roots of Instability in the Middle East', *Middle East Policy* 4/1–2 (Sept. 1995) pp.175–87.
44. For operational definitions see the above sources as well as Maoz, 'The Renewed Controversy...' Appendix.
45. See, Benjamin Miller, *When Opponents Cooperate* (Ann Arbor: U. of Michigan Press 1995).
46. This dataset is described in Robert Summers and Alan Heston, 'The Penn World Trade Data', *Qtly Jnl of Economics* (May 1991).
47. For a more elaborate discussion of these issues see Maoz, 'Strategic Behaviour of Nations, (note 30).
48. See Gary King, *Unifying Political Methodology* (NY: Cambridge UP 1989), and G.S. Maddala, *Limited Dependent and Qualitative Variables in Econometrics* (ibid. 1983) pp.51–4.

Patrons, Clients, and Allies in the Arab–Israeli Conflict

GERALD L. SOROKIN

Since ancient times, states have occasionally formed alliances to pool their military capabilities in the face of foreign policy contingencies. Since the international system is anarchic, alliances are perplexing: if there is no global sovereign to enforce agreements, why do states entrust their security to promises of support from other states? One answer is that states naturally coalesce to balance against potential hegemons by forming alliances that are more powerful than any one state.[1] Alliances are therefore necessary because the stability of the international system and the survival of at least the largest states are of paramount importance. This argument makes sense when applied to major powers, for whom the salient political environment is the global distribution of power. But most states do not operate in the global political and military theatre. Instead, they limit their attention to security challenges within their own geographic regions. Military and political relations in a regional context are therefore different from – and, in many ways, more complex than – global power balancing.

Several notable studies go beyond the global balance of power arguments to examine alliance formation among states in regions like the Middle East. Walt's widely-cited book[2] argues that states balance threat – that is, they look at both the capabilities and the intentions of potential rivals to determine whether alliances are necessary. In Walt's words, 'balance of threat theory predicts that when there is an imbalance of threat (i.e. when one state or coalition appears especially dangerous), states will form alliances or increase their internal efforts in order to reduce their vulnerability'.[3] This prediction suggests three additional questions: (1) what is an alliance; (2) how do states decide whether to rely on alliances or internal means like military personnel and weaponry; and (3) what is the connection between alliances and internal efforts? Walt does not address these questions directly: his definition of alliance blurs the distinction between patron-client relationships and alliances; he does not explain how states decide between alliances and internal means; and, consequently, he implicitly overstates the degree to which alliance policies affect arms acquisition policies.

In this analysis, I demonstrate that alliances have been rare in the Middle East conflict, because states in the region typically prefer to pursue independent security policies using the assistance of outside patrons. Unlike Walt, I limit my use of the term 'alliance' to formal promises of military support. Informal relationships that entail the actual provision of political, economic, and military assistance are 'patron-client' relationships. The difference between alliances and patron-client relationships is not merely semantic. The costs of alliance support are often greater than the costs of aid from a patron, meaning that, where possible, states involved in regional conflicts will form patron-client relationships with outside major powers. Thus, although the desire for security pushes states to seek access to military capabilities, it will lead to alliances only if the allies are expected to be reliable, the states lack access to the means to defend themselves, and the autonomy costs the alliances entail are low.[4]

After discussing the theoretical relationships surrounding alliances and patron-client relationships, I examine the Cold War-era security policies of Israel and Syria, which applied various approaches to managing their conflict, ranging from independent arms-based policies to reliance on major power patrons to alliances with other regional powers. They altered their policies as regional and global political circumstances changed and as the relative effectiveness of existing policies became evident. Far from being a straightforward example of alliance politics, the Arab–Israeli conflict has been characterized by a complex variety of political and military variables. In fact, Israel's desire to remain *unallied*, the dissolution of the alliance between Egypt and Syria, and the changing role of the superpowers are among the most prominent factors underlying the region's political history.

Security Options in a Regional Context

In many ways, a regional balance of power system resembles the global system. It may be bipolar or multipolar, depending on the number of regional powers and the ways they aggregate; arms races and military conflicts occasionally occur. In these respects, theoretical arguments and empirical findings from studies of the global system are relevant to understanding regional conflicts. For example, Kaplan's model of a balance of power system suggests that an alliance is often useful for preventing domination by one state because an aspiring global hegemon cannot defeat a coalition of other major powers.[5] Similarly, an alliance of regional powers may counter a potential regional hegemon.

Walt argues convincingly that threat balancing in a regional conflict differs from balancing in the global context:

> Although the superpowers seek allies in order to balance against those with the largest capabilities, less capable states within a given region, such as the Middle East, seek allies primarily to balance against those who are close by ... Regional powers seek allies against one another both because their neighbors are more dangerous [than global powers] and because their responses can make a difference.[6]

But even though regional powers do not normally balance against actors from outside the system, they often rely on outside states' assistance to achieve their security goals. Specifically, non-regional powers may provide money, military hardware, training, or even active personnel to one or more states in the region. Whether this assistance comes in the form of formal alliances or informal agreements, it creates an additional consideration that regional powers must take into account when assessing threats and capabilities. Not only must states balance against threats posed by their neighbors' current capabilities, they must also anticipate the involvement of outside actors, especially major powers. Therefore, the security dilemma[7] – that actions taken to increase the security of one state reduce the security of others – is even more acute in a regional context than in a global context.

Scholars disagree about what constitutes an alliance. For some authors, including Bercovitch and Walt, virtually any formal or informal military-political agreement among states qualifies as an alliance.[8] I prefer Kegley and Raymond's definition, which says that alliances are 'formal agreements between sovereign states for the putative purpose of coordinating their behavior in the event of specified contingencies of a military nature'.[9] Although informal relationships are important, a formal agreement is likely to have a more significant impact on issues like deterrence. As Siverson and Starr point out:

> Alliances may add precision to state relations and thus make a deterrent threat clearer (and more credible); the aggregation of the military capabilities of several states may also make deterrent threats more credible.[10]

Since violating an informal agreement is likely to be less costly to a state's reputation than violating a written pact, formal agreements should be expected to offer a more credible deterrent.

There is empirical evidence for the importance of formal alliance ties. For example, Huth and Russett find that, although an alliance between the defender and its protege does not increase the probability of extended immediate deterrence success, alliances are strongly related to intervention.[11] Kim shows that formal alliances also have an impact on great power war.[12] Altfeld and Bueno de Mesquita show that the similarity of alliance portfolios, rather than actual alliance ties, predicts third party interventions in wars.[13] In sum, while formal alliances do not play a unique or necessary role in binding states together, the difference between alliances and informal alignments is significant.

The primary argument here is that regional powers often prefer to receive assistance from large states located outside the region. Although asymmetric alliances are one policy option for these states, they are rarely adopted. Much more common are patron-client relationships, which, in Bercovitch's words, 'are based on informal understandings, trust, loyalty, solidarity and shared interests' but 'are not fully legal or contractual'. Instead, the large (global) power provides military, economic, or diplomatic aid to the smaller (regional) power without formally committing to military involvement, neutrality, or consultation.[14] As Lipson suggests, 'informal agreements are often chosen because they allow governments to act quickly and quietly [and because] they are more easily renegotiated and less costly to abandon than treaties'.[15]

In a patron-client relationship, both states normally expect to gain: although the patron gives up economic or military goods, its benefits may include access to new markets for its exports and a broader international political coalition (or, perhaps, a narrower coalition for its primary adversary). These benefits were particularly important to the United States and Soviet Union during the Cold War. The client's costs in such a relationship are often rather small. In fact, the smaller member of a patron-client relationship often has a bargaining *advantage* because of its ability to turn to another patron if it is unsatisfied with its current level of support.[16] In short, a patron-client relationship is likely to involve significantly smaller sacrifices by the client than an asymmetric alliance between a regional power and a global power.[17] If an informal relationship with a patron provides a small state with sufficient security, then a full-fledged alliance is unlikely to exist.

How do regional powers choose among the possible responses to security challenges?[18] A state may respond to a threat posed by its neighbor by either maintaining its current capabilities, augmenting its capabilities, or using force. In the first approach, the state adds no new capabilities in hopes that its existing level is sufficient to deter or repel a possible attack. In the second, it attempts to increase its capabilities in order to improve its ability to deter. There are at least four ways for a state to augment its capabilities: (a) expand the size of its active armed forces; (b) produce additional military hardware domestically; (c) seek additional military hardware through purchases or grants from an external patron; (d) form new alliances or tighten existing alliances to receive promises of greater protection from other states. Finally, in the third approach, the state uses force against its adversary, removing the source of the threat directly instead of attempting to deter an attack.

In evaluating each of these policy options, a state must determine how well equipped it is to adopt the policy, the economic and political costs the policy entails, and the probability that the policy will succeed in deterring attacks and improving security. The advantages of one policy option are often offset by its disadvantages. The problem for policy-makers, then, is a constrained optimization: they want to acquire as much security as possible, subject to limits imposed by their resources and the costs of the policy.[19]

INDEPENDENT VARIABLES CONTRIBUTING TO SECURITY

Four broad independent variables contribute to a state's security policy. The first is its *capabilities*, relative to its adversary's. Empirical studies have shown that acquiring additional capabilities increases states' probability of deterring attacks successfully[20] and of winning wars if deterrence fails.[21] All else being equal, more capabilities – whether their own, their patron's, or their ally's – are preferable to less capabilities.

Although each of the policy options designed to augment a state's capabilities has the potential to increase its security, their likely impacts are unequal. Specifically, because a state is constrained by its population size, level of economic development, and natural resource endowment, the internally-based approaches of expanding the armed forces and producing additional weapons are often insufficient. This is why few small states are truly autarkic militarily.

Patron-client relationships can give the state access to arms that they could not produce domestically and the financial means to purchase arms that would otherwise be unavailable. Yet a client state may still be unable to meet its needs because of such constraints as the level of training of its military personnel and geographic limitations on its ability to project force.

Alliances, especially defense pacts, can provide the greatest increase in capabilities, as long as there exist both the infrastructure and the time necessary for the allies to bring their troops and weaponry to the site of the conflict. Consider the 1991 Gulf War: the United States and other non-regional powers formed an alliance with Saudi Arabia to help deter Iraq from invading Saudi Arabia (and, of course, to compel Iraq to withdraw from Kuwait). By January 1991, the United States and the other members of the coalition had brought enough forces to the Middle East to increase significantly Saudi Arabia's ability to fight against Iraq. Had Iraq attacked Saudi Arabia in August 1990, immediately after it occupied Kuwait, the Saudis would not have been able to rely on the contributions of any non-regional partners. But alliances have another drawback: even if they have the capacity and time to move troops, allies may abandon each other, thus failing to meet their obligations and providing no additional security.[22] This uncertainty about whether alliances will be honored makes them both potentially effective, if an adversary decides not to risk fighting an alliance, and potentially unreliable.

The second variable that affects a state's security policy is external *threat*. This variable is more than the adversary's military capabilities. As Walt argues, 'the level of threat states pose ... [entails their] aggregate power, geographic proximity, offensive powers, and aggressive intentions'.[23] An increase in the level of external threat leads to a reduction in security, all else being equal.

Changes in external threat may be associated in predictable ways with different security policies. The sharper the increase in threat, the greater the urgency to respond to it. Since alliances have the potential to generate large increases in capabilities in a relatively short time, they are likely to be the most effective means of responding to high-urgency threats like the one the Saudis faced after Iraq's invasion of Kuwait. By contrast, gradual increases in threats, or sustained, long-term threats, might be expected to lead to patron-client relationships or internally-based security policies in which the state eventually acquires additional arms or personnel without making the political sacrifices that alliances often entail.

The third variable that affects a state's security policy is the state's *resources*, meaning the political and economic means on which to draw in order to change its policy. Specifically, a state whose government is considered legitimate by both its citizens and the governments of other countries has greater 'political capital' than one that lacks legitimacy. Similarly, a state with a large and growing economy can afford to purchase arms, offer financial incentives to potential allies, and take greater political risks than one that is unable to meet its society's basic economic demands. Resources and capabilities are not identical; resources provide states with the potential to acquire capabilities, but those resources might be devoted to purchases that are not related to military affairs.

The final variable that affects a state's security policy is the *cost* of the security policy. Internally-based security policies have obvious political and economic costs associated with them. Raising and sustaining an army can make leaders unpopular, especially when they impose conscription laws.

Similarly, weapons production can be a drain on the national economy, diverting economic resources from civilian needs.[24]

The costs of a patron-client relationship are somewhat more complex. They depend on the nature of the political demands that the patron makes, as well as the ability of the client to meet the economic burden imposed by the relationship. In many cases, most clearly the United States and Israel, the client's costs are relatively low, in part because of the patron's interest in the political gains the relationship might produce. In other cases, such as the Soviet Union and Egypt, the client's costs were higher, leading ultimately to a dissolution of the patron-client relationship.

The most complex policy from the standpoint of costs is one based on alliances. Much of the alliance literature treats security as a collective good and focuses on the ability of small states to receive a 'free ride' by relying on the military contributions of their allies without paying the economic costs associated with arms.[25] But this is only half of the story: alliances often involve serious political concessions, especially in asymmetric alliances where the smaller state trades autonomy for security.[26] The cost of these trades varies according to the degree of political concessions the larger ally is demanding, the urgency of the threat, and the alternative policy choices available to the state. Even complex, multilateral alliances like NATO involve political concessions from the smaller state. Although the United States contributes a larger proportion of NATO's capabilities (even adjusted for population or gross national product) than any other member, the political costs that its allies bear are often significant. The NATO allies give up much of their decisional latitude because of the US hegemonic position,[27] leaving their leaders less flexibility in foreign policy choices.

Empirical Analysis

Because of the variation in both the content and the context of Syrian and Israeli security policy, the Middle East, between the early 1960s and early 1990s, is an appropriate domain in which to apply a theory of arms acquisition and alliance formation. The countries used a variety of approaches, including independence, reliance on a patron, and close alliance. The factors underlying these choices illustrate some broader tendencies in regional security policy.

Statistical analysis and case studies each offer advantages as empirical methodologies,[28] so I use both approaches to describe and explain the security policies of Syria and Israel. The statistical analysis reveals some systematic patterns in the security policies of both Syria and Israel. As one would expect, their military expenditures rise in response to increases in their adversaries' expenditures. There is also evidence that military expenditures rise when resources rise, but the Israeli results are somewhat ambiguous on this point. The impact of military imports is unclear for both countries. Major changes in the nature of their relations with patrons – due to the Camp David agreement and the emergence of a new Soviet foreign policy under Gorbachev – had a marked impact on military expenditures. Finally, there is evidence of some substitution between Syria and its ally, Egypt, before the Camp David agreement, and then stronger evidence of inter-Arab arms racing after Camp David.

VARIABLE MEASUREMENT

The dependent variable in the theoretical argument is security policy; the independent variables are military capabilities, threat, resources, and costs. Measuring security policy is straightforward, given the definitions of alliances and patron-client relationships I use. If a state signs an agreement to coordinate its military policies with another, then it is in an alliance. If one state provides another with military or economic assistance, then a patron-client relationship exists. The closeness of the relationship may be measured by the quantity of arms transfers and economic aid from the patron to the client each year. Finally, a state that has no close ties to the outside, or severely reduces its existing ties, is following an independent security policy.

There are numerous ways to measure military capabilities, none of which capture all salient aspects. For the purposes of this analysis, I look at changes in levels of military spending.[29] Most of the data come from the annual or biennial publications of the US Arms Control and Disarmament Agency (ACDA).[30] ACDA presents its data in both current year and constant dollars; since I am interested in changes over time, I focus on the constant-dollar data. For Syria, ACDA's data are incomplete, so I supplement them with figures from *The Middle East Military Balance*.[31] I illustrate Israel's, Egypt's, and Syria's military expenditures in Figure 1. All three countries' expenditures rose gradually until the late 1970s, when they increased dramatically, especially in Israel and Syria, and then leveled off in the 1980s.

The threat variable includes the adversary's military capabilities, as well as informal indicators of their intentions. When the adversary's capabilities rise or its intentions appear to be more hostile, then the threat is greater. In the Arab–Israeli conflict, geographic factors are relatively constant, with the important exceptions of the territorial transfers that occurred following the Six Day War of 1967 and the Israel-Egypt peace treaty of 1979.

I use two measures of resources: (1) economic activity, as indicated by real gross or domestic product (these data come from ACDA and the International Monetary Fund and are reported in constant dollars);[32] (2)

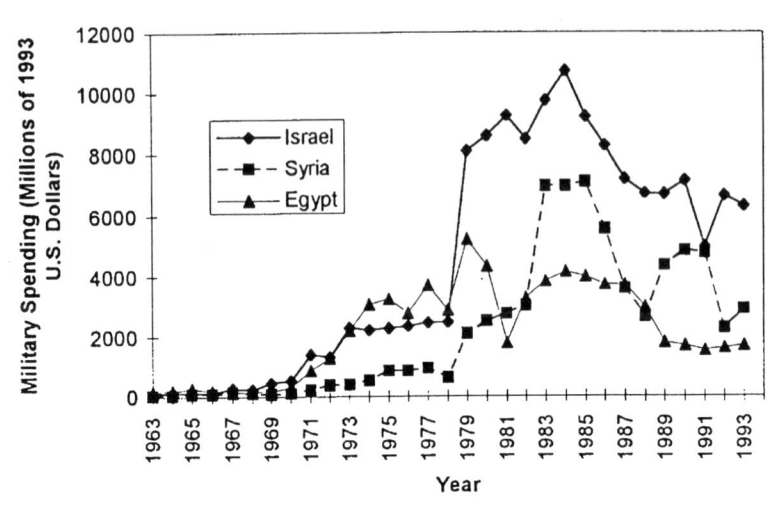

FIGURE 1
MILITARY EXPENDITURES OF ISRAEL, EGYPT, AND SYRIA,
1963-93

Sources: US Arms Control and Disarmament Agency, *World Military Expenditures and Arms Transfers* (Washington, DC: US Government Printing Office, various years 1974–1995); Shlomo Gazit and Zeev Eytan, *The Middle East Military Balance, 1993–1994* (Boulder, CO: Westview 1994); Gazit and Eytan, *The Middle East Military Balance, 1994–1995* (forthcoming).

changes in the internal political situation in the countries. The Israeli government has always been considered legitimate by its own citizenry and by the countries that could serve as its patrons or allies. That it was not considered legitimate by its neighbors or by many of the Arab residents has not effectively reduced its political resources. By contrast, the government of Syria has faced threats of military coups and assassination, sometimes making it difficult to adopt risky policies.

The cost variables are perhaps the most difficult to measure directly. Internal policies, based on expanding the size of the armed forces or producing more arms, involve opportunity costs that are not observable. These security costs involve more than merely adding salaries, raw materials, research and development, etc. In a patron-client relationship or alliance, the exact costs are often hidden from both participants and analysts. But large changes in costs may be apparent. For example, John Foster Dulles might have been willing to make a security guarantee to Israel in the mid-1950s, but only in the context of a regional alliance like the Baghdad Pact.[33] Such an arrangement was not politically feasible for Israel, in part because it would have entailed cooperating with states that refused to recognize its existence, so the cost of such an alliance was too high. By contrast, the military and economic assistance that the United States provided to Israel in the 1970s had only low-cost conditions attached, making the policy more appealing to the Israeli government. A similar change in the costs of Soviet patronage occurred for Syria with the shift in Soviet foreign policy associated with Gorbachev's consolidation of power after 1985. A similar argument may be made concerning alliance costs. After the Camp David Accords, for example, the cost to Syria of continuing its alliance to Egypt involved at least a tacit recognition of the agreement, which had political and military implications that Syria's leadership considered undesirable. Therefore, even though it is not possible to measure precisely the change in the cost of the alliance, it is clear that it rose after Camp David.

Statistical Analysis

Before presenting the case studies of Syrian and Israeli security policies, I present a statistical analysis of the direction and strength of the relationships between the independent variables and each country's military expenditures. Although the dependent variable in the statistical analysis is narrower than the one in the theoretical section, it is an appropriate starting point for testing the hypotheses. First, changes in military spending are evidence of changes in overall security policy, so the statistical results have some external validity on their own. Second, these results serve as the foundation for the case studies later in the study. Finally, my statistical analysis complements previous econometric studies of Middle Eastern military expenditures.[34]

The general statistical equations take the following form:

$$\text{Military Expenditures} = \alpha + \beta_1 (\text{Threat}) + \beta_2 (\text{Resources}) + \beta_3 (\text{Ally's Capabilities}) + \beta_4 (\text{Military Imports}) + \varepsilon \quad (1)$$

The data are presented in constant, 1993 US dollars. The dependent variable is annual military expenditures. The independent variables are all lagged one year to indicate that the impact of such things as adversaries' expenditures and changes in resources is not instantaneous. The threat variable is the sum of military expenditures of the adversary, which for Syria was Israel and for Israel was both Egypt and Syria between 1963 and 1977 and Syria alone thereafter. Resources are indicated by annual real GNP or GDP data. The ally's capabilities variable appears only in the Syrian equation and consists of Egyptian military expenditures. Since the

Syria-Egypt alliance ended in 1978, I estimate an additional coefficient in the Syrian equation for Egyptian military expenditures after the alliance, as well as a dummy variable for the post-Camp David period, in order to determine whether the relationship changes. Finally, military imports include the value of military transfers from all sources, although the vast majority of those transfers come from the patron (the United States for Israel; the Soviet Union for Syria). I illustrate Israel's and Syria's military imports in Figure 2. As the figure shows, both countries' imports rose sharply in the early 1980s, following the peace treaty between Egypt and Israel. As I discuss later, this rise in imports reflected both the changing security situation in the region – Syria was no longer able to rely on promises of Egyptian support, so it imported additional armaments – and the nature of superpower influence both leading to and resulting from Camp David.

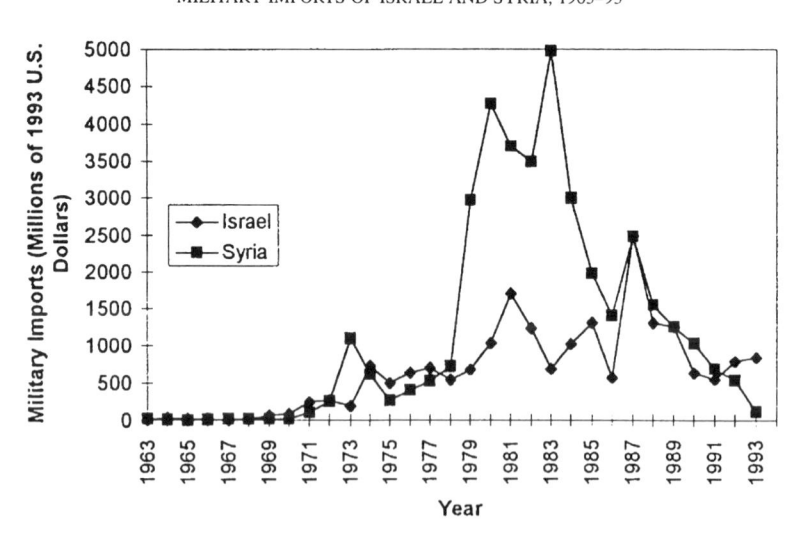

FIGURE 2
MILITARY IMPORTS OF ISRAEL AND SYRIA, 1963–93

Source: US Arms Control and Disarmament Agency, *World Military Expenditures and Arms Transfers* (Washington DC: US Government Printing Office, various years 1974–1995).

SYRIA

Table 1 displays the generalized least squares results for Syrian military expenditures.[35] The results of this regression are consistent with my theoretical argument. First, a million dollar increase in Israeli military expenditures is associated with a $340,000 increase in Syrian spending: evidence of regional arms racing. Second, Syria's real gross national product yields a $100,000 increase in its military expenditures, all else held constant. Third, although there does not appear to be significant evidence of substitution between Egyptian and Syrian arms while they were allies, there is fairly strong evidence of arms racing between them after Egypt concluded its pact with Israel (a million dollar increase in Egyptian spending is associated with an almost half million dollar increase in Syrian spending). Finally, the change in Soviet leadership that followed Gorbachev's rise is associated with a decline of over $1 billion per year in Syrian military expenditures. The change in the nature of Syria's patron-client relationship clearly affected its ability to arm itself. The other variables are not statistically or substantively significant.

TABLE 1
GENERALIZED LEAST SQUARES REGRESSION OF
SYRIAN MILITARY EXPENDITURES, 1963–93

Variable Name	Estimated Coefficient[a]	Standard Error	T-Ratio
Constant	−697.56	119.61	−0.58
Israeli Military Expenditures	0.35*	0.20	1.73
Syrian Gross National Product	0.10	0.08	1.23
Egyptian Military Expenditure	−0.22	0.30	−0.71
Egyptian Military Expenditures Post-Camp David Years	0.46	0.29	1.57
Syrian Military Imports	−0.26	0.35	−0.76
Gorbachev and Post-Cold War Period	−1173.70	1039.70	−1.13
R-squared	0.54		
Adjusted R-squared	0.41		
Standard Error of the Estimate	1007.1		

a. Asterisks indicate variables statistically significant with $p < 0.05$, one-tailed test.

ISRAEL

Table 2 presents the results of a generalized least squares regression of Israeli military expenditures. The results of the regression are also consistent with the theory, although the statistical significance levels of many of the coefficients are low. First, Israel reacts positively to increases in the external threat. This variable is the sum of the predicted Egyptian capabilities, before 1978, and predicted Syrian military capabilities, throughout the period. Each million dollar increase in its adversaries' military expenditures yields an increase of $200,000 in Israel's expenditures, all else held constant.[36] Second, although the results are

TABLE 2
GENERALIZED LEAST SQUARES REGRESSION OF ISRAELI
MILITARY EXPENDITURES, 1963–93

Variable Name	Estimated Coefficient[a]	Standard Error	T-Ratio
Constant	967.63	1261.62	0.77
Egyptian and Syrian Military Expenditures	0.20	0.15	1.37
Israeli Gross National Product	0.06	0.22	0.28
Israeli GNP, post-Camp David	−0.08	0.23	−0.35
Israeli Military Imports	0.03	1.88	−0.02
Israeli Military Imports, post-Camp David	0.07	1.92	0.04
Post-Camp David Period	6684.04*	1715.14	3.90
R-squared	0.75		
Adjusted R-squared	0.68		
Standard Error of the Estimate	818.54		

a. Asterisks indicate variables statistically significant with $p < 0.05$, one-tailed test.

statistically weak, it appears that the impact of resources on military spending changed for Israel with the Camp David agreement. Before Camp David, the coefficient is negative, suggesting that weakness was associated with the need for military spending; afterwards, the impact of GNP goes to zero (the sum of the two coefficients), meaning that resources were not relevant once Israel's ties to its patron, the United States, were stronger. Third, that patron-client relationship shows up in other ways, as well. Israeli military spending rises sharply after the Camp David agreement, when there is an increase of over $6.5 billion per year. This is strong evidence of the impact of the increased commitment from the United States to Israeli security. The marginal impact of arms imports on military expenditures, both before and after Camp David, is statistically insignificant, largely because the other variables capture much of that effect.

Case Studies

The statistical analysis is a useful starting point for testing the theory. But because of measurement problems and the relatively narrow coding of the dependent variable, I complement the statistical results with a more detailed discussion of each of the cases. Together, the two empirical sections add up to a thorough illustration of the relationships among the variables in the theory.

SYRIA

After the break with Egypt that followed the dissolution of the United Arab Republic in 1961, Syria began once again to pursue its own security policy. According to Evron, it was not interested in challenging the territorial status quo with regard to Israel in the mid-1960s. The Syrians preferred 'to avoid a major confrontation with a potentially high cost' because of Israel's military advantage and Syria's general foreign policy interest in avoiding war.[37] Annual Syrian military expenditures between 1963 and 1966 were quite stable, as Figure 1 indicates. Syrian governments before 1966 were interested in legitimizing Syrian independence while remaining loyal to the principle of Arab unity.[38] Therefore, even if the Syrian government had wanted to challenge the status quo regarding relations with Israel, domestic politics made that possibility unrealistic. In 1966, however, the 'old guard' of the Syrian Ba'th party was ousted in a *coup d'etat* by a group of radical neo-Ba'thists. Walt says that the new leaders abandoned the traditional goal of Arab unity [and] proclaimed a radical socialist platform at home and a commitment to violent revolutionary activity abroad, including a "people's war" against Israel'.[39] Therefore, the frequency of border clashes between Israel and Syria grew.

Syria's decision to downplay Arab unity had the ironic effect of permitting it to meet its security needs through a closer alliance with Egypt, which was formalized in the 1966 defense pact. Fundamentally, the alliance was the result of Syria's recognition that if it wanted to pursue a more assertive foreign policy – that is, if it wanted to expand its military needs beyond protecting its existing borders – then it would be better to tighten its alliance with Egypt than to take unilateral action. At the same time, the new Syrian leadership believed an alliance would assist it in consolidating the regime. 'By activating the Arab–Israeli conflict [in 1966], Syrian leaders hoped that Egypt would be forced to devote its attention to the Arab cause instead of interfering in Syrian internal conflicts'.[40]

By solving (at least temporarily) the domestic political competition and diverting efforts away from the goals of pan-Arabism, the neo-Ba'thist coup of 1966 gave the Syrian government more political resources to devote to its security needs. In effect, Syria now had more to offer Egypt in exchange for stronger support since it could mobilize political or military support in pursuit of common interests. More important, Syria took advantage of Nasser's relative weakness to acquire military support cheaply. Walt says that Syria's new leadership 'had great leverage over Nasser because its more radical position threatened the foundation of his political power – his status as head of the Arab revolution'.[41] As Nasser recognized that his political power was becoming more tenuous, he demanded fewer concessions from

Syria in exchange for greater military support. Evron says that Nasser was interested in pursuing two, parallel goals, with the alliance, those of restraining Syria and deterring Israel.[42] Thus, whereas Syria was hoping to increase its security through the alliance, Egypt also intended it as a means of increasing its autonomy with respect to inter-Arab relations. It was this interest in autonomy that impelled Nasser to reduce the price of alliance support and allowed Syria to free ride on Egyptian support.

The period between the Six Day War and the Yom Kippur War included two developments that affected Syrian security policy. First, while Egypt and Israel were engaged in the War of Attrition, Syria and Israel did not clash directly. Second, Asad took power in another military coup, effectively solving the internal political conflicts that had been linked with Syrian foreign policy throughout the 1960s.[43] Nevertheless, Syria increased its military spending in this period (see Figure 1).

The War of Attrition illustrates the negative relationship between the relative cost and the level of alliance support. Since Egypt was preoccupied with border clashes with Israel throughout much of 1967–73, it had less to gain by offering support to Syria than it had had in 1966. Much of its military spending was devoted directly to the War of Attrition; these Egyptian arms were thus not a pure-public good for the purposes of the alliance.[44] Therefore, the price Syria would have had to pay for additional Egyptian support was high and the Syrian-Egyptian alliance was looser than it had been when they coordinated their policies in an effort to deter an Israeli invasion.

The War of Attrition example also illustrates the impact of arms costs. Whereas Israel's military spending – the primary indicator of the threat to Syria's security – rose each year during this period, Syrian military spending rose by almost 25 per cent in 1970, fell by 12 per cent in 1971, and then rose by almost 50 per cent in 1972 (see Figure 1). The Syrian changes in 1970 and 1971 are consistent with Egypt's participation in the War of Attrition. Unlike previous years, when Syria could free ride on Egyptian arms, the high price of the alliance made it necessary for Syria to increase its own arms in 1970. The end of the War of Attrition made free riding less costly, so Syria cut back temporarily on its military spending, even though the external threat remained relatively constant. Then, when the perceived threat continued to rise in 1972, Syria made a much larger increase in its military spending than either Israel or Egypt.

Asad had been the influential defense minister in the neo-Ba'thist government, but he did not gain full control until the end of 1970. In contrast to the Syrian view of the early 1960s, Asad considered the threat from Israel unambiguous.[45] In Moshe Ma'oz's words, 'after he came to power, Asad's major priority was quickly and systematically to build a strong army and prepare it for a war against Israel – for both defensive and offensive purposes as well as to enable him to negotiate with Israel from a position of military strength'.[46]

Although Asad's view of Israel as a serious threat was an important factor in changing Syrian behavior, his domestic political popularity had an even stronger impact, giving him additional political flexibility with respect to foreign policy.[47] This flexibility enabled Syria to tighten the alliance with Egypt, which Asad accomplished by signing an agreement with Egypt to coordinate military policy within two weeks of becoming president.[48] But this effect was counteracted by the high price of the alliance: although Syria had more to offer Egypt in exchange for support, the price of that support was too high to compensate for the increased resources. The large rise in Syrian military spending is also consistent with this high price.

Meanwhile, the patron-client relationship between Syria and the Soviet Union was tightening. In 1972 and 1973, for example, Asad acquired a large amount of arms from the Soviet Union, and the number of Soviet military advisors in Syria rose.[50] But Syria neither had nor wanted a formal security agreement with the Soviet Union before the Yom Kippur War, even though the Soviets seem to have wanted one after Egypt expelled the Soviet advisors in 1972. Moshe Ma'oz says that, while the Soviet 'policy was to help Syria to defend herself against an Israeli attack...at that time the Soviets were not keen to see Asad initiating a war against Israel'.[51] An alliance with the Soviet Union would have restricted Syrian policy choice and might even have been unreliable. Therefore, in Roberts's words, Asad wanted:

> to avoid formal entanglement with either superpower and [believed] that too close a connection with the Soviet Union would be unpopular both inside Syria and with those Arab states upon whose financial aid Syria relied, i.e. Saudi Arabia and the states of the Gulf.[52]

In other words, the price of an alliance with the Soviet Union was unacceptably high in the early years of Asad's presidency, not only because the Soviets were demanding major concessions, but also because Asad wanted to maintain political flexibility. As long as the Syrian leadership was able to acquire sufficient arms without a treaty with the Soviet Union, it was in its interests to remain unallied.

From the end of the Yom Kippur War to the Camp David agreement, Syria's security policy was based largely on increasing its own arms, in spite of its continued alliance with Egypt and its desire for a tighter Arab coalition.[53] The problem was that it was difficult to achieve all of these goals simultaneously. The growing differences among the Arab states made military cooperation unlikely. Ultimately, Syria pursued a largely independent security policy in the mid-1970s, which meant that it was unable to launch a military strike to regain the Golan Heights.

Syrian policy in this period is explained well by the theory. The price of alliance support from Egypt in this period was higher than in the previous period: Sadat had already moved Egyptian policy away from the Soviet Union before the Yom Kippur War; by the mid-1970s, Egypt was friendly with the United States and cooperating in the US-led disengagement talks. These factors meant that Egypt would have required greater policy concessions from Syria in exchange for military support. At the same time, the other side of the relative price of alliance support, the price of arms, became lower in this period. Zeev Ma'oz says that Asad 'invested in the army more than any other Syrian regime had done'.[54] Asad apparently understood that relying on allies meant neglecting the preferences of the Syrian army on whom he depended for support.

Syrian resources clearly rose during the mid- to late-1970s. For one thing, Asad solidified his hold on power; as Zeev Ma'oz says, Syria's 'army seem[ed] to be both willing and able to suppress the opposition'.[55] Moreover, its economy began to grow quickly: between 1973 and 1978, Syrian real GDP rose by two thirds, but Asad diverted resources that might otherwise have gone to social welfare spending in order to increase military spending. And far from threatening Asad's political stability, this diversion of resources reinforced his hold on power.

The period between 1978 and 1990 was dominated by Syria's and Israel's involvement in the Lebanon War of 1982 and its aftermath. Although Syria signed a friendship treaty with the Soviet Union in 1980, the treaty was an affirmation of the patron-client relationship, rather than an alliance, in that the Soviets made no formal commitments to the Syrians.[56] Moshe Ma'oz argues that the treaty reflected Asad's inability to unify the Arab world (other than Egypt) under his leadership; Syria's difficulties in Lebanon; and the renewed alienation between Syria and the United States following the Camp David accords. Moreover, the treaty was designed to increase Syria's ability to achieve strategic parity with Israel unilaterally, which, Asad hoped, would help him deal with rising domestic political opposition.[57] Nevertheless, developments in the Soviet Union after 1985 – the change in leadership, the end of the Cold War, the collapse of the communist economic system – rendered the treaty virtually meaningless as a security guarantee.

Although Syria was involved in Lebanon throughout this period, Israel was its primary security concern. Evron argues that Syria's leaders recognized that their 'isolation during the [1982] war demonstrated the need independently to acquire [a strategic balance] with Israel'.[58] This balance did not necessarily mean equality in military capabilities. But since Syria had no firm alliance ties, and the changes in the Soviet Union made it increasingly difficult for Syria to sustain the patron-client ties, it had to concentrate on keeping pace with Israel on its own. Figure 1 shows that the two countries' arms acquisitions followed roughly the same course after the Lebanon War: their military spending rose until 1984, after which it began to decline. Syria, however, was spending only one third as much on arms in 1988 compared to 1983; Israel was spending about two thirds as much.

Throughout the period, Syria's leaders tried to increase their country's military capabilities while strengthening their own internal political positions. As the statistical analysis shows, internal resources (and, to a lesser extent, external assistance) had an impact on Syria's military expenditures. The loss of Egyptian support both helped and harmed Syria: on one hand, it enabled Asad to adopt a more independent security policy; on the other hand, it left Syria both militarily weaker and strategically isolated. The Soviet willingness to provide large quantities of arms and military advisors helped alleviate the problems produced by the Camp David accords and US support for Israel.[59]

ISRAEL

Israeli security policy is widely discussed and often misunderstood. The assumption is often made, sometimes tacitly but usually explicitly, that Israel relies on its ally, the United States, for security support.[60] The truth is that the two countries have never been allies. In fact, until the Six Day War, France, not the United States, was Israel's patron. Israel's growing reliance on assistance from the United States is an important component of Israel's security policy, as is the fact that Israel never relied on a promise of military intervention from abroad. Israel's security policy diverged from Syria's because of two significant differences between them: Israeli leaders neither faced internal political instability nor had access to a potential regional ally.[61] This meant that its political resources were high and that any alliance it could have considered forming would have been with a non-regional state.

Beginning even before its independence in 1948, Israeli governments tried to balance the goals of state-building and secure borders. The best means of achieving these goals was through the development of an independent security policy with technical and financial assistance from abroad. For example, the Jewish community in Mandatory Palestine built a relatively self-sufficient small arms-manufacturing industry prior to independence.[62] Conscription and universal service in the reserves created an Israeli military that was large, relative to the size of the population, and well prepared to mobilize quickly. Even the taxation system was designed to meet the needs of the military. But Israeli leaders realized that ties with an outside power would be useful, if not necessary, to achieve security. Yaniv says that Israeli leaders 'sought ... a kind of extended deterrence, namely alignment with a great power (preferably the United States, but at times they considered the Soviet Union, Great Britain, or France as an adequate second best), which would so alter the balance of forces in the Arab–Israeli conflict that the Arabs would lose confidence in their ability to vanquish Israel in a military confrontation'.[63] In short, the Israelis understood that their security would depend on acquiring sufficient capabilities through both a domestic military program and ties to outside powers.

Following the Sinai War of 1956, Israel and France began cooperating in what Crosbie calls a 'tacit alliance'.[64] This arrangement was mutually beneficial: France supplied arms and technical assistance to Israel; Israel provided both intelligence and indirect assistance to France for its war in Algeria. This relationship was, therefore, a patron-client relationship that permitted Israel to pursue its security interests without the need for an actual alliance. As long as France considered its interests well served by selling arms to Israel, the price of those arms was relatively low. Moreover, neither France nor the United States would have been willing to make a security guarantee to Israel at that time; Israel had no choice but to provide its own security and acquiring French arms was the best way to do so. By the mid-1960s, Israel began to look to the United States for assistance. Israeli leaders realized that their adversaries were becoming militarily more threatening, the risks associated with relying on France were rising, and the incentives for France to assist Israel were weakening.[65]

By the mid-1960s, at least five major global and regional changes led to the tightening of US–Israel relations.[66] First, the focus of the Cold War widened and the superpowers began to take a more active interest in the Middle East.[67] Second, the United States became more active as a global arms supplier.[68] Third, Israel now had greater military capabilities, which gave it a stronger bargaining position with respect to the United States. Fourth, the Algerian conflict ended, which made Israel less useful to France. This created an arms-supplier vacuum for Israel. Finally, new leaders took power in Israel, France, and the United States, so that many of the assumptions and preferences that had dominated relations were obsolete.[69]

Thus, by the spring of 1967, when the crisis that led to the Six Day War occurred, Israel had been well armed by France but was moving politically closer to the United States. Yet it maintained considerable policy flexibility, as the Six Day War itself demonstrated. In Bar-Siman-Tov's words, 'Israel was forced to make a trade-off between the need to take military action to counter Egypt's concentration of forces in the Sinai and its blockade of the Straits of Tiran, and the necessity of compliance with the U.S. requests that it refrain from preemption'.[70] In an alliance, Israel's range of options would have been more tightly constrained: a major power ally could have prevented Israel from taking action by withholding its forces. As Israel's patron, however, all the United States could do was delay Israel's attack. Israel chose to follow the use-of-force option to promote its security; its loose relationships with France and the United States made that option possible.

From the late 1960s until the present, the United States has pursued two goals in its relations with Israel: first, it has wanted to use Israel as a proxy for its own interests; second, it has tried to mediate in a conflict in which Israel is a major participant.[71] Although these goals are not necessarily consistent, they have led to the same outcome: the United States has made arms acquisition easy and inexpensive for Israel, and made it unnecessary for the Israelis to seek an alliance. But the Israeli-American relationship has been beneficial to the interests of both states. Israel has gained access to modern weaponry, economic aid, and diplomatic support, especially as it became politically isolated regionally and globally. The United States has gained a client that would help achieve its global and regional goals and would satisfy the needs of a variety of domestic political audiences.[72] From both states' points of view, an alliance would have been undesirable. For Israel, it would have meant ceding control over its foreign policy, not just in terms of carrying out military actions but also in terms of negotiating – or not negotiating – with its neighbors. For the United States, it would have entailed making promises that would have been difficult to keep and, therefore, may have hurt its credibility. Nevertheless, even without a formal alliance, there is little doubt that Israel has been the United States's most stable friend in the region, that the United States has been Israel's most reliable patron, and that these ties are likely to continue.

Mandelbaum argues that the increased importance of the United States to Israel was already apparent during the Yom Kippur War: 'The United States was Israel's only reliable political ally and its only source of armaments. Shipments of American military equipment had been hastily dispatched in the middle of the war. The war actually increased Israel's dependence.'[73] Thus, although Israel was now militarily much stronger than it had ever been before – and was beginning to experience huge increases in military assistance – its policy flexibility was not necessarily rising.

Moreover, US-Israeli relations since the late 1960s have not always been harmonious. The United States has been involved in mediating the Middle East peace process, which has placed it in a sometimes awkward position: its primary client state in the region, Israel, is also one of the parties in the conflict. US officials, including William Rogers, Henry Kissinger, Jimmy Carter, and James Baker, have tried to use American influence as a means of putting pressure on Israel to compromise and arrive at agreements on territorial issues with its neighbors. It is probably no coincidence that the United States was most successful as an intermediary between Israel and Egypt after Egypt became its client following the Yom Kippur War. Israel could more easily ignore US pressure when the other side in the dispute was Syria or the Palestinians, who were not as strongly influenced by the United States.

At the same time, Israel was still reluctant to form an alliance with the United States. Mandelbaum points out that in the 1970s, 'the Americans seemed to be willing to offer an alliance only in exchange for concessions – notably Israeli withdrawal from the West Bank – that the Israeli government of the moment, at least, was not willing to make'.[74] So the patron-client relationship was desirable for Israel, but an alliance would have been too costly to justify the security gains it would have entailed. Furthermore, Israeli resources rose steadily throughout the period, permitting Israel to continue increasing its military expenditures, thereby adding capabilities over which it would maintain complete control.

Conclusion

In this study, I have explained when regional powers join alliances, when they rely on patrons, and when they remain fully independent. The theory highlights an important omission in much of the recent work on alliances: by failing to draw clear distinctions between alliances, patron-client relationships, and other security policies, Walt, Christensen and Snyder, and others make predictions about states' behavior that are empirically invalid. Balance of threat theory is a good starting point for predicting when states perceive the need to augment their capabilities because it illustrates the importance of both capabilities and intentions. But it is not a theory of alliance formation. States do not necessarily form alliances when they face an external threat; in fact, most of the relationships that Walt classifies as alliances are either informal regional coalitions or patron-client relationships.

A theory of alliance formation must explicitly compare the costs and benefits of alliances to those of other strategic options states may pursue. In the Middle East, alliances have generally been undesirable for two reasons: (1) access to non-regional patrons that provide low-cost military and economic assistance enables the regional powers to pursue their preferred security policies; (2) political isolation makes potential regional allies rare.

The empirical results in this study support my theoretical predictions. Both Syria and Israel increased their military expenditures fairly steadily, reflecting not only the need to offset the growth in their adversaries' capabilities, but also the growth in their own resources. That Syria relied only slightly on Egyptian arms, and Israel refrained from joining any alliance, reflect the high political risks of abandonment and a reduction in autonomy. But Syria and Israel were far from autarkic: their policies were closely integrated with those of the superpowers, in large part because the superpowers' global rivalry made them attractive clients. There was no need for Syria or Israel to form alliances with the superpowers because the terms of their patron-client relationships were favorable, yielding both high levels of military capabilities and sufficient political autonomy.

Are alliances therefore unimportant in regional security policy? Not at all. In fact, there are at least two areas in which alliances may be expected to play a prominent role in a regional security structure. First, in times of extreme urgency, such as the Persian Gulf crisis of 1990–91, a non-regional power may be brought in on short notice to assist the threatened state or states. That the United States and Israel or the Soviet Union and Syria never formed an alliance is partly due to the absence of crises of that nature for Israel or Syria. It is also due to the nature of the ongoing relationships that the regional powers had with their major power patrons.

The second role that alliances can play in the context of regional security structures relates to states that share a common regional adversary. These states might consider an alliance a useful, if imperfect, instrument for establishing security and promoting their foreign policy goals.[75] In the case of Egypt and Syria up to the late 1970s, the common adversary was Israel. But Israel was primarily a status quo power, rather than a state that posed a direct threat to the survival of either Syria or Egypt, so the alliance was not always beneficial to the promotion of Syrian or Egyptian goals. Regionally-based alliances of this type might be useful in the future as part of a Middle East security structure, especially if the majority of regional actors are interested in preserving the status quo against potential threats from a dissatisfied neighbor.

Irrespective of the role of alliances, the most important finding here is that long-term patron-client relationships are not only alternatives to alliances, but often supersede them in terms of effectiveness and desirability.

By focusing on the subtle distinctions among security policies, this analysis helps produce a better understanding of alliances' roles, especially in the context of the Cold War when Israel lacked potential regional allies and both Israel and Syria had access to major power patrons. During the post-Cold War period, the United States has increased, rather than reduced, its activities as a regional patron. Moreover, it is conceivable that the United States will agree to make alliance commitments to Israel – and, perhaps, other regional actors – as part of a series of peace agreements. With reductions in the external threat within the region and the costs of alliance ties, a change in security policy might be worthwhile.

I wish to thank John Conybeare, Paul Huth, Jim Lindsay, and Zeev Maoz for their comments, and Dirk Deam for his assistance with gathering and analyzing the data. Financial support was provided by an Old Gold Summer Research Fellowship and a CIFRE grant from the University of Iowa.

NOTES

1. See, for example, Hans J. Morgenthau, Politics among Nations (NY: Random House 1948); Morton Kaplan, *System and Process in International Politics* (NY: Wiley 1957); Kenneth N. Waltz, *Theory of International Politics* (Reading, MA: Addison-Wesley, 1979); Emerson M.S. Niou, Peter C. Ordeshook, and Gregory F. Rose, *The Balance of Power: Stability in International Systems* (CUP 1989).
2. Stephen M. Walt, The Origins of Alliances (Ithaca, NY: Cornell UP 1987). See also George Liska, *Nations in Alliance: The Limits of Interdependence* (Baltimore, MD: Johns Hopkins UP 1962); Robert L. Rothstein, *Alliances and Small Powers* (NY: Columbia UP 1962); Thomas J. Christensen and Jack Snyder, 'Chain Gangs and Passed Bucks: Predicting Alliance Patterns in Multipolarity', *Int. Organization* 44/2 (Spring 1990), pp.137–68; James D. Morrow, 'Arms versus Allies: Tradeoffs in the Search for Security', Ibid. 47/2 (Spring 1993), pp.207–33.
3. Walt (note 2) p.263.
4. Glenn H. Snyder, 'The Security Dilemma in Alliance Politics', World Politics 34/4 (July 1984), pp 461–95; James D. Morrow, 'Alliances and Asymmetry: An Alternative to the Capability Aggregation Model of Alliances', *American Jnl of Political Science* 35/4 (Nov. 1991), pp 904–33; Gerald L. Sorokin, 'Arms, Alliances, and Security Tradeoffs in Enduring Rivalries', *Int. Studies Qtly* 38/3 (Sept. 1994), pp.421–46.
5. Kaplan (note 1). See also Niou, Ordeshook, and Rose (note 1).
6. Walt (note 2) pp.161, 163.
7. See Snyder, 'Security Dilemma' (note 4).
8. Jacob Bercovitch, 'Superpowers and Client States: Analysing Relations and Patterns of Influence', in M. Efrat and J. Bercovitch *Superpowers and Client States in the Middle East: The Imbalance of Influence*, (London: Routledge 1991) defines an alliance as 'a collaborative agreement between two or more states to join together, for a stipulated period, to pursue common political economic or security interests' (p.1). Walt writes that 'an alliance is a formal or informal arrangement for security cooperation between two or more sovereign states' (p.12).
9. Charles W. Kegley Jr and Gregory A. Raymond, *When Trust Breaks Down: Alliance Norms and World Politics* (Columbia: U. of S. Carolina Press 1990) p.52.
10. Randolph M. Siverson and Harvey Starr, *The Diffusion of War: A Study of Opportunity and Willingness* (Ann Arbor: U. of Michigan Press 1991) p.41.
11. Paul Huth and Bruce Russett, 'What Makes Deterrence Work? Cases from 1900 to 1980', *World Politics* 36/4 (July 1984), pp.496–526; Huth and Russett, 'Deterrence Failure and Crisis Escalation', *Int. Studies Qtly* 32/1 (March 1988) pp.29–45.
12. Woosang Kim, 'Power, Alliance, and Major Wars, 1816–1975', *Jnl of Conflict Resolution* 33/2 (June 1989), pp.255–73; Kim, 'Power Transitions and Great Power War from Westphalia to Waterloo', *World Politics* 45/1 (Oct. 1992) pp.153–72.
13. Michael Altfeld and Bruce Bueno de Mesquita, 'Choosing Sides in Wars', *Int.Studies Qtly* 23 (1979) pp.87–112.
14. Bercovitch (note 8) p.15. Among the many studies of patron-client relationships in the Middle East are: Yaacov Bar-Siman-Tov, *Israel, the Superpowers, and the War in the Middle East* (NY: Praeger 1987); Gabriel Sheffer, 'American-Israeli Relations: An Israeli Assessment and Perspective', in Efrat and Bercovitch (note 8); Nitza Nachmias, *Transfer of*

Arms, Leverage, and Peace in the Middle East (NY: Greenwood 1988); Pedro Ramet, *The Soviet-Syrian Relationship Since 1955* (Boulder, CO: Westview 1990); Efraim Karsh, *Soviet Policy towards Syria since 1970* (London: Macmillan 1991); David Schoenbaum, *The United States and the State of Israel* (NY: OUP 1993).
15. Charles Lipson, 'Why Are Some International Agreements Informal?' *Int. Organization* 45/4 (Autumn 1991) p.518.
16. Abba Eban, *The New Diplomacy: International Affairs in the Modern Age* (NY: Random House 1983) makes the following argument: 'The capacity of small countries to assert their independent interest and judgment against those of powerful allies [or patrons] is a feature of the modern diplomatic era, and the Israeli-American dialogue is merely the most conspicuous example of a general tendency. The huge disparity of power does not imply that the smaller partner has no independent options' (p.218). See also Nachmias (note 8); Sheffer (note 14); Bernard Reich, 'Israel in US Perspective: Political Design and Pragmatic Practices', in Efrat and Bercovitch (note 8).
17. According to Morrow, 'Alliances and Asymmetry' (note 4) symmetric and asymmetric alliances differ according to the goals their members are trying to achieve. In a symmetric alliance, both members pursue either security or autonomy; the capabilities contributed by their alliance partner makes it easier for them to defend or to alter the status quo, depending on their goals. In an asymmetric alliance, the larger member provides security to the smaller member in exchange for additional autonomy. The small state's new security comes from the large state's promise of military involvement, neutrality, or consultation. The promise of support should increase the small state's deterrent and war-fighting ability. The large state's autonomy might take the form of access to military bases or waterways that could enable the larger ally to pursue changes in the status quo that would be difficult without the alliance.
18. Benjamin A. Most and Harvey Starr, *Inquiry, Logic and International Politics* (Columbia: U. of S. Carolina Press 1989); Siverson and Starr (note 10).
19. See Sorokin, 'Arms, Alliances, and Security Tradeoffs' (note 4).
20. Paul K. Huth, *Extended Deterrence and the Prevention of War* (New Haven, CT: Yale UP 1988).
21. Geoffrey Blainey, *The Causes of War* (NY: Free Press 1973); Bruce Bueno de Mesquita, *The War Trap* (New Haven, CT: Yale UP 1981).
22. Snyder, 'Security Dilemma' (note 4); Michael Mandelbaum, *The Fate of Nations: The Search for National Security in the Nineteenth and Twentieth Centuries* (Cambridge: CUP 1988).
23. Walt (note 2) p.22.
24. In some cases, internal policies may be beneficial to the popularity of a government or may even serve as an economic stimulus. These are extreme examples of low-cost internally-based policies. For a discussion of the relationship between state-building and military policy, see Michael N. Barnett, *Confronting the Costs of War: Military Power, State, and Society in Egypt and Israel* (Princeton UP 1992).
25. For a review of this literature, see Todd Sandler, 'The Economic Theory of Alliances', *Jnl of Conflict Resolution* 37/3 (Sept. 1993), pp.446–83.
26. Morrow, 'Alliances and Asymmetry' (note 4).
27. John R. Oneal and Mark A. Elrod, 'NATO Burden Sharing and the Forces of Change', *Int. Studies Qtly* 33/4 (Dec. 1989), pp.435–56.
28. See Harry Eckstein, 'Case Study and Theory in Political Science', in F.I. Greenstein and N.W. Polsby (eds.) *Handbook of Political Science*, Vol.7 (Reading, MA: Addison-Wesley1975); Alexander L. George, 'Case Studies and Theory Development: The Method of Structured, Focused Comparison' in P.G. Lauren (ed.) *Diplomacy* (NY: Free Press 1979); Christopher H. Achen and Duncan Snidal, 'Rational Deterrence Theory and Comparative Case Studies', *World Politics* 41/2 (Jan. 1989), pp.143–69.
29. Data on military personnel are also available. Although the personnel data are probably more reliable than the expenditures data, I focus on expenditures since they tend to be more sensitive to changes in security policy.
30. The most recent publication is US Arms Control and Disarmament Agency, *World Military Expenditures and Arms Transfers 1993–1994* (Washington, DC: US GPO 1995). It contains

data for 1983–93. Earlier data come from previous issues of *WMEAT*, beginning with the 1974 issue, which contains data going back to 1963. The data for 1983–93 are reported in 1993 dollars in the most recent issue. For 1963–82 data, I convert the figures from previous issues of *WMEAT* to 1993 dollars according to the ratios between the figures for overlapping years. The figures are not completely reliable, however, because of (a) the difficulties of estimating military expenditures, and (b) sudden, sharp changes in exchange rates. For example, according to figures from the IMF's *International Financial Statistics Yearbook 1991* (Washington, DC: IMF 1992), Syria's official exchange rate rose to 11.225 pounds per US dollar in 1988, after having been 3.925 since 1976.

31. Shlomo Gazit and Zeev Eytan, T*he Middle East Military Balance, 1993–1994* (Boulder, CO: Westview 1994); Gazit and Eytan, *The Middle East Military Balance, 1994–1995* (forthcoming). The MEMB figures tend to be close to the ACDA figures, but since they are all reported in current-year dollars, they are difficult to work with in a longitudinal study.
32. See IMF, *International Financial Statistics Yearbook*, Vol.44 (Washington, DC: IMF 1991); IMF, *International Financial Statistics*, 47/11 (Washington, DC: IMF, Nov. 1994). I use the IMF data for Syrian GDP because the IMF reports a single series, in 1985 prices, for 1961–90, and then a series in 1990 prices for 1987–93. I merge the two scales and then convert the prices to 1993 dollars, according to the exchange rates and price deflators reported by the IMF and ACDA. ACDA's Israel GNP data series is complete for 1963–93, while the IMF's GDP data begin only in 1968, so I use ACDA's figures. The correlation between the two series is .96 for the years covered by both publications.
33. Eban (note 16) p.204 says that the Baghdad Pact 'had the distinction of being offensive to the Soviet Union, Egypt and Israel, in equal degree and for contrasting reasons'. See also Schoenbaum (note 14).
34. See, for example, James H. Lebovic and Ashfaq Ishaq, 'Military Burden, Security Needs, and Economic Growth in the Middle East', *Jnl of Conflict Resolution* 31/1 (March 1987), pp.106–38; Alex Mintz and Michael D. Ward, 'The Evolution of Israel's Military Expenditures: 1960-1983', *Western Political Qtly* 41/3 (Sept. 1988) pp.489–507.
35. I use generalized least squares to correct for the autocorrelation in the error terms that arises from the use of annual data.
36. Although this variable is not statistically significant with $p<.05$, it is in the expected direction and is comes close to statistical significance.
37. Yair Evron, *War and Intervention in Lebanon: The Israeli-Syrian Deterrence Dialogue* (London: Croom Helm 1987) p.181.
38. Yaacov Bar-Siman-Tov, *Linkage Politics in the Middle East: Syria Between Domestic and External Conflict, 1961–1970* (Boulder, CO: Westview 1983).
39. Walt (note 2) p.88.
40. Bar-Siman-Tov, *Linkage Politics* (note 38) p.171.
41. Walt (note 2) p.88.
42. Evron (note 37) p.182.
43. Bar-Siman-Tov, *Linkage Politics* (note 38).
44. See Sandler on private, purely public, and impurely public goods.
45. Ramet (note 14).
46. Moshe Ma'oz, *Asad: The Sphinx of Damascus* (London: Weidenfeld 1988) p.86.
47. Bar-Siman-Tov, *Linkage Politics* (note 38).
48. M. Ma'oz, *Asad* (note 46).
49. Ibid.
50. Ramet (note 14); Karsh (note 14); David Roberts, 'The USSR in Syrian Perspective: Political Design and Pragmatic Practices', in Efrat and Bercovitch (note 8).
51. M. Ma'oz, *Asad* (note 46) p.86.
52. Roberts (note 50) p.214.
53. Evron (note 37).
54. Zeev Ma'oz, 'The Evolution of Syrian Power, 1948–1984', in M. Ma'oz and A. Yaniv (eds.) *Syria under Assad* (London: Croom Helm 1986) p.76.
55. Ibid.
56. Had there been a formal commitment, the Syrian-Soviet friendship treaty would have been

considered an entente by the coding rules of the Correlates of War Project. The defense pact between Syria and Egypt was never formally canceled, but it was clear that the two countries no longer cooperated on military matters. The rest of the Arab League members were, at best, unreliable military allies.
57. M. Ma'oz, *Asad* (note 46) pp.147–8, 179.
58. Evron (note 37) p.194.
59. M. Ma'oz, *Asad* (note 46).
60. See, for example, Walt (note 2) p.95.
61. Walt asserts that Israel and Jordan were allies in 1970 when Jordan was being threatened by Syria. In addition to not fitting my definition of an alliance, this relationship was not intended to augment Israeli security directly.
62. Barnett (note 24).
63. Avner Yaniv, 'A Question of Survival: The Military and Politics Under Siege', in idem (ed.) *National Security and Democracy in Israel* (Boulder, CO: Lynne Rienner 1993) p.91.
64. Sylvia K. Crosbie, *A Tacit Alliance: France and Israel from Suez to the Six Day War* (Princeton UP 1974). See also A.F.K Organski, *The $36 Billion Bargain: Strategy and Politics in U.S. Assistance to Israel* (NY: Columbia UP 1990).
65. Bar-Siman-Tov, *Israel* (note 14).
66. Gerald L. Sorokin, 'Alliance Formation and General Deterrence: A Game-Theoretic Model and the Case of Israel', *Jnl of Conflict Resolution* 38/2 (June 1994) pp.298–325.
67. William B. Quandt, *Peace Process: American Diplomacy and the Arab-Israeli Conflict since 1967* (Washington: Brookings 1993).
68. Nachmias (note 14).
69. Bar-Siman-Tov, *Israel* (note 14); Alan R. Taylor, *The Superpowers and the Middle East* (Syracuse UP 1991).
70. Bar-Siman-Tov, *Israel* (note 14) p.91. See also Quandt (note 67).
71. Mandelbaum (note 22); Taylor (note 69).
72. Eban (note 16).
73. Mandelbaum (note 22) p.283. Note that the term 'political ally' refers to a relationship that does not involve specific security guarantees. See also Organski (note 64); Dan Horowitz, 'The Israel Concept of National Security', in A. Yaniv *National Security and Democracy in Israel* (Boulder, CO: Lynne Rienner 1993).
74. Mandelbaum (note 22) p.308.
75. See Sorokin, 'Arms, Alliances, and Security Tradeoff' (note 4).

War and Peace as Rational Choice in the Middle East

MARTIN SHERMAN and GIDEON DORON

> The subject matters of the social and natural sciences are profoundly different. The difference does not obliterate certain possibilities and necessities
> Kenneth Waltz

A. Introduction

Armed conflict has never been a rare phenomenon in the Middle East. However, in the post-World War II era in particular, the region has experienced burgeoning violence on scale seldom precedented. Virtually every state in this tempestuous area has, at one time or another, been involved in armed hostilities against one or another of its neighbours. Six major military conflagrations (1948–49, 1956, 1967, 1970, 1973, and 1982) traditionally focused international attention on Israel as the pivotal regional belligerent. More recent events, however, have established Iraq as an additional 'epicenter of conflict' (chiefly, the 1980–88 Iran–Iraq War and the 1990 Iraqi invasion of Kuwait). Moreover, both Egypt and Syria have been involved in several large-scale military actions to which Israel was not at all party. (For example, the 1966 Egyptian military involvement in Yemen; the 1977 Egyptian–Libyan border disputes; Syria's recurring attempts to take control of Lebanon by military means, prior to Damascus' final attainment of dominance over the country in 1990). Likewise, recurring violence, such as the hostilities between the two Yemeni states in the 1970s has flared in the Arabian peninsula from time to time.

In the interim between these and other violent incidents, the adversaries have not infrequently signed formal ceasefire agreements, non-aggression pacts, or fully-fledged peace treaties, only to violate them when the incumbent regime in one of the signatory-states, perceived maintaining its contractual undertaking as no longer being in its interest – as in the case of the Iraqi violation of the 1975 Algiers and Baghdad agreements with Iran, five years after their ceremonious conclusion.

Several explanations have been provided for this apparent regional propensity to violence. One of the more common *endeavors* identifies the 'intrusion' of *Israel* – as a *discordant*, alien political element – into an area, largely religio-culturally homogeneous, as the major cause of instability. But the singling out of an 'alien' Israel as the alleged source of conflict can not account for the military clashes which frequently occur in the region between protagonists of *similar* religio-cultural make-up such as those cited above.

Another frequently-employed explanation focuses on the aftermath of the colonialist presence in the region which resulted in arbitrarily-drawn borders between newly-formed political entities. The design of these nascent sovereign units was insensitive to the claims of tradition and exigencies of emerging political aspirations. Indeed, disputes over borders and territorial claims often characterize much of the past and present inter-state relationships throughout the area.

Yet a third version relates the violence to the political strategies and foreign policies of the pre-World War II Great Powers (particularly Great Britain and France), and later to the post-World War II superpowers (the USA and the USSR), during the Cold War period. Accordingly, the regional states were seen as no more than local bases for these major powers in their quest for global domination.[1]

Finally, there are numerous case-studies which treat each incident of regional conflict as a unique occurrence, independent of any general explanatory principle, and thus causally unrelated to other events.

The approach adopted here to explain the incessant occurrences of state-instigated violence in the Middle East is qualitatively different from that of the more conventional historical accounts. Instead of treating the Middle East as a region entirely unique (hence requiring uniquely-tailored explanations entirely dependent on regional specifics), it proposes a general, deductively deduced, theoretical scheme in which the events and processes in the area are analyzed and explained as specific manifestations of a broader principle of international relations that identifies the *internal political structure* of states' domestic regime as one of the major underlying causes of inter-state violence in general, and of the frequently recurring military conflict in the Middle East in particular.[2] In a nutshell, the main thrust of the arguments developed herein, is that since all the sovereign political units in the region (with the notable exception of Israel) are essentially non-libertarian, and since, in an anarchic international environment, such regimes can be shown to have an inherently high propensity to violence, it is to be expected that the actual manifestation of such violence will accordingly be high.

In deriving these arguments, we generate a conceptual link between two major, and seemingly contradictory paradigms of international relations.[3] On the one hand, the *realpolitik* paradigm which perceives *all* states (irrespective of their internal regime-type), as having *similar* national interests (of enhancing their national power and security) which, in the conduct of their foreign policy, they all pursue in *similar* vein. On the other hand, in the *domestic constraints* approach, the nature of a state's domestic regime is seen as a substantial determinant of its international behaviour. Accordingly, states of *dissimilar* regime-types should conduct their foreign policy in a *dissimilar* fashion.

We show that a link can be forged between the apparent incongruities in these two approaches by adopting a decision-theoretic modelling technique. This demonstrates that when the *element of uncertainty* is introduced into the decision-making situation in a methodologically rigorous manner, the differing domestic constraints, formulated in classic Kantian terms, can be translated into differing expected utility maximizing (EUM) rational actor risk-preferences. These EUM rational actor utility profiles will thus differ in shape. Consequently, a logically-consistent framework is created in which the *seemingly-uniform realpolitik* aspiration of an egotistical pursuit of national interest (i.e. of maximizing expected utility), expresses itself in *different* policy choices, each of which maximize expected utility for actors of various utility profiles (i.e. for regimes of different domestic structures and hence of differing domestic constraints).

In the ensuing three sections (B,C and D) we assemble the decision-theoretic elements of the analytical apparatus employed to explain the different patterns of conduct observed in the international system in general and in the Middle East sub-system in particular. Subsequently, Sections E to G explore the theoretically-deduced predictions regarding *dyadic, monadic and regional* contexts and evaluate their explanatory power *vis-à-vis* empirical findings pertaining to these differing levels of aggregation with special emphasis being placed on the relevance for Middle Eastern events. In Section H we establish the possibility of deriving a *theoretical principle of asymmetry* for the characterization of the disparate conditions under which dictatorships and democracies initiate inter-state violence, and the pertinence of this principle for the Middle East. The concluding Sections (I, and J) discuss various policy-oriented implications of the theory, focusing on their specific significance for the on-going conflictual realities in the region.

B. Paradigms of International Relations: Thesis, Antithesis and Synthesis.

The organizing principles assumed to govern the international behavior of states are of consequence both to those engaged in the theoretical study and the actual conduct of foreign policy. For clearly, in given circumstances, different sets of principles are very likely to imply different policy initiatives and responses. What may be appropriate in the light of the interpretation of events in terms of one paradigm, may not be so in case of an alternative paradigm.

To underscore this point, let us revert to the distinction between the *realpolitik* and the *domestic constraints* paradigms. Clearly, the basic terms of references adopted regarding the nature of the international system, determine whether the point of departure for policy formulation is that, a-priori, such policy should be perceived as 'regime-insensitive' in accordance with the former paradigm or as 'regime-sensitive' in accordance with the latter.

For the Middle East this is an issue of consequence. Indeed, as a political milieu in which the regime-structure is of a pronounced 'non-libertarian' nature, it matters profoundly whether or not this fact should be accorded significant weight as determinant of foreign policy, both for the international community toward the region as a whole, and for the individual Middle Eastern states themselves in their intra-regional dealings.

It is thus of significance to note that although there is substantial logic in the *realpolitik* arguments, accumulating empirical evidence seems to militate, at least partially, in favor of the alternative regime-sensitive *domestic constraint* view. For example, a regime-insensitive perspective is powerless to account for the almost universal (and almost universally acknowledged) absence of war between libertarian regimes.[4] Neither can it offer an explanation for additional empirical findings such as those of Schweller's that all preventive wars have been begun by non-libertarian regimes; an observation which seems to indicate that not only the propensity to *participate* in wars, but also the propensity to *initiate* them is a regime-sensitive variable.[5]

These empirical observations are, of course, of considerable significance, but there are also analytical arguments for the belief that, in essentially the same circumstances, regime-types of differing structure will behave *differently*. One of the earliest and more eloquent expositions of this position was set out by Immanuel Kant in his 1795 essay on 'Perpetual Peace'.[6] Of one type of regime, he writes:

> [A state governed according to] a constitution . . . [which] is republican . . . established . . . by principles of the freedom of the

members of a society (as men); secondly, by principles of dependence of all upon a single common legislation (as subjects); and thirdly, by the law of their equality (as citizens) ... gives a favorable prospect for the desired consequence i.e. perpetual peace. The reason is this: if the consent of the citizens is required in order to decide that war should be declared (and in this constitution it cannot but be the case), nothing is more natural than that they would be very cautious in commencing such a poor game, decreeing for themselves all the calamities of war.

Kant enumerates these self-inflicted calamities as 'having to fight, having to pay the costs of war from their own resources, having painfully to repair the devastation war leaves behind, and ... load themselves with a heavy national debt ...'. In contradistinction to this, of the opposite type of regime Kant warns:

... on the other hand, in a constitution which is not republican, and under which the subjects are not citizens, a declaration is the easiest thing in the world to decide upon, because war does not require the ruler, who is the proprietor and not a member of the state, the least sacrifice of the pleasures of his table ... He may therefore resolve on war as on a pleasure party for the most trivial reasons, and with perfect indifference leave the justification which decency requires to the diplomatic corps who are ever ready to provide it.

This Kantian differentiation of behavioural propensity of states as a function of their regime-type, runs counter to the logic of classic *realpolitik*. This apparent 'conceptual clash' prompts the question of whether it may be feasible (or indeed, necessary) to create a integrative analytical framework capable of incorporating in a logically consistent manner, the seemingly irreconcilable elements of regime-sensitive and insensitive-approaches. It is to this question of that we now turn.

C. Regime Type as a Determinant of International Conduct

In similar vein to Bueno de Mesquita we treat the executive authority of a regime 'as if' it were a single EUM decision-maker.[7] Furthermore we utilize the fact that Kant's characterization of the disparate predilections of different regimes types lends itself conveniently to schematic representation in terms of basic decision theory in the way shown in Table 1.

In Table 1 (opposite), a decision to choose option I represents a preference for the maintenance of the status quo, while a choice of option II indicates a preference for a risky attempt to change the status quo by means

TABLE 1
DECISION-MAKING SITUATION INVOLVING CHOICE BETWEEN
CERTAIN AND UNCERTAIN INITIATIVES

		Outcomes	
Decision	I	0	0
Options	II	+X	–X
Probabilities		p_1	p_2

of force, which may result in high rewards or costly failure. Thus, positive and negative values of X denote, respectively, the gains and the losses involved in a successful and an unsuccessful attempt to force a change in the status quo existing between two states, while p_1 and p_2 represent the respective probabilities of each such outcome.

Under the assumption (presently to be discussed in detail) that the disparity between p_1 and p_2 is not extreme, a choice of option I would be consistent (at least schematically) with the 'cautious', risk-averse behaviour attributed by Kant to a 'republican' regime and, which following Bueno de Mesquita and Lalman, we shall relate to as a 'libertarian' or a 'democratic" regime'.[8] Similarly, under the same assumption regarding p_1 and p_2, the choice of option II, would be consistent with the risk-acceptant behavioural characteristics implicit in Kant's 'non-republican' regime to which we shall relate as a 'non-libertarian' or 'dictatorial' regime.

Note that the assignment of risk averse and risk acceptant characteristics to libertarian and non-libertarian regimes respectively, is not an *assumption* but an *inference* drawn from the Kantian arguments regarding the disparate domestic accountability of these regime types, on the one hand, and the disparate effects it has on their attitudes toward risk-taking in their international policy, on the other. It is this non-trivial inference, that the difference in accountability generates different risk preferences in libertarian and non-libertarian regimes which is the crux of the model. Accordingly, the conclusions as to the pursuant behaviour of the model's regime-types are not tautological re-statements of self-evident truths, but substantive logical deductions which follow from this inference.

Suppose next that an EUM decision maker is confronted with the schematic decision situation depicted in Table 1 involving a choice between a certain outcomes and a risky option with uncertain outcomes of equal probability, that is $p_1 = p_2 = 0.5$. Clearly, a choice of option I would imply a *risk averse* EUM decision maker with a utility curve concave toward the X-axis; while a choice of option II would imply a *risk acceptant* EUM decision maker with a utility curve convex toward the X-axis. Figures 1 and 2 below illustrate the differences between these two types of decision makers and the reasons for their disparate choice behaviour.

FIGURE 1

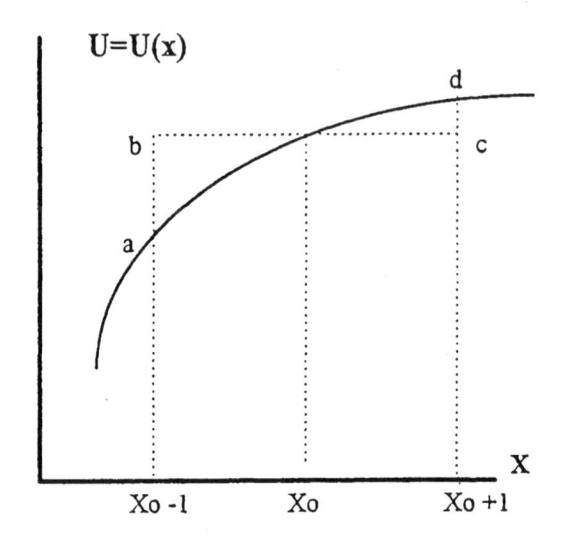

FIGURE 2

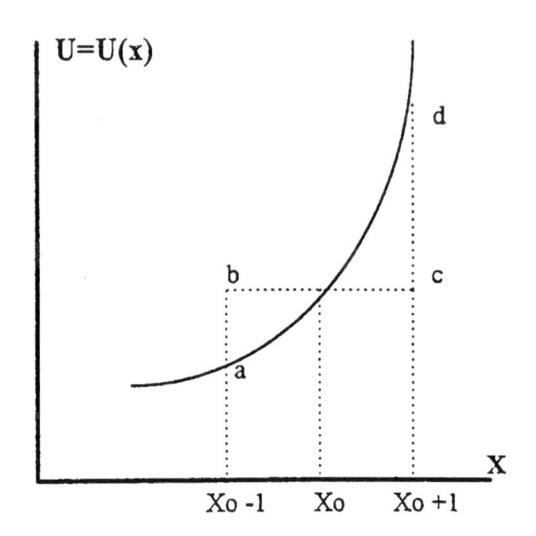

Figure 1 above shows that for any given level of pay-offs, say Xo, a decrease of one unit (x = Xo–1), will cause a decrease in utility U(x), (ab), which is greater than the corresponding increase in utility (cd) due to an increase of one unit in pay-off (x = Xo+1). Conversely, Figure 2 shows that a unit decrease in the pay-off will cause a correspondingly smaller decrease in utility than the increase therein due to a unit increase in pay-off. Thus, when the two decision makers are confronted with the two options as presented in Table 1 (i.e. either preserving the status quo – at x = Xo – *or* choosing a option involving equal probability of unit loss or unit gain), the one in Figure 1 will always opt for the risk-free option (option I) while the other will always prefer to take a risk (option II). For by doing so, they both maximize expected utility – although each of them attains this by means of a different choice.

The crucial aspect of this divergence of choice preference is that it occurs despite the fact that (a) there in no discrepancy between the perceptions of the two EUM decision-makers as to the pay-offs and the probabilities of the various outcomes and hence (b) both decision makers perceive both options as having equal (i.e. zero) expected pay-offs. This point underscores some of the methodological and substantive rationale for introducing into the model-building process the stringent *ceteris paribus* proviso implicit in the postulation of equal probabilities for losses and gains of equal magnitude, generating the zero expected *pay-off* (as distinct from expected *utility*) for both options. For if these probabilities or pay-offs were to deviate significantly from parity, then both risk-averse and risk-acceptant EUM decision-makers may choose the same alternatives thereby obscuring the effects of their very different attitudes toward risk.

At first glance the assumption of equal probabilities of equal losses and gains may appear to be overly contrived and restrictive (even unacceptably unrealistic), because it does not reflect the richness of the empirical world. It can however be shown that, given the analytical objective of exploring the effects of disparate risk preferences, which on the basis of Kantian arguments, are inferred to be induced in the international behavior of libertarian and non-libertarian regimes, this is in effect, the least restrictive and most illuminating assumption. There are several reasons for this, both methodological and substantive. Because of their importance in the establishment of the model's epistemological rationale these are elaborated on below:

- First, as we have just pointed out, if, in the construction of the model, these probabilities or pay-offs were to deviate significantly from parity, then both risk-averse and risk-acceptant EUM decision makers may choose the same alternatives thereby obviating the ability to demonstrate the effects of their very different (Kantian-inferred) attitudes toward risk. However, such a deviation would not eradicate the inherent disparity in risk preference, but merely distort or attenuate its manifestation; much as the existence of friction does not undermine the validity of Newton Laws of Motion. However, as an external influence, it does impose a distorting effect on the 'pure' manifestation of the theoretically predicted phenomena.

- Second, strict arithmetical parity is not an absolute imperative, since not all deviation therefrom would necessarily eradicate the manifestation of the propensity to divergent choice patterns due to the disparate risk preference. Indeed, for *any* given risk averse (acceptant) utility profile, there exits a δ such that for the range of probabilities, $p = 1/2 \pm \delta$, the same definite preference for the certain status quo (uncertain risky option) over the uncertain risky option (certain status quo) by all risk-averse (acceptant) EUMs, will prevail. The precise value of δ will of course depend on the precise mathematical specification of the utility profile. In particular it will depend on the value of the second derivative of the utility function, namely $\delta = F\{U''(x)\}$ for any given $U = U(x)$. (Clearly, a similar analysis may be performed *vis-à-vis* the divergence from parity by the pay-offs, $\pm X$).

- There is thus an inherent 'trade-off' as to the generality of the assumptions that can be made *vis-à-vis* the pay-offs and the probabilities thereof, on the one hand, and utility profiles on the other. By assuming equality of pay-offs and probabilities one can make unrestricted assumptions as to the features of the utility curves and thus allow the inclusion of all risk-averse (concave to the X-axis i.e. all $U = U(x)$ with $U''(x) < 0$) and all risk acceptant (convex to the X-axis i.e. all $U = U(x)$ with $U''(x) > 0$) profiles into the analysis.

- Accordingly, once the *general principle* of divergent, regime-dependent risk preference has been established on the basis of the assumption of equal probabilities and pay-offs, it is possible to relax this assumption and allow for both the probabilities and the pay-offs to vary. This however does not affect the conceptual rationale of the model or the underlying regularity of disparate risk-propensities it is intended to elucidate. For whatever configuration of probabilities or pay-offs are assumed, the underlying propensity of any risk-averse (risk-acceptant) EUM for the certain status quo (uncertain risky option) will be greater than for any risk acceptant (averse) EUM even if the manifestation of this propensity is overridden by the specifics of the situation – just as in physics, the manifestation of the motional propensities of moving objects implicit in the Laws of Gravity may be overridden in certain circumstances by the specifics of the situation, say, by the Laws of Aerodynamics which allow the flight of Jumbo jets in apparent defiance of the Law of Gravity.

- Thus, to contest the validity of the model because of the 'unrealistic assumption' of equal probabilities and pay-offs would lead to the threat of epistemological disqualification of a wide range of intellectual constructs and hypothetical fictions throughout various fields of scientific endeavour. These include, for example, the useful concepts of 'homo economics', 'perfect markets', 'frictionless surfaces' and 'rays of light', together with the many real-world applications (and practical benefits) derived therefrom.

- Moreover, the model does not base its epistemological validity on a claim to the empirical veracity of its assumptions in any *specific* case. Rather, it should be considered primarily as a *systemic* analogue and as such, it is designed to elucidate system-wide phenomena, on an 'as if' basis, with epistemological validity *in spite* of the (purposeful) lack of empirical veracity of its assumptions. Thus, an analogue model of a market system comprising hypothetical consumers and firms, all assigned utility- or profit-maximizing characteristics respectively, does not purport to give an accurate factual account of the precise psychological motivations of the vendor and purchaser in any given commercial interaction, but is intended to provide an 'as if' account of the overall, system-wide functioning of the market mechanism. So too, an analog model of *an international system* comprising libertarian and non-libertarian regimes, all assigned risk-averse or -acceptant characteristics respectively (as a result of their disparate accountability) does not purport to give an accurate factual account of all the prevailing specifics in any given case of an interaction between two regimes.

- The empirical relevance (as opposed to the epistemological validity) of an analog-model (whether of the market system or of the international system) should be judged on its ability to account for (and predict) empirical phenomena on an overall systemic level (such as the inverse relation between demand and price or between war and libertarianism) and not by its inability to embrace the full richness of empirical detail in any specific case.

- Furthermore, unless one is willing to eschew any aspiration to generality, the assigning of *any* specified probability (or pay-offs) that differ significantly from parity would raise almost insurmountable obstacles both for the structural rationale of the model and for its empirical applicability. As for the former, there is no a priori basis for ascribing divergent regime-differentiated perceptions regarding the pay-offs or probabilities of outcomes, without making substantial and arbitrary assumptions as to the reasons why such disparate perceptions should be attributed to the disparate regime-types. With regard to the latter, in the light of an almost universal absence of war between democracies, any deviation from the assumed parity would require a seemingly even more difficult task of providing a reason for why democratic states should be loathe to engage in wars even though they have a good chance of winning them, or why dictatorial regimes should be eager to engage in wars that they have a good chance of losing.

- Finally, it is feasible to conduct the whole analysis in a very similar fashion, *independently* of assumptions of any kind regarding the specific value assigned to the probabilities. This may be done by probability-independent criteria such as the Minimax (or Maximin), the Maximax or the Hurwicz Optimism-Pessimism Criterion. Thus in Table 1 above, a choice of Option I would indicate Minimaxer (or Maximiner) behavior instead of EUM risk-averse behavior; while a choice of Option II would indicate Maximaxer behavior instead of EUM risk-acceptant behavior. Note that the assignment of Maximaxer (Minimaxer) behavioral characteristics to non-libertarian (libertarian) regimes would, as before, be an inference which follows from the Kantian distinction between the accountability of these two regime-types. In the case of the application Hurwicz Optimism-Pessimism Criterion, an α-value of $\alpha > 1$ or $\alpha < 1$ would be assigned the decision maker instead of risk averse ($U''(x) < 0$) or risk acceptant ($U''(x) > 0$) characteristics. The substitution of these probability-independent criteria for the probability-dependent EUM criteria will not change the analysis, or the conclusions drawn therefrom, in any significant way and the consequent libertarian/non-libertarian preferences in Tables 1–3 will remain unaltered.

Note also, that in an alternative deductive-oriented analysis, emphasizing a *game-theory* rather than a *decision-theory* perspective, Bueno De Mesquita and Lalman seem to overlook (or at least, gloss over) the significance of many of these aspects of risk analysis and disparate risk preferences. This disregard reflects a general laxity in their treatment of risk preference, especially in their lack of rigor in distinguishing between expected pay-offs and expected utility. Hence, there is much confusion as to whether their 'expected utility maximizer' is indeed maximizing expected utility in a risk sensitive manner, or merely maximizing expected pay-off, as if insensitive to the level of risk associated with his actions.[9]

Framing the Kantian characterization of different regime-type behaviour in the decision-theoretic format, provides a device for assigning differently-shaped utility curves to different regime types. Specifically, the implication is that dictatorial (non-libertarian) regimes should be ascribed utility curves convex to the X-axis and be schematically represented as risk acceptant EUM-decision-making entities, while democratic (libertarian) regimes should be ascribed utility curves concave to the X-axis, and be schematically represented as risk averse EUM-decision-making entities.[10]

D. Modelling the International System: Internally Disparate Ideal-Type Sovereignties in Environmental Anarchy

In our scheme we postulate, in accordance with the 'as if' approach adopted hitherto, an 'idealized' international system. The basic units comprising this system are sovereign entities, called 'states'. Since these entities are by definition 'sovereign', they are immune to sources of authority external to themselves. Thus, the system which they comprise must also be, by definition, 'anarchical', that is devoid of any hierarchical structure regarding the ranking of the authority of units in it.

In terms of empirical approximations, such a system would thus be differentiated from a 'quasi-hierarchical' Soviet bloc-like system in which the supposedly sovereign units included in it, subordinated their national and international policies to the dictates of Moscow. By contrast, the post-World War II Middle East, with the sole exception of present day Lebanon, whose political process has been largely determined by Damascus, could be considered a good approximation of an anarchical system.

Now, in accordance with the *realpolitik* paradigm, these sovereign entities are assumed to behave in a manner commonly (indeed necessarily) ascribed to states in their anarchic milieu, namely, they each strive to pursue their own egotistic national interest. In our decision-theoretic context, pursuit of this interest is taken to be the aspiration to maximize expected utility from available policy options in which the relevant pay-offs are defined in terms of national power and security.

Furthermore, all the regimes included in this theoretical system are assumed to be either 'indisputably democratic' or 'indisputably dictatorial'. To avoid becoming embroiled in a semantic dispute as to what precisely constitutes a 'democracy' and a 'dictatorship', each of the regimes is defined in terms of a set of five parameters, as follows:

i. The legitimacy of overt, legal political opposition to the incumbent executive authority.

ii. The effective limitations imposed on the power of the executive – that is, the degree to which there exists effective separation of powers, or alternatively an effective system of checks and balances.

iii. The degree of public participation in the political routine and the extent to which this participation determines the composition of the executive.

iv. Limits on the possible use that can be made of state resources by an incumbent executive to further his own ends (as opposed to those of the state).

v. The independence of the communication media from control by the incumbent executive.

A regime in which all five parameters are manifested to a maximum degree is defined as 'indisputably democratic'; a regime in which they are manifested to a minimum degree is defined as 'indisputably dictatorial'.[11]

Note, that we have purposely evaded the problems of operationalizing these parameters which can all, in principle, be conceived of as quantifiable variables ranging between two polar values. However, as will be seen, this does not detract from the methodological validity of the approach adopted, which draws on diagnosing, identifying and correlating *clearly discernible qualitative* (or at least *'order-of-magnitude'*) differences in both the dependent variables (international behaviour) and the independent variable (regime types), rather than measuring graduated variation in these variables.

Accordingly, in all the regimes included in the 'idealized' international system postulated above, these five parameters are either 'maximally' or 'minimally' manifested. Thus for example, in these regimes, there is either total government control over the media or total absence of such control. Similarly, there is either total prohibition of overt opposition or complete toleration thereof.

Clearly, in the real-world international system, it is unlikely that the empirical domestic attributes of actual regimes will exhibit all (or any of) these five parameters to their theoretically most extreme degree. However, in the Middle East, such regimes as Iran, Iraq, Libya, Syria, Saudi Arabia, the Gulf states, Yemen, Egypt and Jordan could be considered as acceptable approximations of the 'dictatorial' category having relatively low scores on all five parameters. Note that in terms of the model, these regimes would be categorized in a single group on the basis of the *general* parameters of their internal system of power structure and dispensation, in spite of the fact that the *specifics* of their domestic political structures vary considerably.[12] Only Israel (and to a certain degree, pre-1970 Lebanon) may be classed as approximations of a 'democratic' state, and assigned relatively high parameter scores.

It is reiterated that the design of an international system comprising only two distinct regime-types, is a hypothetically fictitious construct. As previously stressed, like concepts of 'perfectly competitive markets' and 'frictionless surfaces', it does not purport to mirror the reality of the empirical world. Rather, it is employed as an analytical tool in an effort to formulate potentially useful, simplified abstractions regarding the phenomena under consideration. In this regard, it is of course consistent with the exigencies of scientific method as prescribed by Conant,[13] since this schematically constructed universe is purposefully 'directed toward the lowering of the degree of empiricism involved in solving problems'.

Indeed, in this respect, the methodological thrust of the current endeavor runs counter to much of the common practice and conventional wisdom in political science where, as Waltz[14] points out, 'students . . . have tried to get closer to reality . . . [and] to increase the empirical content of their studies'.

Accordingly, the issue to be addressed herein, is whether the hypothetical simplifications and abstractions set out above and that draw on both the *realpolitik* paradigm (which assigns EUM-characteristics to all foreign policy formulators) and domestic constraint paradigm (which imposes different utility curve profiles on policy formulators in different regimes), can indeed be fashioned into a useful analytical implement, capable of accounting for observed empirical phenomena pertaining to the relationship between the domestic political structure of the state on the one hand, and its conduct in the international system on the other, in a manner which reconciles the apparently contradictory perspectives of the traditional paradigms. It is to this that we turn next.

E. The Dyadic Analysis: Twosomes Tranquil and Turbulent

Let us consider a potential dyadic confrontation between two regimes. Suppose that, as suggested in Table 1, in any such conflict, the prospective EUM-rational protagonists weigh the expected utility to be derived from the maintenance of the status quo relative to that associated with a risky decision to attempt to change it. As stated before, stringent *ceteris paribus* conditions are imposed on the analysis which can therefore be taken to represent the schematic conflict situation prevailing in our postulated ideal international system. In such a system then, there are three possible types of dyadical conflict configurations:

> Dictatorship vs Dictatorship *(Dict – Dict dyad)*;
> Dictatorship vs Democracy *(Dict – Dem dyad)*;
> Democracy vs Democracy *(Dem – Dem dyad)*.

In the case of the Dict – Dict dyad, when both participants are confronted with the decision situation depicted in Table 1, the preferred choice for both will be option II, thus making violence inevitable. The Iran–Iraq War of the 1980s would be an archetypal illustration of military conflict between two 'indisputable dictatorships' for whom violent disruption of the status quo is likely to be the preferred mode of pursuit of their national interests.[15]

By contrast, in the case of the Dem-Dem dyad, the preferred choice of each participant will be option I, implying no motivation for either of the parties to attempt a forcible violation of the status quo. Accordingly, while wars do occur in dyads composed of risk acceptant dictatorships, the mutual behavioural propensities of the risk-averse democratic protagonists generate a situation where there are no wars in dyads composed of exclusively such regimes. This is of course a theoretical derivative that conforms not only to the highly robust empirical findings as to the general absence of war between democracies but also tends to be supported by post-1945 realities in the Middle East, where Lebanon. up until the mid-1970s, was the only regional regime, apart from Israel, which was perceived by some scholars as manifesting democratic traits.[16] Indeed, from 1948 and until that time, there were no serious state-instigated border clashes between these two regimes. Note that the relative fragility of Lebanon cannot be invoked as a reason for the lack of dyadic violence between the two countries without simultaneously invoking inherent traits of non-belligerent restraint in democratic Israel, which manifestly did not exploit its overwhelmingly greater might to attack its much weaker neighbor as did a dictatorial Iraq in its 1990 invasion of the Kuwaiti sheikdom.

Of course alternative explanations are possible to account for Israel's refraining from the instigation of large-scale violence against Lebanon, based on the specifics of the dyadic participants and the regional environment. We claim neither exclusivity nor superiority for the explanation provided by the model in this (or any other specific) case, but merely point out that the general prognosis of the model is consistent with the specific empirical event discussed.

A slightly more complex case is the Dict-Dem dyad. When confronted with the pertinent decision situation, the proclivity of the democracy will be to opt for the maintenance of the status quo (option I). However, the dictatorship will prefer the course represented by option II, and attempt a forcible change of the status quo. This will impose violence on the dyad even though the democracy would prefer to refrain therefrom. Thus the preference of its dictatorial adversary will dictate its involvement in violent conflict, either in reaction to the dictator's aggressive initiative in implementing its choice of option II – as in the case of the Syrian and Egyptian offensive against Israel in October 1973;[17] or as a preemptive measure to forestall it, once the intentions to launch an aggressive move become clear – as in the case of Israel's preemptive strike against Egypt and Syria in 1967.[18]

With regard to the latter instance, and in the light of an earlier remark regarding the propensity of differing regime types to initiate war, it should perhaps be underscored that while Israel was indeed, the first to strike against its adversaries, it is, as Schweller points out, inappropriate to categorize this action as 'preventive war' initiated by a democracy. For it was the Arab military decisions and military initiatives that constituted the *causis belli* for the preemptive attack, and as such, should be considered aggressive action to which Israel was obliged to respond.[19] Indeed the foregoing analytical derivation of the greater predilection of dictatorships to initiate violence as a means of changing the status quo, can be adapted slightly to theoretically corroborate Schweller's finding that virtually 'all preventative wars' were initiated by non-libertarian regimes. Substantively, Schweller employs the term 'preventative war' to denote the use of large scale violence as a response to unfavorable aspects immanent in a prevailing status quo – chiefly the decline of one's own power relative to potential adversaries.[20] In this regard, it is interesting to note that Schweller presents the destruction of the Iraqi nuclear facilities in the 1981 Israeli strike as the only deviant case involving the initiation of inter-state preventative action by a democratic regime.[21] This, however, is rather a contentious example to quote of a 'preventative war' since: (a) it is questionable whether an operation of such restricted scope involving a single raid on a single objective and which, as Schweller himself comments, carried 'little (if any) military risk', qualifies as 'war'; and (b) a case can be made for the claim that the Israeli action constituted not an '*preventative*' effort to disrupt a prevailing status quo, but a '*preemptive*' measure to preclude a drastic and qualitative change in it, which would have resulted had Iraq attained nuclear capability.[22]

With regard to the definition of 'preventative' action, purists may object that if there is an on-going relative decline (i.e. an on-going change) in the prevailing circumstances, the term 'status quo' is somewhat inappropriate. This is however a difficulty that can be circumvented by using the term 'status quo' to include gradual, continuous change in prevailing conditions. Thus, as an effort to bring about abrupt, qualitative change in these conditions, a 'preventative war' can be considered as an attempt to violate such a 'status quo' by means of force. This adaption of the original premise would not change, in any significant way, the analysis conducted hitherto. Table 1 presented above (p.77) would thus be transformed into Table 2 presented below:

Where: $-\varepsilon$ is the gradual deterioration which would occur during the short time interval, T, in which an attempt to cause abrupt change (such as a preventative war) would induce a large, rapid improvement (X) if successful, or deterioration (–X) if not, with $X \rangle\rangle \varepsilon$.

TABLE 2
DECISION-MAKING SITUATION INVOLVING CHOICE BETWEEN
CERTAIN AND UNCERTAIN INITIATIVES

		Outcomes	
Decision	I	$-\varepsilon$	$-\varepsilon$
Options	II	$+X$	$-X$
Probabilities		p_1	p_2

Clearly, when confronted with the decision situation in Table 2, the order of preference of risk-averse (libertarian) and risk acceptant (non-libertarian) EUMs would remain unchanged. Thus, the former would opt for option I and abstain from violence despite the gradual decline in its power (presumbably endeavoring to address this decline in more pacific fashion such as internal reforms or alliance formation); while the latter would opt for option II and initiate a 'preventative war'.

Note that there is clearly a threshold value for $\varepsilon = \varepsilon_0$ beyond which even a risk adverse EUM will opt for the risky option. This value of ε_0 is the decrease in pay-off that would generate a corresponding decrease in utility, ΔU, equal to the difference between perceived utility associated with the current status quo and the perceived expected utility associated with the risky option. Thus the threshold value, ε_0, is such that:

$$\Delta U = \Delta U(\varepsilon_0) = U(0) - \{1/2*U(X) + 1/2*U(-X)\}$$

This calculation of the threshold value relative to the status quo is very similar to the basic technique for premium calculation in the theory of insurance. Interpreting Schweller's empirical findings in the light of this concept of a democratic 'deterioration threshold', would appear to indicate that in practice it has not yet been breached.

Clearly, for a risk-acceptant non-libertarian regime, instead of a 'deterioration threshold' there will be a theoretical 'amelioration threshold', ε_0, such that:

$$\Delta U = \Delta U(\varepsilon_0) = \{1/2*U(X) + 1/2*U(-X)\} - U(0),$$

beyond which such a regime will forgo the risky option.

The existence of such threshold levels defines the 'bargaining space' between two regimes. For example, in the case of a Dem-Dem dyad, the respective 'deterioration' thresholds determine the range in which the non-violent resolution to a clash of interests will take place; while in the case of a Dict-Dem dyad, the 'amelioration' and 'deterioration' thresholds respectively will determine whether the bargaining structure is 'resolvable' or not. If there is an overlap of the ranges defined by the thresholds, the dispute will be amenable to non-violent resolution; if not, it will not be.

Consequently the model also provides a rigorous framework for accommodating the analysis of non-violent disputes and for the definition of the boundary, delineating the realm of violent and non-violent disputes involving a democratic participant. (Non-violent interactions in Dict-Dict dyads are accounted for by the non-zero value of the systemic constant, $1 - P_c$, defined in Section F hereunder. Accordingly, it will be seen that it would be incorrect to interpret the model as presenting violence in a Dict-Dict dyad as deterministically inevitable. Rather it is treated as a stochastic event, the probability of which is dependent on the system-anarchy parameter assigned to the idealized international system specified in Section D above).

In general then, in a Dict-Dem dyad, the violence-inhibiting properties of a democracy implicit in its concave utility curve, will not be manifested, as they will be overridden by the violence inducing properties implicit in the dictator's convex utility curve. Consequently, in the terms of the model, only when a dictatorial regime is a member of a dyad, can one expect violence. This conclusion constitutes a theoretical affirmation of both Rummel's observations that the presence of at least one 'non-libertarian' regime is a necessary condition for the occurrence of violence between two states.[23] It also supports Schweller's claim of 'overwhelming empirical evidence' that 'every preventative war ... has been initiated by a non-democratic state' irrespective of whether the opposing side was democratic or authoritarian.[24]

F. The Monadic Analysis: The Arithmetical Aberration vs Substantive Significance

In this section it is shown that the deductive scheme can also account for the empirically observed results regarding propensity-to-war on the *monadic* level. In particular an explanation is offered for the observed fact that in spite of there being no wars between democracies (i.e. in Dem-Dem dyads), empirically they are found to be, as individual monads, no less war-prone than are non-democracies.[25]

To show this, suppose that the probability of a state being confronted with options as presented in Table 1 is independent of its regime type. This probability, P_c, is thus an expression of the likelihood of a potentially violent clash of interests arising between two sovereign states, each pursuing its own egotistical national self-interest in an anarchical system. Note that there is no a priori reason to assume that P_c will be regime-sensitive, unless one makes far reaching a priori assumptions as to the linkage between domestic structure and international behavior, in general; and as to the propensity of certain types of regime to *coordinate* with, or even *subordinate* their interests to those of other regimes, in particular.

Thus, the likelihood that a clash of interests between two states may arise is (in contrast to the preferred mode of resolution of such a clash) independent of the state's internal political structure. Consequently, the number of times that such a decision situation arises in a dyadical context will not depend on the composition of the dyad. It should be noted that this assumption seems to be borne out empirically. Maoz, for example, while re-affirming the lack of war in Dem-Dem dyads, found that 'dispute behavior is not affected by regime type'.[26]

Thus, assuming that in our idealized system the probability of a clash of interests arising in an encounter between two states is P_c (which as argued, is not a function of regime-type), then the probability that a given dictator will be involved in violence will also be P_c. This is because of the dictatorial preference for violence (option II) – regardless of the nature of the adversary. For a democracy the probability of a clash of interests arising in an encounter with another state will also be P_c, but the probability that this will result in violence is:

$$P_c \times P_{dict} = P_c \times \frac{N_{dict}}{N_T}$$

where: P_{dict} is the probability of a encounter with a Dict.
N_{dict} is the number of Dicts. in the system.
N_T is the total number of states in the system.

or

$$P_c \times (1 - P_{dem}) = P_c - P_c \times P_{dem} = P_c - P_c \times \frac{N_{dem}}{N_T}$$

where: P_{dem} is the probability of an encounter with a Dem.
N_{dem} is the number of Dems in the system.

Note that $P_{dict} + P_{dem} = 1$ by the definition of the idealized international system in which regimes are either indisputably democratic or indisputably dictatorial. Thus, under strict *ceteris paribus* conditions, the difference between the propensity to violence of a dictatorship and a democracy is:

$$P_c \times P_{dem} = P_c \times \frac{N_{dem}}{N_T}$$

Now, because empirically, the number of democracies in the international system in general, and in the Middle East sub-system in particular, is far less than the number of dictatorships, the difference between the propensity to violence of a dictatorship, and that of a democracy, expressed by the above product of two small numbers (each less than unity), will be even smaller and hence hard to detect. The Middle East sub-system would thus appear to provide robust corroboration of this analytical derivative, where the phenomenon of a lone democracy, Israel, surrounded and outnumbered by non-democratic regimes, being a highly war-prone regime, conforms well to the foregoing theoretical prognosis.

G. The Regional Analysis

The foregoing analysis can also be applied to empirical work regarding regime-related international behaviour conducted by Maoz, who has extended the *dyadic* context to a *regional* one. In this context, the relevant unit of analysis is no longer the participating duo, but the 'politically relevant international environment' (or PRIE). Accordingly, the PRIE of a state A, is defined such as to include: (a) all states (or colonies, principalities, or mandated territories thereof) which are contiguous to A; (b) all major powers with global reach capacity; and (c) all regional powers with regional reach capacity.[27] Maoz finds that the political make-up of the PRIE of a democratic state significantly influences the probability that it will be involved in conflict, with higher democratization inducing a lower probability of conflict. By contrast, the political make-up of the PRIE of a non-democratic state has no apparent effect on their conflict behaviour.[28]

This finding is consistent with, and indeed necessarily implicit in the foregoing theoretical development. For from the definition of a PRIE, it is clear that for any given state, what has been designated as P_c, is the probability of its involvement in a dispute of the type depicted in Table 1 within its PRIE. For a non-democratic state, the probability that the dispute will develop into violent conflict is also P_c, which is independent of the regime-type composition of the PRIE. However, in the case of a democracy, the probability of dispute developing into violent conflict is:

$$P_c \times (1 - P_{dem}) = P_c - P_c \times P_{dem} = P_c - P_c \times \frac{N_{dem}}{N_T}$$

Thus, the probability is indeed dependent on the regime-types comprising the PRIE. Clearly then, in line with Maoz's observation, as the number of democracies increases in the PRIE (N_{dem}), the probability of a democracy being involved in violent conflict decreases; and in a PRIE composed entirely of democracies, ($N_{dem} = N_T$), the probability of violent conflict is negligible, since:

$$P_c \times (1 - P_{dem}) = P_c \times \frac{(1 - N_{dem})}{N_T} = 0$$

The tranquil stability of Western Europe over the last half century, would appear to vindicate such an inference and provides stark contrast for high incidence of war in the Middle Eastern PRIE with its pronounced dictatorial, hence turbulent, composition.

H. The Propensity to Preempt

It is, nonetheless, manifestly clear that democracies do in fact initiate inter-state violence. For example, Israel launched a preemptive strike against the armies of Egypt and Syria in 1967. Likewise, the American-led coalition launched a violent strike against Iraq in 1991 without the USA having actually been subjected to direct prior attack. The foregoing theoretical analysis can also be of value in identifying some generic principle for distinguishing between the circumstances which induce democracies on the one hand, and dictatorships on the other, to embark on inter-state violence.

Consider a decision situation involving a schematic choice between policy *responses* – as opposed to the choice between policy *initiatives* dealt with hitherto. Suppose now that a severe threat to the prevailing status quo is perceived to arise by a EUM decision maker confronted by such response choices. Suppose further that it is perceived that the threat can be removed by preemptive action involving a certain sacrifice of fixed amount. This decision situation is depicted schematically in Table 3 below.

Note that the negative value 2X in Table 3 represents the severe perceived threat to the prevailing status quo, while the negative value of X represents the magnitude of the certain sacrifice required to eliminate the possibility of the perceived threat. Thus, a choice of option I indicates a willingness to forfeit a fixed, certain sacrifice (–X) involved in preemptive action required to eliminate the threat of a possible extremely negative result (–2X).

On the other hand, a choice of option II indicates a propensity to eschew preemptive action and a willingness to risk the possibility that the perceived threat will not materialize.

Note that as in the previous instance depicted in Table 1 – similar *ceteris paribus* conditions are, for similar reasons (see Section C), imposed on the decision situation depicted in Table 3. Namely, the assumption of equal probabilities for the outcomes of the uncertain option and of equal expected

TABLE 3
DECISION-MAKING SITUATION INVOLVING CHOICE BETWEEN
CERTAIN AND UNCERTAIN RESPONSES

		Outcomes	
Decision	I	–X	–X
Options	II	0	–2X
Probabilities		p_1	p_2

pay-off, (–X), associated with both options is again made, thus allowing the pure effect of the disparate risk preferences to be isolated from any extraneous influence.

Now consider figures 3 and 4 below in which the status quo is defined as a given level of pay-off, X_0.

In the case of a utility curve concave to the X-axis, associated with democracies and shown in Figure 3, the decrease in utility (ab) resulting from a fixed unit sacrifice of pay-off ($x = X_0 - 1$) is less than half of the decrease (cd) associated with a loss of 2 units of pay-off ($x = X_0 - 2$). Hence, for such a EUM decision maker, option I is the preferred one, having expected utility greater than that of option II. In Figure 4, in the case of a utility curve convex to the X-axis which is associated with dictatorships, the

FIGURE 3

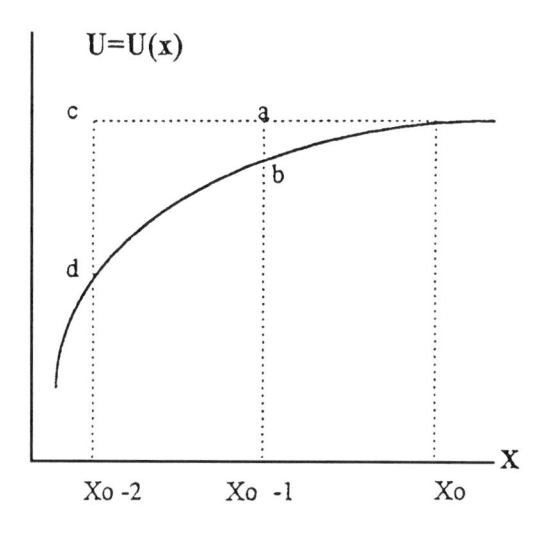

FIGURE 4

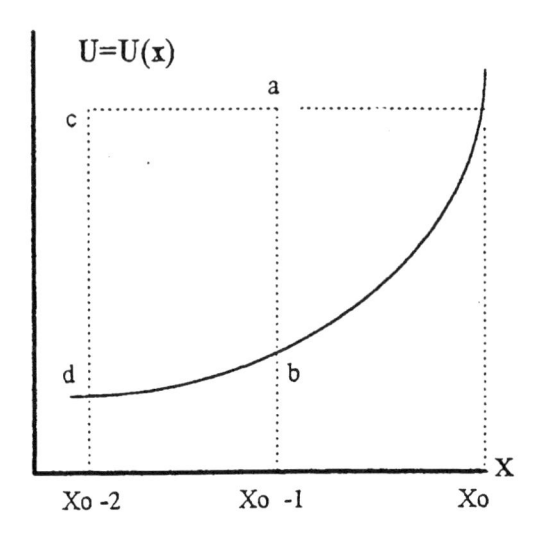

[Figure: Utility function U=U(x) curve showing points a, b, c, d at x-values Xo-2, Xo-1, Xo]

decrease in utility (ab) associated with fixed unit sacrifice of pay-off ($x = X_0 - 1$) is more than half the decrease (cd) associated with a loss of 2 units of pay-off ($x = X_0 - 2$). Hence, for such a EUM decision maker, option II is the preferred one, having expected utility greater than that of option I.

The implication of this theoretical development is that a democracy would have a greater proclivity than dictatorships to initiate violent preemptive action in order to remove a grave threat to the existing status quo. More specifically, this means that, according to the model, risk-averse libertarian regimes have a lower pre-emption threshold than risk-acceptant non-libertarian ones.

Thus in Table 3, for a given level of threat, $-2X$, the preemption threshold for a libertarian regime, X_{th}, will be at $X_{th} = -X - \delta < X$, where:

$$U(-X - \delta) = 1/2\{U(-2X) + U(0)\}.$$

By contrast, for a given level of threat $-2X$, the preemption threshold for a non-libertarian regime, X_{th}, will be at $X_{th} = -X + \delta > X$, where:

$$U(-X + \delta) = 1/2\{U(-2X) + U(0)\}$$

Note that the implication is *not* that, in the real-world, violent pre-emption by risk-acceptant dictatorships is entirely unfeasible; nor that the initiation of violence for reasons other than preemption by risk-averse democracies is totally inconceivable in specific empirical situations. Rather the inference to be made is that because of their inherent differences *vis-à-vis* their attitude to risk, risk-averse democracies have, other things being equal, a greater propensity to pre-empt than do risk-acceptant dictatorships.[29]

Moreover, it should be stressed that the schematic representation in Table 3 does not signify that all real-world decisions to pre-empt are necessarily 'risk-free' – the expected pay-off (as distinct from the expected utility) of the decision to preempt may indeed be greater than the expected pay-off of the decision to refrain therefrom. However, Table 3 does encapsulate the essential rationale of such a decision. For in principle the purpose of preemption is to remove a threat to the prevailing status quo and not to launch an initiative to *improve* it, as represented in Tables 1 and 2. Thus, the best perceived outcome is the status quo itself (i.e. 0 in Table 3). Accordingly, if it is perceived that a decision to preempt involves a possibility of failure with a negative pay-off of an order of magnitude approaching that of the threat which the preemption is designed to remove, the decision to preempt will be *irrational* for any EUM, no matter what his risk preference. Thus, unless preemption is perceived to be significantly less risky than the decision to gamble on the materialization of a severe threat, it will not be a viable rational-policy option.

This derivation of regime-differentiated propensities to violence in order to defend (or restore) a prevailing status quo, is of not inconsiderable significance. For instance, it provides a cogent and coherent explanation for dictators such as Gamal Abdul Nasser or Saddam Hussein underestimating the vigor of democratic response to their violation of the status quo in the Sinai Peninsula and the Persian Gulf respectively.[30] But perhaps of wider significance, is the fact that the theoretical conclusions are borne out by Maoz's findings that democracies are generally 'considerably more sensitive' to radical changes in their PRIEs than are non-democracies.[31]

It would thus appear that the theoretical constructs which have been adopted, generate a rather elegant *principle of asymmetry* in distinguishing between the proclivities of dictatorships and democracies to resort to violence. According to this principle, dictatorships have a greater propensity to initiate violence as a means of *changing* the prevailing status quo, while democracies have a greater propensity to embark on violence to *maintain* the prevailing status quo or to restore it once it has been violated.

I. The Policy Oriented Implications

As shown, when the element of uncertainty is introduced into the decision-making situation in a methodologically rigorous manner, the differing domestic constraints, formulated in Kantian terms, can be translated into differing EUM rational actor risk-preferences, and hence differing EUM rational actor utility-profiles. Consequently, the seemingly-uniform *realpolitik* aspiration of maximizing expected utility will express itself in different policy choices, each of which maximize expected utility for actors of different utility profiles. Hence a logically-consistent conceptual framework is created in which the *realpolitik* pursuit of the national interest will be conducted differently by regimes of differing domestic constraints, thereby producing an integrative synthesis, reconciling the two apparently-antithetical paradigms of international relations.

However, beyond the general consequence of this result, the analytical scheme developed also generates several policy implications of significance for the Middle East. These implications draw their claim to real-world validity and pertinence from the fact that the hypothetical analog- system, designed in the foregoing sections, produces theoretical results which indeed parallel observed empirical results in the real-world system. It thus provides a cogent 'as if' account for these phenomena. Hence, if further theoretical conclusions can be inferred from the hypothetical analog, these should also be considered valid and pertinent inferences for the real-world system, which the analog-system has been shown to parallel.

An example, regarding the implications for the formulation of deterrence policy will serve to illustrate the point. Consider two states A and B. Suppose that B is deliberating a policy choice of either option I or II in Table 1 *vis-à-vis* A, while A is interested only in preserving the status quo (i.e. option I). Both A and B estimate that if B opts for the status quo, this will involve neither costs nor gains for either of them. Similarly, they both estimate that if B attempts to change the status quo, A will react and attempt to prevent this. In the context of Table 1, +X represents what both A and B perceive to be the gains that will accrue to B if it is successful in achieving a change in the status quo, whilst −X represents the costs that both perceive will be incurred if B fails. In other words: −X is a measure of the deterrent element incorporated in A's retaliatory reaction to a possible attempt by B to change the status quo to its advantage.

Clearly, if the perceived gains are of equal order of magnitude relative to the perceived losses, and the likelihood of incurring them is also perceived to be roughly equal, than any decision maker with a concave utility curve will be deterred by the deterrent element immanent in the possible loss associated with option II, and thus opt for the maintenance of the status quo.

Therefore, from the point of view of A, it is of profound significance whether B's utility curve is concave or convex. For in the former case, the threat of inflicting a loss of −X on B would be sufficient to deter it from any attempt to disrupt the status quo, while it would not be so in the latter case.

Thus, if as it has been argued, concavity of the utility curve is associated with democracy and convexity with dictatorship, it follows that a democracy would be deterred from any attempt to alter the status quo under the specified parameters, while a dictatorship would not be. Conversely, under the same assumptions, any decision maker with a convex utility curve will not be deterred by the possible loss involved in option II, which will be his preferred course of action.

Hence, if A is a democratic policy formulator, several interesting conclusions suggest themselves:

i. As a state which is interested in preserving the status quo, it matters profoundly, even in a EUM *realpolitik* context, whether its potential adversary is a democracy or dictatorship.

ii. If the adversary is a democracy, it will be easier (i.e. require less resources) to dissuade it from attempts to disrupt the status quo than if it were a dictatorship.

iii. A policy which may be perceived as sufficiently robust to deter a democracy from any attempt to violate the status quo, will in fact be insufficiently so, if A's adversary is a dictatorship.

iv. If A is a democracy, then in order to deter B from attempting to change the status quo, it must increase either the mutually-perceived (by both A and B) potential costs such a move may entail, and/or the likelihood of incurring such costs over and above the levels that A would perceive as being sufficiently daunting to deter a democracy (or itself) from such an attempt.

Note that these are policy aspects that are not well elucidated in game-theoretic approaches such as those of Bueno de Mesquita and Lalman, where, because the issue of disparate risk preference is dealt with less explicitly – and therefore less rigorously – the analysis is at times coerced into almost tautological circularities, such as assuming that democracies are likely to be dovish in order to explain their mutually dovish interactions.[32]

Point iv. suggests the existence of an inherent potential for a democracy to miscalculate in formulating deterrent policy against dictatorships – even when there is no discrepancy between the protagonists' perceptions of the consequences of possible outcomes or of their probability of occurrence. For when such policy is designed on the basis of the evaluations of the adversary's expected reactions, under the assumption that the cost/benefit calculus one applies oneself, will also be applied by the said adversary, then definite potential for error is introduced – even when both parties concur entirely in their evaluations of the significance of potential future results and of the likelihood thereof. Such an error would lead a democracy to believe that a dictatorship would be deterred from attempting to violate the status quo, in circumstances where this is in fact not the case. The result would either be a *deterrence failure* in cases where intentions to change the status quo are suspected and *strategic surprise* when they are not.[33]

In this regard Janice Gross Stein has deftly described the flaw in the Israeli decision-makers assessment of Egyptian readiness in 1973 to violate an existing status quo, despite Cairo's awareness of the magnitude of the costs involved therein.[34] Similarly, the marked willingness of non-libertarian regimes to risk heavy losses seems to call for some reassessment of the value of a nuclear deterrence of the kind Israel is alleged to possess especially within frontiers that may seriously reduce second-strike capability.[35]

J. Conclusion

For the Middle East, the implications that follow from the foregoing theoretical developments would seem to militate in favor of a thorough reappraisal of much of the conventional wisdom on which the Arab-Israeli 'peace process' has been founded since 1991. For if: (1) regional violence is a function of the regime-types comprising the regional political environment; (2) the greater the degree of non-libertarianism in the region, the greater the potential for violence; (3) with the exception if Israel, nearly all the regimes in the Middle East may be categorized as having a pronounced non-libertarian nature,[36] then, in order to induce regional stability, international efforts should be directed towards bringing about democratic reforms in the non-libertarian Arab regimes rather than extracting territorial concessions from the libertarian Israeli regime. For the model suggests that this would contribute little to establishing the required structural conditions for a stable and durable peace.

Indeed, the inferences implicit in the internal logic of the models would seem to prescribe the adoption of a robustly assertive defence posture by libertarian regimes in a predominantly non-libertarian environment such as the Middle East. For the diagnosis is that a non-libertarian adversary will choose to eschew option II in Table I in favor of option I, only if the libertarian regime conveys the perception that should any attempt be made to disrupt violently the prevailing status quo, it has the capacity and the resolve to inflict upon the prospective non-libertarian aggressor outcomes significantly more disagreeable than those which would suffice to deter an adversary of a more libertarian nature.

This of course entails a far more somber and foreboding perspective of regional realities than that on which the present 'peace process' with its vision of a harmonious New Middle East is predicated.[37] Indeed, it would appear that before such a vision of European Union-type harmony and co-operation can be initiated, a restructuring of the current political edifice, involving substantial liberalization of the incumbent regimes in the region, needs to be implemented. This would seem to be an apparently necessary pre-requisite for the creation of a political climate in which non-violent means become the preferred mode of dispute resolution. For without EU-type regimes' with EU-type cost/benefit calculi, the vision of EU-type harmony seems to be inappropriately premature.

In this regard it should be underscored that any paradigm for some exogeneously initiated process for a *long term, durable* reduction on inter-state conflicts of interests (such as negotiations under third party auspices or any other endeavor of external origin), runs counter to the assumption (and reality) of international anarchy in the global system in general, and in the Middle East sub-system, in particular. As we have pointed out, any assumption that the interests of *sovereign* entities, which by definition perceive and pursue these interests independently of each other, can some how, on a long term basis, be co-ordinated with, or subordinated to, those of other sovereign entities, necessarily implies imposing *hierarchical* elements of some kind, on a system (or sub-system) inherently *anarchic*. This of course does not obviate the possibility of *short term, random* congruence of national interests and resultant *ad hoc* alliances and cooperative action between sovereign states. However, this should not be confused with *purposeful, steady-state* reduction of system anarchy and of the inherent potential for the divergence of national interests.

Thus, the model argues that while conflicts of interest are inevitable in an anarchic system, democratic regimes are far more likely to resolve them by non-violent means (such as in the USA-Japanese trade dispute, where the most radical measure proposed was sanctions), while dictatorial regimes are more likely to resolve them by violence (such in the case of the Iraqi invasion of Kuwait). Thus, even without evoking Samuel Huntington's emotive and ominous imagery of Islam's 'bloody borders' in his foreboding prognosis of a imminent 'Clash of Civilizations',[38] it would appear that, until the sovereign units in the region undergo meaningful democratization, the order of the day will be: SI VIS PACEM, PARA BELLUM.

NOTES

1. For a discussion of the changing regional interests of the United States and the Soviet Union see Gideon Doron, 'Peace or Oil: the Nixon Administration and its Middle East Policy Choices', in Leon Friedman and William Levanttrosser (eds) *Cold War Patriot and Statesman* (Westport, CT: Greenwood Press 1993) pp.119–37.

2. Throughout this study we shall adopt Rummel's usage of the term 'violence' in the formulation of his 'Libertarian Propositions'. The term will thus incorporate all forms of the overt, state-to-state use of force (including war), in the conduct of a regime's official foreign policy. See Rudolph Rummel, 'A Test of Libertarian Propositions on Violence', *Jnl of Conflict Resolution* [hereafter *JCR*] 29 (1985) pp.419–55.
3. See Bruce Bueno De Mesquita and David Lalman, *War and Reason: Domestic and International Imperatives* (New Haven: Yale UP 1992), pp.15–19.
4. See for example, Peter Wallensteen, *Structure and War* (Stockholm: Raban and Sjoren 1973); Melvin Small and David Singer, 'The War Proneness of Democratic Regimes 1816–1965', *Jerusalem Jnl of Int. Relations* 1/4 (1976) pp.50–69; Erich Weede, 'Democracies and War Involvement', *JCR* 28/4 (1984) pp.649–64; Rudolph Rummel, 'Libertarianism and International Violence', *JCR* 27/1 (1983) pp.27–71 and, Rummel (note 2); Steve Chan, 'Mirror Mirror on the Wall - Are Freer Countries More Pacific?' *JCR*, 28 (1984) pp.617–48; Michael Doyle, 'Liberalism and World Politics', *American Political Science Review* 80 (1986) pp.1151–63; Francis Fukuyama, 'The End of Ideology', *National Interest* 16/2 (1989) pp.3–18; Zeev Maoz and Nasrin Abdolali 'Regime Type and International Conflict, 1816–1976', *JCR* 33 (1989) pp.3–35; Stuart Bremer, 'Dangerous Dyads: Conditions Affecting the Likelihood of Interstate War 1816–1965', *JCR* 36 (1992) pp.309–42; and Zeev Maoz and Bruce Russet, 'Alliances, Contiguity, Wealth and Political Stability: Is the Lack of Conflict among Democracies a Statistical Artifact?', *Int. Interactions* 17 (1992) pp.245–67 and, 'Normative and Structural Causes of Democratic Peace, 1946–1986', *American Political Science Review* 87 (1993) pp.624–38.
5. Randall Schweller, 'Domestic Structure and Preventative War: Are Democracies More Pacific?' *World Politics* 44 (1992) pp.235–69.
6. Immanuel Kant, 'Perpetual Peace' (1795) in L.W. Beck (ed.) *On History* (NY: Bobbs-Merrill 1963) pp.94–5.
7. Bruce Bueno de Mesquita, *The War Trap* (New Haven, CT: Yale UP 1981) p.20.
8. Bueno de Mesquita and Lalman (note 3) p.145.
9. For example Bueno de Mesquita and Lalman sometimes (such as on pp.40–7),use α, τ, φ to denote *independent* variables (units of pay-off which generate utility s.t. $U = U\alpha, \tau, \varphi$)), while in other instances (such as on p.165), they glide nonchalantly in the use of the same variables to denote the *dependent* variable (utility itself). This is of course only meaningful if one assumes a specific linear utility curve (i.e. $U(x) = x$), implying a risk indifferent decision-maker, and implicitly precludes risk averse and risk acceptant decision-makers from the model, which is clearly an impediment that severely restricts the applicability of the theory they develop. The confusion between the actual cost or gain on the one hand, and the utility that this cost or gain generates on the other, recurs several times throughout Bueno de Mesquita and Lalman's work.
10. Note that it is possible to arrive at identical results by different methods. For example Sherman, using analytical techniques similar to those employed in micro-economic models of consumer choice under external constraints, demonstrates, in a formally deductive manner (entirely independent of the Kantian arguments presented above), that the five defining parameters of the disparate archetypal regimes as specified in Section D will, under strict *ceteris paribus* conditions, interact to induce a relatively greater (lesser) propensity to risk in non-libertarian (libertarian) regimes. Consequently, under the assumption of a EUM executive decision making unit, this interaction of defining parameters will induce greater convexity, and greater concavity (towards the X-axis) in the utility curves of non-libertarian and libertarian regimes respectively. See Martin Sherman, *Despots, Democrats, and the Determinants of Inernational Conflict* (London: Macmillan forthcoming, 1997).

Likewise, the risk-averse characteristic of libertarian regimes is confirmed by Kilgour who, using a game-theoretic approach in crisis decision making models, cites empirical corroboration of the view that, 'decisional constraints [in libertarian regimes] serve mainly to preserve the status quo making any movement away from it . . . less preferred'. (D. Marc Kilgour, 'Domestic Political Structure and War: A Game Theoretic Approach', *JCR* 35/2 (1991) p.278. Furthermore, Kilgour, whose definitive regime parameters are, to a large degree, similar to those specified in Section D of this work, goes on to state that 'the existence of an effective opposition [a feature which by definition is characteristic of democratic regimes only] seems not only to reduce the probability that a state will wish to foment a crisis, but also the values of all outcomes that might follow the crisis' (Kilgour, p.280). These two elements – the propensity for the maintenance of the status quo, and the proclivity to reduce the spread of possible outcomes – capture the very essence of risk averse behaviour.

In similar vein, Doyle identifies aversion to risk as feature of libertarian international behaviour. In his study of Liberalism and World Politics he points to the 'exercise of democratic caution' in the conduct of the foreign policy of libertarian regimes (Doyle, note 4, p.1162).

Other scholars see the externalization of internal democratic norms as the reason for more subdued, and circumspect international behavior of libertarian regimes . Maoz and Russett (note 4) for example summarize the essence of this approach in the following manner: 'Since democracies emphasize peaceful competition, persuasion, and compromise ... these notions are used by democratic governments in dealing with other states' (p.246). Clearly the externalization of such norms will generate international behavior that would be consistent with risk aversion – or at least inconsistent with risk acceptance.

Thus the risk-averse attributes of democratic regimes and the counter distinction between these attributes and risk characteristics typical of non-democracies is not a concept uncommon in the mainstream literature of international relations. The present study, however, focuses on articulating this feature, and its policy-oriented implications, more explicitly and with greater formal decision-theoretic rigor than has been done previously.

11. See Sherman (note 10).
12. Iran and Saudi Arabia, for example, are theocracies; Iraq, Syria, Libya, Yemen and Egypt are essentially 'revolutionary' one-party or military regimes; and Kuwait, the United Arab Emirates and Jordan are oligarchical kingdoms.
13. James Conant, *Modern Science and Modern Man* (NY: Columbia UP 1952) p.62.
14. Kenneth Waltz, *Theory of International Politics* (Reading, MA:Wesley 1979) p.68.
15. Christine M. Helms, *Iraq: Eastern Flank of the Arab World* (Washington DC: Brookings 1984) p.186.
16. For example, Eric Nordlinger, *Conflict Regulation in Divided Societies* (Cambridge, MA: Harvard UP 1972).
17. Indeed, this Egyptian initiative could be considered an archetypal example of a 'preventative' war, discussed in some detail hereinafter, and schematically depicted in Table 2.
18. The conditions under which the theoretical model will predict the use of preemptive violence by a democracy are discussed in section H below.
19. See Schweller (note 5) pp.264–5, see also Ben Mor, *Decision and Interaction in Crisis: A Model of International Crisis Behavior* (Westport, CT: Praeger 1993).
20. Schweller (note 5) p.236.
21. Ibid. p.264–5.
22. The relatively high propensity of democracies to preempt in order defend prevailing status quo situations is discussed in Section H, as is the qualitative analytical distinction between 'preventative' action as an *initiative* designed to disrupt prevailing circumstances involving an on-going deterioration of the initiator's relative power; and 'preemptive' action as a response designed to forestall the radical disruption of the prevailing circumstances, considered immanent in a perceived threat of an aggressive initiative by potential adversary. These differing types of actions are schematically portrayed in decision-theoretic terms in Table 2 and Table 3 respectively.
23. See Rummel (note 4) 1983 p.67 and (note 2) pp.421 and 441.
24. Schweller (note 5) p.249.
25. See Chan (note 4) p.642 and Maoz and Russet (note 4) p.245.
26. Zeev Maoz, *Domestic Sources of Global Change* (Ann Arbor: U. of Michigan Press 1996) p.157.
27. Ibid. pp.139, 168–9.
28. Ibid. p.161.

29. However, in actual fact, it is possible to make a far more unequivocal assertion than this. For, under the eminently reasonable assumption that a desirable status quo will not induce the initiation of violence, the motivations for the initiation of interstate violence (as opposed to armed response to a direct attack) may be broadly classified into two major categories: (a) 'preventative motives' – i.e initiatives launched to impose a change on an undesirable status quo (broadly defined to include on-going, prevailing trends); (b) 'preemptive motives' – i.e. initiatives launched to remove a threat to a desirable status quo, or to restore it once violated (in cases which do not entail direct attack on the initiator, such as the US-led initiative in the 1990–91 Gulf War).

    Now as not only the model's prognoses, but the empirical evidence seems to indicate that the motivations of the first type i.e. 'preventative motives', as defined above, are confined to non-libertarian regimes (Schweller) it would indeed seem that libertarian motivations are restricted to the second type i.e to 'preemptive motives' as defined above.

    Note the model does not relate to all possible manifestations of violence, but explicitly restricts itself to violence between states mutually perceived, at least ex ante, as sovereign. Thus, phenomena such as colonial conquest by libertarian regimes are not included within the scope of the analysis, which relates to an international system of type specified in Section D in which non-sovereign political entities are inadmissible. In such a context, colonies (as non-sovereign entities) are admissible only as territory under the sovereignty of an empire. Thus the conquest by one empire of territory under rule of another would be considered an inter-state conflict. Such conflicts should be distinguished conceptually from conquest of domains perceived 'unclaimed' by some other acknowledged sovereign state. However, since such events have not been of relevance over the last half century, their exclusion from the scope of the analysis, would appear to be but a minor deficiency in the modern context.

30. On Nasser's miscalculations see Mor (note 19) and Shlomo Aronson, *Conflict and Bargaining in the Middle East* (Baltimore: Johns Hopkins UP 1978) pp.56–74. On Saddam Hussein's mistaken perceptions see, Efraim Karsh 'Survival at all Costs: Saddam Hussein as Crisis Manager' in Barzilai, Klieman and Shidlo, *The Gulf Crisis and its Global Aftermath* (London: Routledge 1993) pp.51–66

31. Maoz (note 26) pp.161 and 166.

32. Bueno de Mesquita and Lalman (note 3) p.156.

33. See Sherman (note 10) and Efraim Kam, *Surprise Attack: The Victim's Perseptive* (Cambridge, MA: Harvard UP 1988).

34. Janice Gross Stein, 'Calculation, Miscalculation and Conventional Deterrence I:The View from Cairo' and ibid. II: The View from Jerusalem' in R. Jervis, R.N. Lebow and J. Gross Stein (eds.) *Psychology and Deterrence* (Baltimore: Johns Hopkins UP 1985) pp.34–88.

35. For example, see Seymour Hersh, *The Samson Option: Israel's Nuclear Arsenal and American Foreign Policy* (NY: Random House 1991).

36. Note that points (1) and (2) are not only theoretical derivatives of Section G but also are empirically supported by Moaz's findings as to the influence of the composition a given PRIE. Point (3) expresses no more than a observation of empirical realities in the Middle East.

37. For a detailed exposition of this vision – see Shimon Peres, *The New Middle East* (Beni Berak: Stimazki 1993 in Hebrew).

38. Samuel Huntington, 'The Clash of Civilizations?', *Foreign Affairs* 72/3 (Summer 1993) pp.22–49.

Great Powers and Regional Peacemaking: Patterns in the Middle East and Beyond

BENJAMIN MILLER

With the end of the Cold War many things have changed in world politics, most notably in US-Russian relations and in Russia's behaviour in foreign affairs. Yet, some recent diplomatic positions and actions of Russia in the domain of regional conflict management and resolution are quite reminiscent of past Soviet conduct in this domain. At the same time, some of the US reactions remind us of earlier American attitudes dating back at least to the Cold War era. Thus, there is much in common to President Boris Yeltsin's call in June 1994 for an international conference on the North Korean nuclear crisis, the Russian proposal in early 1994 to reconvene an international conference to resolve the Arab–Israeli conflict, and to the Russian broker urging the West during the Sarajevo crisis of February 1994 to treat his country as an 'equal partner'. Despite the warming of US-Russian relations in the last few years, the US reaction to these ideas has been somewhat lukewarm. At the same time, there is a growing worry in the West that Russian treatment of the ex-Soviet republics resembles earlier imperialist tendencies of both the Soviet Union and Tsarist Russia *vis-à-vis* its weak neighbors. These coercive tactics can be contrasted with US hesitations about using force in its own backyard against Haiti, its reluctance to impose a settlement on the weak party in the Bosnian conflict – the Muslims, and its relatively benign leadership of the post-Gulf War Middle East peace process. I will argue that such diplomatic positions and actions by the US and Russia reflect, at least to some extent, a continuation of certain patterns demonstrated during the Cold War, most notably in the Middle East. Since these patterns were not caused by the Cold War, they are likely to continue in the post-Cold War era so long as the causal factors which have led to their emergence in the first place are going to be in effect.

Thus, these causal factors are likely to affect the prospects for great power concerted diplomacy *vis-à-vis* the numerous regional conflicts in the post-Cold War period.

Indeed, the seemingly growing possibility of the formation of a great power concert for dealing with regional conflicts in the post-Cold War era has recently attracted considerable interest among international relations scholars.[1] The major question explored by most recent studies has been the willingness of the great powers to work together with regard to promoting the resolution of regional conflicts. Yet, great power approach to regional peacemaking has two distinct aspects: the preference of a unilateral or a multilateral path *vis-à-vis* the other great powers; and the attitude toward the small states in the region: coercive or benign. The lack of a clear-cut distinction between these two dimensions by studies of great-power concerted diplomacy (the second aspect especially has been overlooked) has precluded a useful explanation of this phenomenon. I propose a model of great power approach to regional peacemaking including both dimensions.

The explanation will be based on the combined effects of two factors. One factor is derived from a realist perspective, while the other (the type of domestic regime of the great power) stems from a liberal approach. The model is examined with regard to the different approaches of the superpowers to the resolution of the Arab–Israeli conflict during the Cold War era. Indeed, the Middle East is an appropriate region for such an analysis because of the intensity and persistence of the Arab–Israeli conflict during the Cold War era. Moreover, there were some notable superpower attempts at resolving this regional conflict, either unilaterally or multilaterally,[2] probably more than in any other region during the post-1945 era. After introducing the model, I shall elaborate below why the selection of the Middle East as the case-study is justified in terms of the model and for the purpose of examining it empirically.

The starting point for the following discussion will be that great powers have different approaches toward regional conflict resolution. Indeed, as I will show, there were persistent differences between the US and Soviet approaches to regional conflict resolution during the Cold War, notably with regard to the Middle East. The persistent differences between the superpowers with regard to the question whether or not to cooperate show the limitations of one of the most common explanations of why superpower cooperation in regional conflict resolution failed during the Cold War – namely, ideological antagonism. This explanation should lead us to expect a similar behaviour on the part of both superpowers, namely, rejection of cooperation with the ideological rival. Yet, as this study shows, only one of the powers persistently rejected cooperation in Middle East regional peacemaking while the other superpower persistently favored it. Moreover, the continuities in attitudes from the Cold War era despite the ending of the ideological conflict may also testify to the inadequacy of the ideological explanation, and seem to suggest that the explanation of great power approaches to regional peacemaking has to be based on factors that carried over to the post-Cold War era.

Like the ideological explanation, systems theory[3] also cannot satisfactorily account for the variation in the great power approaches (as well as for the continuities in their attitudes following the end of bipolarity). On the contrary, this theory expects that states located similarly in the international system will tend to behave similarly irrespective of their internal attributes. The superpowers of the Cold War era should especially conform to this expectation because of the highly intense effects exerted by bipolar systems on great power behaviour. However, when the great powers behave differently in a certain domain under the same international system, we must turn to explanatory factors other than polarity. Moreover, there is an indeterminacy in the neorealist analysis of certain outcomes.[4] For example, despite the crucial importance that structural theory attributes to the effects of polarity on international outcomes, it is not clear from that literature whether one should expect more great power cooperation in bipolarity or in multipolarity.[5] Consequently, instead of focusing on polarity, it might be useful, as some studies have recently suggested, to integrate the effects of systemic and domestic factors.[6]

Accordingly, the explanation presented here is based on the combined effects of a power-related factor, namely the relative capabilities of the great powers vis-à-vis each other, and a unit-level element – the type of domestic regime of the great powers. Each of the two factors is related to one of the two dimensions of the great power attitude toward regional peacemaking. More specifically, whereas relative capabilities account for the great power preference of a multilateral or a unilateral path in the region vis-à-vis the other great powers, the attitude to the small regional states is shaped by the type of the great power's domestic regime. I introduce the two dimensions of the great power approach toward regional peacemaking in the first section. The next two sections discuss theoretically the effects of relative capabilities on the inclination toward a multilateral or a unilateral approach and of the great power domestic regime on the attitude toward small states. The following two sections provide an empirical application of the main propositions to US and Soviet behaviour in Middle East diplomacy in the Cold War era. The last section and the conclusions discuss seemingly deviant cases and apply the model to the post-Cold War Middle East, respectively.

The Dependent Variables: Great Power Approaches to Regional Conflict Resolution

For the purposes of this study, peacemaking may be defined as a strategy pursued by an external power, based mainly on diplomatic, although possibly also on economic and military measures, and designed to promote conflict resolution between parties to a regional conflict. This study discusses the situation where the great powers are genuinely interested in promoting the resolution of a regional conflict – if only in order to prevent its escalation and enhance international stability. Such a focus on negotiated conflict resolution by diplomatic means has to be distinguished from crisis management, on the one hand, and from military intervention by one of the great powers in a regional state, on the other. Both crisis management and unilateral military interventions are beyond the scope of diplomatic peacemaking and thus are excluded from the model discussed here. They differ from peacemaking in terms of both objectives and means. The objective in peacemaking is resolving the fundamental issues in a regional conflict but this is usually not the goal in crisis management and military interventions. Crisis management is the attempt to balance between protecting one's vital interests and avoiding war but without necessarily settling the underlying issues in a conflict.[7] Thus, the situation discussed in this study should be differentiated from a crisis situation among the great powers themselves which might arise from the escalation of a regional war to a dangerously high probability of a resort to military force directly involving the great powers. As for a military intervention of a great power, it may be designed as part of a peacemaking strategy (in which case it constitutes peace enforcement), but it may frequently be unrelated to peacemaking.[8]

As for the means employed, although peacemaking might also make use of military power (including the threat or use of force), the difference is that it is only one of the means in a wide range of policy tools available to peacemakers, and not necessarily the most useful or prevalent of these tools in many cases of conflict resolution and regional reconciliation. This is in contrast to the obvious centrality of military force in both crisis management (primarily threats of force) and military interventions. An additional difference between peacemaking on the one hand and crisis management and military interventions on the other concerns explanatory factors. Under conditions of crisis and threat of war that are typical of both crisis management and military intervention, realist factors such as polarity and balances of capabilities and interests are the dominant explanatory factors, but this is not the case to the same extent with regard to peacemaking which often extends beyond the time of a specific regional crisis into noncrisis situations.[9] Such is the theoretical logic behind the argument of this model that domestic factors must be included in explaining attitudes toward peacemaking and conflict resolution which take place beyond the time of a certain military crisis.

Indeed, even in a situation of peacemaking, the approaches of different great powers to the resolution of a regional conflict may vary on two major aspects:

First, a great power may either be inclined to cooperate with the other great powers in regional peacemaking, act jointly with them, and pursue concerted diplomacy in the region – or, conversely, it may attempt to pacify the region on its own, and to exclude the other great powers from its peacemaking efforts, in order to reap unilateral benefits in the region. These approaches are termed multilateral-cooperative[10] versus unilateral-exclusionary.

Second, whatever the approach of a great power to cooperation with other great powers in the region, it may also adopt two distinct attitudes with regard to the small states involved in the regional conflict. These attitudes are termed accommodative and coercive. The accommodative approach emphasizes negotiated diplomacy for promoting regional conflict resolution; the local actors actively participate in the negotiating process and can voice their concerns and bargain among themselves and with the great powers. The talks between the great powers and the small actors tend to be of a persuasive nature, characterized by compromise and give-and-take rather than sheer *diktat* by the great powers to the smaller states. Indeed, accommodative diplomacy attempts to advance peace and stability in the region (whether unilaterally or multilaterally) while minimizing the encroachment on the local states' sovereignty and autonomy. Great-power mediation in a regional conflict is a major manifestation of what is called here accommodative peacemaking. Indeed, mediation is 'an intervention of a third party in a conflict with the stated purpose of contributing to its abatement or resolution through negotiation. It is an intervention acceptable to the adversaries in the conflict, who cooperate diplomatically with the intervenor.'[11] In contrast, in the coercive[12] approach the great powers impose a regional order on the small states.[13] A situation where several great powers cooperate with regard to resolving a regional conflict in a coercive manner may be termed condominium. In the context of regional conflict resolution, a condominium refers to a collusive definition of great power interests, geared toward jointly imposing on weaker states terms for peaceful regional settlement that the great powers have worked out on their own.[14]

Relative Capabilities and the Choice of a Unilateral vs. Multilateral Path

Systems theory assumes that there is a tendency for rough equality in great power capabilities and accordingly focuses on the effects of changes in the number of the great powers.[15] Yet, even among great powers that are roughly equal in overall capabilities, there may be differences in capabilities or resources in certain issue areas or regions. We may thus distinguish between relatively superior and inferior (or weaker) powers *vis-à-vis* these issues or regions. In case of such inequality in great power capabilities, there are likely to be differences between the orientations of the superior and the inferior powers with regard to regional conflict resolution.

Indeed, in contrast to systems theory, hegemonic theories highlight the important effects of power asymmetries among great powers on international behaviour and outcomes.[16] Yet, in the terms used here, while one variant of hegemonic theories underlines the benign or multilateral-accommodative character of hegemonic leadership,[17] another variant advances a unilateralist-coercive type of hegemony.[18]

This study will advance a more differentiated conceptualization of hegemony which depends on relative capabilities (regarding the unilateral-multilateral aspect – that is, the approach to the other great powers) but also on domestic regimes (with respect to the coercive/ accommodative dimension – namely, the approach to smaller powers).[19] Let us start with the unilateral-multilateral question.

THE UNILATERAL-MULTILATERAL QUESTION

Proposition 1: All other things being equal, a great power that is superior or dominant in a certain region *vis-à-vis* other great powers will tend to exclude them from international diplomacy in the region involved, and will prefer to pursue unilateral peacemaking, to the extent that it can reasonably believe that its resources enable it to play the role of an exclusive broker. This belief can be derived from a no-choice situation for the small powers who enjoy very limited maneuvering room (this is typical of a coercive order). Another major source for the belief in such an ability is the local parties' preference for a unilateral brokerage by that power, because the small powers believe that the superior resources of the leading power can both advance a regional settlement more effectively than other agents and provide side payments to the local parties (this is characteristic of an accommodative management). The dominant great power will, in turn, be interested in unilateral management because, beside benefiting from the collective goods of growing regional and international stability, it will be able to gain some important unilateral benefits from brokering the regional settlement, such as a growing political influence and a secure position in a stabilizing region, greater economic advantages (preferential access to raw materials and markets), and enhanced international prestige.

In contrast, those weaker great powers which are interested in regional stability, will prefer a multilateral framework in which they will be able to take part alongside the leading power in the resolution of regional problems. Their inclusion also conveys a recognition on the part of the dominant power of their equal great power status, at least on the issues involved.

Having said that, it is worthwhile underlying the 'all other things being equal' qualification to this proposition. Thus, the general state of great power relations and the degree of ideological polarization among them may condition the degree of the dominant power's inclination toward unilateralism. In other words, the better the overall relations and the lower the ideological polarization between the great powers, the greater the tendency of the dominant power to move away from a pure unilateral-exclusionary preference and toward a position of a 'multilateral leader' or a 'first among equals,' and vice versa.

Type of Domestic Regime and the Choice of Accommodative vs. Coercive Strategy

I propose that the preference for a certain strategy with regard to small states depends on unit-level attributes of the great power. The logic of the second (state or unit-level) image suggests that there is a congruence between the internal environment of states and their behaviour in international affairs. When it comes to a choice between an accommodative and a coercive strategy, two factors internal to the state exert an influence. The first is the dominant *ideology*, political culture or world view of a great power, which affects its *willingness* to pursue one of the two strategies. The ideological factor is a necessary condition for the pursuit of an accommodative approach but it is insufficient by itself to ensure a minimal use of coercive measures. Indeed, even more important is the second factor, namely, the domestic political *structure*, which affects the *ability* of a great power to adopt this strategy, and thus may impose a constraint on it.[20] The relevant distinction in this context is one between liberal democracies and authoritarian states. I will propose that because of the combination of the factors of willingness and ability, liberal democracies will prefer an accommodative approach, while authoritarian states will tend to a coercive strategy.

DEMOCRACIES' BELIEF IN SELF-DETERMINATION AND THE INCLINATION TO AN ACCOMMODATIVE APPROACH

Proposition 2: All else being equal, liberal democracies are relatively more concerned about the right of small nations to self-determination and are relatively less likely to favor a coercive regulation of the domestic and foreign affairs of other nations. Such an acceptance of pluralism in the international arena reflects the maintaining of pluralism at home. An authoritarian great power, conversely, is more likely to favor centralized decisionmaking, the conformity of small states, and a hierarchical organization of international affairs led by a dominant great power or a great power condominium. This distinction draws on the well-documented argument in the alliance literature that pluralist societies tend to establish pluralistic alliances, whereas centralist-hierarchical powers form monolithic blocs.[21] These are 'ideal types,' but they broadly reflect the differences between the Western and Eastern blocs from the late 1940s until the late 1980s.

Indeed, the difference between a democratic and an authoritarian regime with respect to the principle of self-determination conditions their attitudes toward small states. As a result, all other things being equal, a democratic great power is somewhat less inclined to coerce small states,[22] whether on its own or in collusion with other great powers. This is especially true if the small state is also democratic, because democratic states regard each other's government as a manifestation of 'the will of its people', and thus as more legitimate than nondemocratic regimes.

More specifically, with regard to the dependent variable of this study, we expect democratic great powers to pursue mediation frequently as a major avenue of regional peacemaking.[23] This is because mediation accords well with the way democracies resolve conflicts at home, that is, via give-and-take, compromises, negotiations and bargaining among the parties.[24]

In contrast, an authoritarian power is more favorably disposed to impose its preferred policy on small states or to negotiate with the other great powers behind closed doors, over the heads of its small clients, once it perceives that this will best serve its interests. This is especially true with regard to a communist great power because communist ideology has traditionally preferred the establishment of centralized-hierarchical movements and called for the members to obey a single authoritative leadership. Consequently, all the members of the communist alliance faced threats to their autonomy from the leader.[25]

'STRONG' STATES, 'WEAK' STATES, AND THE ABILITY TO ADOPT A COERCIVE APPROACH

Yet, the unwillingness of democratic powers to exercise coercion in principle is not always translated to an accommodative approach to small states in practice (e.g. because of perceived threats to important interests). Indeed, a great power's *ability* to engage in coercion of small states may be more significant than its *willingness*. The major factor affecting such ability is the domestic structure and its effects on the capacity of small states to oppose coercion by mobilizing support for their cause within the polity of the great power.

Krasner's distinction between 'strong' and 'weak' states[26] is a good starting point for discussing how domestic political structure affects the likelihood of a great power adopting a coercive approach toward small states. Domestic structure refers to the relationship between a state and its society, and the organization of the state and societal groups. If a state is 'weak', it is unable to manipulate the behaviour of domestic groups, interest groups are often successful in attaining their objectives, there is a multiplicity of access points to the government and state power is fragmented. Thus, pluralist democracies are 'weak' states, while authoritarian states are 'strong' ones. It should be stressed that the terms 'strong' and 'weak' in this sense are not to be confused with overall great power capabilities, and a pluralist domestic structure is not a sign of actual weakness (thus, pluralist great powers are 'weak' states). In terms of the above distinction, the United States is a 'weak' state (and 'strong society') whereas the USSR was a 'strong' state (and 'weak society').[27]

Proposition 3: 'Weak' states will be less capable than 'strong' states to coerce their small allies, whether on their own or through a great power condominium.

In an open society the 'weakness' of the state structure makes possible the 'penetration' of external ideas and agents. Accordingly, those small allies of the democratic power that can mobilize powerful domestic resources within its political system, are capable of influencing its policymaking process and especially of limiting seriously its ability to coerce them. Furthermore, transnational linkage groups can be formed between the great power's small allies on the one hand, and agencies of its government or interest groups in its political system on the other.[28] Such linkage groups may prove effective in influencing the great power's foreign policy, especially when influential constituencies in its political system are sympathetic to the concerns of the small ally.[29] This is particularly true regarding the 'penetration' of the great power political system by lesser allies through sympathetic ethnic, religious, or cultural groups.[30] To the extent that small allies, with the help of their supporters, are able to mobilize public and legislatures' support for their positions, they become participants in the domestic democratic game. The internationalization of this game via the presence of linkage groups will increase the bargaining power of the small ally *vis-à-vis* the great power government,[31] and will enable the small ally to preclude great power coercion in more cases than could be expected according to a *realpolitik* analysis based exclusively on the asymmetry in capabilities between the great power and the small ally.

Thus, linkage groups are important because they can affect the ability of different polities to pursue a coercive approach with regard to small allies. The greater importance of the domestic structure in comparison with the normative-ideological element affecting willingness should lead us to expect that those small states which are unable to mobilize support for their cause within the polity of the great power will not always be able to count on the goodwill of democratic great powers for avoiding coercion, especially if the small states are proximate to the great power and thus are located in its exclusive sphere of influence. Such proximity makes great power coercion easier and also, all other things being equal, the stakes for the great power in proximate small states seem to be higher than in remote small states. This might explain past US coercive interventions in Central America (e.g. the CIA-sponsored overthrow of a democratically-elected leftist regime in Guatemala 1954).[32] At the same time, in accordance with the model presented here, the growing domestic political power of Hispanic-American lobbies is likely to make it more difficult for the US to exercise coercion in this region in the future to the extent that these lobbies will oppose such coercion. Similarly, past cases of US coercion of small states beyond Latin America (like the overthrow of a democratically-elected leftist regime in Iran 1953, and coercive interventions in Africa and Southeast Asia) are not only outside the formal scope of this model because these are not cases of regional peacemaking, but they can also be explained by the logic of the model because in these cases there were relatively weak lobbies in favor of the small state. Moreover, as could be expected from the normative dimension of the model, and as opposed to the common image of the US as a coercive power, especially in Latin America, recent studies[33] show that the US resorted quite frequently to mediation as a major method of regional peacemaking, including in Latin America;[34] and this pattern of behaviour differed markedly from Soviet behaviour in its own sphere of influence.[35]

Indeed, the active role of transnational linkages in the foreign policy of a pluralist state with its 'penetrated', open political system, stands in striking contrast to the weakness of such linkages in a centralist closed political system, wherein the decisionmaking process, especially in foreign affairs, is centralized-hierarchical, which reduces the constraints on such systems' ability to coerce small allies. Thus, the inclination of an authoritarian great power to a coercive approach results from a combination of its 'strong' domestic structure and the related lack of respect for the right of self-determination of smaller nations. At the same time, democratic great powers will not be able to behave coercively toward small states where groups favoring those states are politically influential in the great power domestic political system.

THE COMBINED EFFECTS OF RELATIVE CAPABILITIES AND STATE ATTRIBUTES ON GREAT POWER APPROACH TOWARD REGIONAL PEACEMAKING

The combination of the two causal factors discussed above – relative power and domestic regime – yields four possible great power orientations toward regional peacemaking. The orientations are presented in the following table.

TABLE 1
GREAT POWER APPROACHES TOWARD REGIONAL PEACEMAKING
ACCORDING TO RELATIVE CAPABILITIES AND DOMESTIC REGIMES

	Domestic Regime	
	Pluralist Democracy	**Authoritarian**
Superior	1 Unilateral Accommodative	2 Unilateral Coercive
	(US in the Middle East)	
Relative Capabilities		
Inferior (weaker)	3 Multilateral Accommodative	4 Multilateral Coercive
	(the West Europeans in the Middle East)	(USSR in the Middle East)

Approach 1 is typical of pluralist democratic great powers which are more powerful than their competitors at least in some regions or issue-areas. This approach consists of a disinclination to collaborate with other great powers (because of relative strength), but also a relatively tolerant attitude to small states (due to the democratic-pluralist regime of the great power), especially if they are also democratic. As I will show, this was the overall US approach toward the Arab–Israeli conflict in the Middle East in the Cold War era, because Washington has enjoyed superior diplomatic and economic resources in that area which have enabled it to play a unilateral role of an 'honest broker' and to exclude the Soviets from the international diplomacy of this important region, while maintaining a generally tolerant and non-coercive attitude toward its ally Israel.

Orientation 2 characterizes the conduct of authoritarian great powers in situations or areas where they enjoy superior capabilities. Their conduct is intolerant both with regard to cooperation with great power rivals and to small state autonomy. This orientation has no example in the Cold War Middle East, but it is manifested in the Soviet attitude toward its exclusive sphere of influence in Eastern Europe in the Cold War era. The opposite of this approach is inclination 3 which combines both cooperation with other powers and respect for the rights of small states. It is typical of democratic powers which are weaker in comparison to other great powers. Such, for example, has been the general approach of the Western Europeans during the Cold War era with regard to an international conference to resolve the Arab–Israeli conflict. As relatively weak external powers in the Middle East (in comparison to both superpowers), they were closer to the Soviet position of a multilateral forum (which should include either the five permanent members of the Security Council or the four powers: the US, Soviet Union, Britain and France) rather than to Washington's preference for a unilateral strategy for resolving the Middle Eastern conflict under an exclusive US leadership. Yet, as democratic states, the Europeans were closer to the American position with regard to the non-coercive nature of the international engagement in the resolution of this regional conflict.

Authoritarian powers, when they are relatively weak as compared to other great powers, tend to prefer a condominium (inclination 4), that is, great power collaboration which will jointly impose peace in third areas. As discussed below, such was the overall inclination of the Soviet Union in the Middle East during most of the Cold War period.

The next two sections apply the theoretical propositions to superpower behaviour in the Cold War Middle East, and thus illustrate two of the four orientations proposed by the model: unilateral-accommodative and multilateral-coercive. But first a few words why the selection of the Middle East as the case study makes sense.

THE MODEL AND THE SELECTION OF THE MIDDLE EAST AS THE CASE STUDY

The reasons why it makes sense to examine the model with regard to the Middle East are the following:

1. During the Cold War the Middle East met the condition of a 'situation where the great powers are genuinely interested in promoting the resolution of a regional conflict – if only to prevent its escalation and enhance international stability' (p.106 above) much more than any other Third World region. This is because of the high-interest, high-danger character of the region for both superpowers. Thus, repeated great power attempts (unilateral or multilateral) at regional conflict resolution took place much more frequently and recurrently and over an extended period of time in the Middle East than in any other region. These attempts were also higher on the foreign policy agenda of both superpowers than similar attempts in other regions, as manifested by the involvement of high-level policymakers, summit negotiations (notably, in 1972 and 1973) and investments in foreign aid and arms deliveries which were related in one way or another to peacemaking. Thus, only the Middle East provides considerable empirical data on great power regional peacemaking which also allows a comparative analysis between the approaches of the superpowers and an examination of patterns and continuities over a lengthy period of time.

2. As I will discuss below, because of the special advantages of the US in the region, a distinction between an inferior and a superior great power in regional peacemaking has been much more notable in the Middle East than in any other region. Thus, it allows us a useful investigation of the proposition concerning the effects of relative power on cooperation with other great powers in regional peacemaking.

3. The Middle East is also remarkable because in regional peacemaking undertaken by the US there was a potential clash between *realpolitik* considerations and domestic politics in a pluralist democracy which allows us to examine the effects of domestic factors on the attitude of democratic great power to small allies when there is such a clash.

The absence or the much weaker presence of these characteristics in other regions makes a full-blown comparative investigation of the utility of the model in other regions much less useful.

THE SUPERPOWER APPROACH TO CONFLICT RESOLUTION IN THE
MIDDLE EAST IN THE COLD WAR ERA

The Effects of Relative Capabilities on the Choice of a Unilateral or Multilateral Approach to Peacemaking

In accordance with the theoretical argument, we need to look at power-related factors for explaining why it should necessarily have been the Soviet Union that was inclined to prefer a multilateral approach to regional conflict resolution, whereas the US tended toward unilateral diplomacy.

PAX AMERICANA IN THE MIDDLE EAST?

Although at times the US cooperated with the USSR with regard to conflict resolution in the Middle East (the prime examples being the cosponsorship of UN resolutions 242 following the Six Day War and 338 at the end of the 1973 war, and the subsequent co-chairmanship of the Geneva conference, and also the 1 October 1977 joint statement),[36] such cooperative ventures were sporadic, constituted the exception rather than the rule, and were quickly abandoned in favor of the dominant US approach to regional conflict resolution – a unilateral-exclusionary one. Since 1967, the US has undertaken a long series of unilateral diplomatic efforts intended to promote the resolution of the Arab–Israeli conflict under exclusive US auspices. A short survey of such unilateral American initiatives includes:

1. The diplomatic initiatives made in 1970–71 by the State Department in the first Nixon administration, dubbed Rogers I, II, III, and IV.[37] The last three initiatives especially marked a departure from the collaborative superpower framework of the two-power talks on conflict resolution in the Middle East begun in March 1969.

2. Kissinger's unilateral, step-by-step 'shuttle diplomacy' produced the disengagement accords of 1974 between Israel and Egypt (Sinai I, January 1974) and between Israel and Syria (May 1974). American exclusionary brokerage also generated the Sinai II interim accord between Israel and Egypt (September 1975).[38]

3. US unilateral mediation culminated under the Carter administration with the achievement of the Camp David accords (September 1978) and the Egyptian-Israeli peace treaty (March 1979).[39] These steps marked a major departure from the collaborative superpower approach manifested in the 1 October 1977 joint statement.

4. Reagan's 'fresh start' initiative of 1 September 1982 drew upon the Camp David accords while calling, more specifically, for some form of association between the West Bank, Gaza, and Jordan.

5. The Shultz plan of 4 March 1988 suggested that an international conference precede bilateral negotiations between Israel and a Jordanian-Palestinian delegation. The US was seemingly ready to accept a Soviet role in the conference but it was expected to be a symbolic role while the US would, in fact, play the role of the regional broker.[40]

6. A similar US approach has continued in the post-Cold War era with the diplomatic efforts made by the Bush administration in the wake of the Gulf War, culminating in the convening of the Madrid peace conference in October 1991 (although it was formally cosponsored by the US and Russia as a manifestation of post-Cold War cooperation, the US played by far the role of the leading broker). This approach basically continues under the present Clinton administration with regard to the peace negotiations between Israel and the Palestinians and Syria.

The objective American advantages in the Middle East as compared to the limitations to the Soviet capacity to contribute to regional peacemaking helped make the unilateral-exclusionary approach the dominant inclination in US Middle East policy in the Cold War era. Thus, regional circumstances conducive to American-led brokerage have led even cooperatively inclined policy-makers (such as Rogers-Sisco and Carter-Vance) to pursue unilateral diplomatic initiatives in the region.

The dominant strand in American policy in the Middle East in the Cold War era has been based on the assumption that superior US capabilities for influencing events in the region would ensure the success of unilateral mediation. The US has enjoyed superior non-military (economic and diplomatic) resources in the region *vis-à-vis* the USSR.[41] Although since the mid-to-late 1960s the USSR achieved impressive overall military capabilities, [including some power projection capability to the Middle East], Washington has been able to offer the regional countries much more aid in the economic and technological fields. Its superior economic resources have enabled America to promote peacemaking in the region by providing small states with positive inducements in the form of financial assistance and technology transfers in addition to 'honest brokerage.' Thus, considerable financial resources have been spent by the US through foreign aid to those Middle Eastern states which cooperate in the US-led peace process. Accordingly, following the 'step-by-step' agreements, and later the Camp David accords between Egypt and Israel, these two states top, by far, the list of recipients of US foreign assistance.[42] Furthermore, the US has enjoyed a diplomatic leverage in the Middle East that the Soviets lacked. Israel has been the superior military power in the region, at least since the 1956 Suez War; yet Soviet leverage over Israel was limited because it did not maintain diplomatic relations with the Jewish state since the 1967 war until the end of the Cold War. Even before 1967, relations had been very strained, at least since the mid-1950s. In contrast, the US has had, at least potentially, substantial leverage over Israel because of the great Israeli dependence on American military and economic aid and diplomatic support; a dependence further enhanced by the fact that Israel lacked any real option of realignment.

Consequently, once Arab states realized that they could not recover the territories occupied by Israel in 1967 by force because of Israeli military predominance, one could reasonably have expected, as did Kissinger,[43] that Arab leaders would turn to the US as the chief arbiter of the Arab–Israeli dispute. Only the US, it seemed, could bring about a settlement that would satisfy the Arabs' territorial demands. Developmental and technological needs could only reinforce their inclination to the US. Manipulation of its foreign assistance and its pivotal diplomatic position could help Washington extract concessions from the local antagonists for attaining regional accommodation under *Pax Americana*. Israel, in particular, could be expected to prefer an exclusive US brokerage rather than a participation of the Soviet Union with its (until the late 1980s) widely perceived pro-Arab orientation.

Indeed, the source of Soviet diplomatic strength in the Middle East – its alliance with radical Arab states – constrained Soviet diplomacy in the peace process by presenting a dilemma. If the Soviet Union had tried to exercise a moderating influence on its allies, such pressures might have antagonized them. As a result, some of them might even have turned to the US, which appeared better able to deliver Israeli concessions in the event of an active peacemaking process and an Arab willingness to compromise (a scenario that was realized with regard to Egypt). If, on the other hand, Moscow had maintained its support for the Arab maximal position, it might have kept the radicals' friendship in the short run, but it would not have been able to help them achieve their long-term objectives because of Israel's military superiority and the Soviet fear of escalation of local hostilities to a global confrontation.[44] At the same time, if Moscow's Arab allies had continued to be intransigent, the Soviets would not have been able to contribute to the peace process.

The US, for its part, was ready to engage in such a peace process because *Pax Americana* would stabilize this turbulent region, and mitigate the main US dilemma: the tension between the ideological and political commitment to Israel versus the need to maintain good relations with the Arabs to ensure an uninterrupted flow of oil from the Persian Gulf. Furthermore, peace and stability in the Middle East could reduce the likelihood of a superpower clash resulting from a local war. *Pax Americana* would also ensure US predominance in the region by peaceful means.

Indeed, an explanation based on US comparative advantages in the Middle East can best account for the progress in the Arab–Israeli peace process achieved under American leadership from the aftermath of the 1973 war to the late 1970s. Especially important in this respect is Kissinger's strategy in the Middle East throughout the Nixon and Ford years.[45] Indeed, Kissinger was the most significant exponent of the policy of Pax Americana, whose basic objective in the Middle East was to expand Washington's influence at the expense of Moscow's. At a minimum, he hoped that Egypt would defect from the Soviet camp and enter the US orbit. His maximal goal was to guarantee US hegemony in the Middle East and to exclude the Soviets from any major role in the area, although Kissinger was ready to concede to the USSR a purely symbolic role, manifested in joint superpower declarations on the Middle East (notably, at the May 1972 and June 1973 superpower summits). Such vague public statements, and also engaging the Soviets in secret summit agreements on the Middle East, (like the 'general working principles' negotiated by Kissinger and Gromyko during the May 1972 summit)[46] were intended to satisfy the Soviets' desire for formal recognition as a coequal superpower. Kissinger hoped that such a satisfaction would encourage the Soviets to pursue a more moderate policy in the Middle East (e.g. slow down the arms supply to the Arabs) and, as a result, both strain Soviet-Arab relations and frustrate the Arabs' military option. Thus, Kissinger's symbolic moves *vis-à-vis* the Soviets, in fact, formed an integral part of his strategy to deny them a major role in the region. The appearance of superpower collaboration was essentially a device to enhance US influence with the Arabs.

At the same time, Kissinger was in favor of ensuring Israel's military superiority, so that the Arabs would realize that Soviet arms could not bring about the recovery of the occupied territories. He also embarked upon a 'back-channel' communication with Egypt in the early 1970s, and thus helped start the process of Cairo's realignment from the Eastern to the Western camp. But this exchange was not accompanied by what he saw as a 'premature' responsiveness to Arab demands.[47] Only when the Arab position became more flexible, could the American ally, Israel, be expected to reciprocate. Most importantly, the credit for this newly-won flexibility would then be given to Israel's patron and the US would thus emerge as the regional peacemaker.

The major effect of Kissinger's strategy was the July 1972 expulsion of the Soviet advisors from Egypt following the vague US-Soviet declarations of May 1972 (although Kissinger could not anticipate the precise form and timing that this effect would take). These statements created the impression of Soviet support for the status quo in the Middle East and thus alienated Sadat from the Soviets. The resulting explusion was a serious blow to the

Soviet standing in the Middle East and the beginning of a rift between Moscow and Cairo. Indeed, after the 1973 war, Kissinger presided over Egypt's realignment and the progress in the Arab–Israeli peace process.

The exclusion of the Soviets from any effective involvement in the peace process could be seen as beneficial not only from a narrow Cold-War standpoint but also in the view of those local actors interested in reaching a settlement. Thus, in the aftermath of the 1973 war not only Egypt and Israel but also Jordan supported US-sponsored negotiations. Most interestingly, 'even President Assad of Syria indicated a willingness to let Kissinger try his hand, although his skepticism was considerably greater than Sadat's.'[48] Sadat's support of diplomatic progress, moreover, appeared to be forthcoming only when the US single-handedly presided over the peace negotiations as during 1974–75 and 1978–79.

THE SOVIET APPROACH TO PEACEMAKING IN THE MIDDLE EAST:
A PARTICIPANT OR A SPOILER?

During the Cold War a common contention among Western analysts regarding Moscow's Middle East policy was that it stood for 'no war, no peace'. The advocates of this contention, though accepting that the Soviets did not favor the breakout of a regional war, claimed that the Soviets were equally opposed to an Arab-Israeli peace settlement because peace would undermine Moscow's influence in the Arab world.[49] In the absence of a conflict with Israel, it was maintained, Arab states would not turn to Moscow anymore because they would no longer need the major Soviet comparative advantage: a willingness to provide massive arms shipments to the Arabs.

This section shows that far from obstructing any efforts at peacemaking in the Middle East, as claims the 'no peace no war' thesis, the Soviets were in fact genuinely interested in peacemaking in the region and in collaborating with the US for that purpose, albeit under certain conditions. The role of the 'spoiler' which they occasionally played resulted from the unwillingness of the US to recognize and accept these conditions, and the US preference for an exclusionary approach.

Many analysts have noted that one of the motivations behind Soviet foreign policy during the Cold War era was an eagerness to be recognized as an equal of America. Such

> preoccupation with the establishment of status equal to that of the US in global security matters . . . gives the USSR a limited stake in cooperative arrangements which recognize this status and legitimize it. The Soviet aspiration to equality in the hierarchy of prestige in international politics may be achieved, in other words, not only by

conscious challenge to the position of the previous hegemon, but through acts whereby the United States consciously concedes to the USSR status commensurate with its growing power to affect outcomes in the Third World.[50]

Numerous Soviet statements since the early 1960s, cited by Jonsson,[51] have highlighted their desire to fulfill the traditional great power role of taking part in the resolution of international conflicts, including even those which were far from its frontiers.[52] Since the Middle East is not remote from the Soviet Union-indeed, it is much closer to its borders than to the US – it should not be surprising that the Soviets especially insisted on their inclusion in the Middle East diplomatic process.[53] Thus, the Soviets persistently proposed a wide range of joint political and military actions with Washington in the area of regional conflict management and resolution. There have been five main Soviet attempts in the diplomatic field:

1. In the late 1940s and early 1950s, Moscow tried to participate in the peacemaking and peacekeeping activities of the UN machinery in the Middle East.[54]

2. Throughout the 1950s, but especially in 1957–58, Moscow requested to join a revised version of the Tripartite Statement of the three Western powers concerning arms control and the maintenance of peace in the Middle East.[55] This, however, was in the heyday of the Cold War, and the West sought to preclude any Soviet 'penetration' of the Middle East and thus completely rejected any diplomatic role for the USSR, even if ostensibly for peacemaking purposes. However, the idea of Soviet participation (along with the US) in superpower guarantees of the borders between Israel and its Arab neighbours has become, since the mid-1950s, a consistent theme of the Kremlin's Middle East peace proposals.[56]

3. Following the Six Day War, the Kremlin has expressed an interest in working jointly with the US, notably in the two-power talks[57] and also during the 1972 and 1973 summits,[58] to reach a comprehensive Arab-Israeli settlement (albeit under certain conditions to be described below).

4. In the 1970s, in the aftermath of the Yom Kippur War, Moscow sought to play the role of cochairman of the Geneva Peace Conference along with Washington.

5. In the 1980s, the Soviets succeeded in mobilizing the Arab world and the majority of the UN members for supporting an international conference on Middle East peace with active Soviet participation. The idea of an international conference was a major element in the Soviet Middle East

peace plans advanced under Brezhnev in 1981, Chernenko in 1984, and Gorbachev in 1986.

Basically, the idea of a multilateral framework to resolve the Arab–Israeli conflict was designed to promote Moscow's general aim to be recognized as an equal of Washington in the Middle East. Thus, the Soviets sought to prevent separate deals between Israel and individual Arab states (most notably Jordan) that would be brokered exclusively by the US.[59]

In addition to diplomatic peacemaking, the Soviets have expressed a readiness to support their equal great power status by a military presence for peacekeeping or even peace-enforcement purposes. Thus, in December 1947 they proposed that US and Soviet troops take part in an international force which would assist in implementing the UN partition resolution (this resolution, which was opposed by the Arabs, called for the establishment of a Jewish and an Arab state in the territory of Palestine, then under British control).[60] At the end of both the 1956 and 1973 wars, the Soviets suggested sending joint US-Soviet forces to enforce the UN-sponsored ceasefires.[61] Finally, Brezhnev offered to contribute Soviet troops to the UN forces which would be deployed in demilitarized buffer zones separating Israel and its neighbours following a territorial settlement to be reached in an international conference.[62]

Because of the intensity of the conflict in the Middle East, an Arab–Israeli peace was expected to be an 'armed peace';[63] and one of the often-mentioned measures for preserving such a peace was great power guarantees.[64] Indeed, the Soviets consistently advocated this means of ameliorating the regional security dilemma. Superpower guarantees would ensure the Soviets the long-awaited, formally legitimized presence in the Middle East[65] and recognized equality with the US. Moscow also supported a superpower role in enforcing the peace because it

> would make the Soviet Union less dependent on unstable regimes in the Arab world by providing it with an additional, more solid and secure means of participating in the politics of the region.[66]

Thus, analysts have reached the conclusion that the Soviets have been interested in joint diplomacy with the US in order to resolve the Middle East dispute and jointly guarantee the peace. This interest has been contingent, however, on US willingness to reciprocate, and has been valid only to the extent that the peaceful settlement would not reduce Soviet influence in the Arab world.[67] A rigorous examination of the 'no war, no peace' hypothesis with respect to Soviet Middle East policy during 1967–72 concludes that 'the Soviet leadership sought a peace settlement based on superpower collaboration that would simultaneously reduce the probability of military confrontation with the US in the Middle East, advance the cause of détente, and create a more stable base of influence for the USSR in Middle Eastern affairs.'[68]

This Soviet inclination to pursue a joint collaborative approach with Washington stemmed mainly from the Soviets' desire, as the relatively-weaker great power in the Middle East, to be recognized as an equal superpower. Indeed, the Soviets often preferred joint US-Soviet diplomacy in the Middle East (with an equal role for each of the two superpowers) to the involvement of all five permanent members of the Security Council.[69] This inclination was reinforced by an additional incentive related to the overall economic weakness of the Soviets vis-à-vis the West: even after attaining impressive military capabilities, the Soviets remained inferior to the US in overall economic resources; thus, cooperation in regional peacemaking could enhance American readiness to provide Moscow with much-desired trade benefits and technology transfers. Joint regional diplomacy could also strengthen domestic support in the US for arms control,[70] in which the Soviets had an economic interest (in order to save money by reducing defense spending and also to raise the likelihood of Western economic assistance).

To sum up, the US, at least at first glance, has had the potential to manage the Arab–Israeli dispute unilaterally. On the other hand, because of their inferior economic and diplomatic resources in the region, and the related quest for a recognized equal great-power status, the Soviets needed to resort to collaboration with the US in order to promote the stabilization of the Middle East.

As Smolansky observes, 'throughout all the convulsions of Moscow's Middle East policy since 1955, the one common theme that emerges is the Kremlin's quest for full superpower status and consequent recognition that its interests must be considered in whatever regional arrangements are reached'.[71] Smolansky argues, moreover, that only some kind of peaceful arrangement would have enabled the Soviet Union to gain the great power status and international legitimacy it aspired to achieve through being recognized as the equal collaborator of the US in settling regional disputes.[72] Similarly, Eran suggests that: 'The achievement of such a status in the region by the Soviet Union would mean, at long last, the formalization and legitimization of Soviet Middle Eastern involvement by the international community.'[73]

However, the different approaches of the superpowers to peacemaking in the Middle East were not confined to the choice between a multilateral versus an exclusionary strategy (i.e. between cooperation and non-cooperation), but included also a second dimension, that of disagreement over the approach toward small states (accommodative or coercive). While the first difference may be explained by relative capabilities, the second stems from state-level regime factors.

Domestic Factors and the Preference for an Accommodative or Coercive Approach toward Small States

According to the proposition advanced earlier, an authoritarian power is both willing and able to pursue a policy of coercion of small states, either on its own or in a condominium with other great powers. This proposition is confirmed by the Soviet position on the issue of peacemaking in the Middle East. Indeed, the Soviets seemed to prefer a superpower collusion in the Middle East behind closed doors[74] and without the presence of unruly allies. Some analysts argue that the Soviets have sought a superpower condominium in the Middle East as a joint imposition of peace.[75] This view is shared by some US policymakers. According to Nixon and Kissinger, the Middle East was one of the major areas in which the Soviets wanted to establish a superpower condominium based on an imposed solution to the Arab–Israeli dispute.[76]

With regard to the Soviet proposals of an international conference for settling the Middle East conflict, the Soviets were interested in reaching a superpower understanding on the outline of a regional settlement, and then using the international conference to enforce a comprehensive arrangement on the local parties. For such enforcement, the Soviets demanded, somewhat similarly to the view of many of the Arabs (especially the Syrians), that the multilateral plenary supervise the work of the bilateral subcommittees and, on a number of issues, supersede them. Thus, Moscow sought a multilateral, hierarchical framework in which it would first reach an agreement with the US and then the two superpowers would persuade their respective Middle Eastern clients to accept it.[77] This orientation corresponds to the concept of an 'imposed peace.' Breslauer suggests three major indicators of the Soviet commitment to peacemaking in the Middle East[78] which are associated with a coercive approach: a readiness to take some distance from maximal Arab positions; a desire to collude with the US behind closed doors; and insider testimony about Soviet pressures on the Arabs to accept a diplomatic settlement of the dispute.[79] Another indicator of a coercive Soviet approach is the restraints that the Soviets imposed on their arms supply to the Arabs. This is seen especially in Moscow's refusal in 1971–72 to ship sophisticated weapons to Egypt that would have enabled Sadat to launch a major offensive against Israel (especially MiG-23s and Scud surface-to-surface missiles).[80] Such Soviet unwillingness severely frustrated Sadat, as he repeatedly makes clear in his memoirs.[81]

The Soviet emphasis on military measures for enforcing the peace is also associated with the idea of a condominium and with a policeman role. As Eran puts it:

> Moscow intends that any Arab-Israeli settlement be tied to the establishment of an international regime – one may call it Soviet-American condominium – which from time to time would require international policing; Moscow wishes to become co-gendarme of any Arab-Israeli settlement with the United States.[82]

Similarly, Breslauer concludes that 'the Soviets sought to bring about an armed peace based upon Israeli withdrawal from occupied territories, Arab recognition of and normalization of formal relations with Israel, and a coequal superpower role in enforcing the peace.'[83]

Yet, such an idea of a condominium or an imposed solution in the Middle East has been persistently and forcefully rejected by the US foreign policy elite, in a manner consistent with its pluralist nature. This rejection had to do not only with an ideological unwillingness to take part in a condominium, but especially with a domestic political inability to do so. The theoretical argument stressed the domestic opposition in a pluralist democracy to the pursuit of a coercive strategy at the expense of small allies, especially those that have powerful domestic resources within the great power's polity, as has been the case with Israel's standing in the US.[84] Accordingly, the opposition of both Israel and pro-Israeli elements in the US to any initiative that smacked of a great power condominium at the expense of Israel was instrumental in obstructing such initiatives, as will be demonstrated by the following two examples: the joint US-Soviet statement of October 1977, and the first Rogers plan of December 1969.

The 1977 joint superpower communiqué contained important Soviet concessions to the US position on the terms of the Middle East peace settlement;[85] nonetheless, as soon as it was made public, it became the target of sharp criticism by Israel and Israel's friends in the US.[86] In order to calm the strong domestic and Israeli opposition, President Jimmy Carter, together with Israeli Foreign Minister Moshe Dayan, produced a working paper on 4 October 1977 that diluted the impact of the superpower communiqué.[87] As Quandt points out, both Arabs and Israelis felt that

> Carter had backed down in the face of domestic and Israeli pressures ... Although Carter never wavered in thinking that he had held firm, the widespread perception, caused by the joint statement with Israel, was that the United States had abandoned the position it had just worked out with the Soviets.[88]

The failure of the joint superpower peacemaking in 1977 was derived from the strength of domestic and allied opposition motivated by fears of

Israel's supporters that US cooperation with the Soviets in peacemaking in the Middle East would necessarily be coercive and harmful to Israel. The effectiveness of this opposition in the US, in turn, influenced Sadat to try another road to peace, namely to travel to Jerusalem in November 1977 rather than to wait endlessly for the convening of the Geneva Peace Conference.[89]

An additional brief example will further highlight the point: namely, the strong domestic opposition to Rogers I, the December 1969 collaborative superpower attempt to resolve the Arab–Israeli conflict. Secretary Rogers's speech on 9 December outlined his proposal, which had been worked out in collaboration with the Soviets during the two-power talks in 1969.[90] The plan called for an Israeli withdrawal from almost all of the occupied territories in exchange for an agreement by the Arabs to some contractual arrangement guaranteeing a permanent peace with Israel. Rogers's speech triggered an outcry from Israel's supporters in Congress and in the Jewish community; this powerful protest, in turn, led to signals from Nixon to Jewish leaders that the US would not impose a settlement on Israel. As a result of the domestic pressure, the president also backed off from the strong language in the plan about the necessity for Israel's withdrawal from the occupied territories and pledged to continue delivering necessary military hardware to Israel.[91]

Another example of failed coercion is not connected to attempts at a superpower condominium but rather to an attempt at a unilateral coercive American strategy. This is the reassessment crisis of Spring 1975.[92] The Ford administration decided to reassess its policy toward Israel following Secretary Kissinger's abortive effort of March 1975 to mediate an interim agreement between Israel and Egypt. The new policy included several punitive measures in the form of implicit threats as well as limited sanctions.[93] Yet, 'in pursuing its coercive posture ... the administration could not remain totally oblivious to a number of domestic factors and constraints, particularly Congress, which ultimately severely narrowed its margin of maneuverability.'[94] Most notably, 76 senators responded favorably to an initiative of the pro-Israeli lobby and sent a strongly worded letter to the president, urging him to be 'responsive to Israel's economic and military needs.'[95] The letter coincided with the findings of public opinion polls, which persistently reported the presence of a large and solid base of popular support for Israel in the US. As Ben-Zvi points out, 'taken as a whole, these manifestations of public and Congressional dissent clearly indicated that the administration lacked the necessary base of domestic support for the effective pursuit of coercive diplomacy.'[96] As a result, the administration decided to soften its strategy toward Israel by incorporating important positive inducements into its policy such as the provision of large-scale economic and military aid and advanced arms as well as significant diplomatic commitments. Due to the addition of these incentives, Israel signed the second Sinai agreement in September 1975.

Because of the greater influence of domestic and transnational politics in a pluralist democracy, the effectiveness of US pressures on Israel, at least in noncrisis situations, was considerably diminished.[97] Accordingly, in its unilateral diplomatic initiatives, the US has tended to an accommodative approach toward Israel. Indeed, one could argue that there have been fewer American attempts at coercing Israel[98] than could be expected from a *realpolitik* analysis of the combination of the divergence in US and Israeli interests and the high Israeli dependence on Washington. The divergence in interests was based on the persistent tension between the US commitment to Israel and the US interest in maintaining friendly relations with Arab states both because of the Western dependence on Arab oil and in order to contain Soviet penetration of the Middle East during the Cold War. Moreover, the US could be more frequently tempted to exercise coercive diplomacy *vis-à-vis* Israel not only because of the high asymmetry in the distribution of overall capabilities between the US and Israel but also because Israel has been highly dependent on American diplomatic, economic and military assistance, especially in the post-1967 era. In addition, Israel did not have a viable realignment option during the Cold War because of the consistent Soviet preference for an anti-Israeli alliance with the Arabs. The explanation for such a recurring gap between realpolitik expectations and actual US behaviour is both the unwillingness of the US to rely on coercion as its preferable strategy *vis-à-vis* small allies, especially democratic ones like Israel, and the strength of the support for Israel in US domestic politics.

Summary and Seemingly Deviant Cases

This study has shown that in the domain of regional peacemaking, there were persistent differences between the superpowers despite their similar location in the bipolar international system. A Cold War analysis would also lead us to expect a mutual rejection of cooperation by both superpowers based on their ideological antagonism.

Yet, it was shown that, contrary to these approaches, it is helpful to consider the combined effects of two factors, which conditioned the *differences* in the superpower approaches to regional peacemaking in the Middle East: relative capabilities and domestic regime. Thus, a careful synthesis of realist and liberal causes can be productive if the outcomes explained by each of these factors are clearly specified.

Having said that, the model does not exclude the possiblity that under certain conditions the Soviet Union would behave accommodatively towards its own allies (as it did during long periods *vis-à-vis* Egypt and Syria, two of its principal clients in the region) while the US may exercise coercion against small states as was the case with regard to Lebanon (l958, 1982–83), Iraq (the Gulf crisis of 1990–91 and later under both the Bush and Clinton administrations) or Iran (under the Clinton administration).

First, this may happen when the dependent variable is not peacemaking, because the model claims explicitly to address this bounded phenomenon rather than all great power-small state relations. Indeed, all the cases mentioned above did not take place in the context of regional peacemaking but are rather related either to the Cold War or the containment of regional aggressors. Second, the Soviets could be expected to accommodate their clients so long as the US tried to exclude them from the peacemaking process, as indeed it tried to do during most of the Cold War era. The Soviet accommodative attitude to their clients took place precisely because of the relatively weak Soviet standing in the region and the US attempt to exclude Moscow from the peacemaking process. The Soviet preference for coercive multilateralism could be carried out only in the context of an American agreement to collaborate with Moscow. In the absence of such an American willingness, the Soviets tried to compete by establishing close relations with anti-American forces such as revolutionary Egypt, Syria and Iraq.

Third, the Americans may exercise coercion against a small state when there is a combination of a perceived threat to important US interests and the small state does not have powerful allies inside the American domestic political system, and thus it is unable to establish transnational alliances which would constrain US coercive capability. The normative factor of respect for the right of other states to self-determination in a democracy is a necessary condition for an accommodative approach towards small states, but it is insufficient by itself to preclude the exercise of coercion. The probability of imposed solutions by a democratic great power is minimized only when the domestic structural element also works against coercion. Israel is a good case in point because of the large-based domestic support for Israel in the US. Accordingly, as against many *realpolitik* predictions that in the post-Cold War era Israel would cease to be a strategic asset and thus the US would be more able to exert pressures on it, the US support of Israel only increased, especially since the Clinton administration came to power. The reason is that despite the end of the Cold War, the domestic political factors and the value-related elements did not lose their appeal. This has been especially notable under the Clinton administration because of its domestic political dependence on pro-Israeli groups and also its moral-ideological bias towards Israel. Moreover, both the domestic political factor and the ideological consideration seem to work in favor of Israel also among many Republicans in Congress. In contrast, Lebanon, Iraq or Iran did not have such powerful constituencies in the American domestic system and thus the US was able to use coercion against them.

Conclusions: Implications for Present and Future Peacemaking in the Middle East and Beyond

What are the implications of the proposed model for great power approaches to regional peacemaking in the post-Cold War era? The end of the keen ideological polarization between the superpowers, and especially the political and economic reforms initiated under Gorbachev towards more democratization and liberalization, made the Soviet Union (and later Russia) since the mid-to- late 1980s a much more acceptable partner in American eyes for joint conflict resolution in the Third World, including in the Middle East.[99]

Yet, the expectation of the model is that so long as there are power differences among the great powers, the strongest will be inclined toward a more unilateral-exclusionary strategy than the weaker powers. Thus, so long as the US remains the sole superpower, it might be expected to behave in a much less multilateralist manner than the Europeans, the Japanese or the Russians. This is expected to be the case especially in the Middle East because following its victory over radical Iraq in the 1991 Gulf War the US emerged as the clear-cut external hegemon in the region.[100] While the Russians have disengaged from the Middle East since the end of the Cold War, the US has shown its commitment to defend its interests in the region. The defeat of Iraq has weakened the standing of the radical anti-American forces in the region. Together with the Soviet collapse, it has meant that for the foreseeable future there is no real option for an ex-Soviet client like Syria to join an anti-US alliance in the Middle East. If Syria wants to get the Golan Heights back from Israel, it must turn to the US. Moreover, the inability of Arab states to defend Kuwait has shown how highly many states in the region, especially the oil-rich Gulf states, depend on the US for their security. The Gulf War has also shown the limitations that the US can pose, under certain crisis conditions, to the freedom of military action of Israel as was manifested in the deployment of US Patriot missile batteries in Israel as a substitute (in addition to US-led coalition air raids on the Iraqi army) to an Israeli military response to the Iraqi Scud missile attacks. The local states are also highly dependent on American aid, investments and technology transfers for their economic development. Thus, the growing vulnerability of both the Arabs and the Israelis and their rising dependence on the US have increased the ability of the US to serve as the sole 'honest broker' in the Middle East.

Indeed, it was not so much a concert of great powers that has multilaterally dealt with the Gulf Crisis or the Arab–Israeli peace process. Rather, it was the US which, for better or worse, managed and brokered these conflicts in the last few years.[101] Although since the end of the Cold War the US has shown a growing readiness to pursue a multilateral approach towards its traditional junior partners – the West Europeans, this took place especially with regard to a post-Cold War *European* crisis – the Bosnian war. Even here the US excluded the Europeans from crucial aspects of the peacemaking in Fall 1995, including during the Dayton negotiations of a peace agreement, but the exclusion of the Europeans was more notable with regard to the Arab–Israeli peace process. Indeed, the Europeans have felt frustrated since the beginning of the post-Gulf War Middle East peace process because of their exclusion from the major developments in this process and the unilateral American leadership.[102] Despite the European efforts to get involved in the economic track of the peace process and their generous financial assistance to the Palestinians, the Europeans have been almost completely excluded from the American-led peace process: the two major agreements between Israel and the Palestinians (Oslo A and Oslo B) as well as the non-belligerency agreement between Israel and Jordan were signed in Washington. The Jordanian-Israeli peace agreement was signed on the border between the two states but it was a clear-cut US-sponsored show.

The main source of weakness of the Europeans in the Middle East compared to the US is that they lack a common foreign and defense policy. The 15 members of the European Union have different interests and positions on many issues of foreign policy. The inferior position of the Europeans in the Middle East disposes them toward a multilateral approach, and accordingly they call for active European participation in leading the peace process alongside the US and Russia (the official co-sponsors of the process). Thus, there is a certain equivalence between the Soviet demand for inclusion in the Middle East peace process during the Cold War and the European call for an active involvement in the process in the post-Cold War era. The exclusion of the Europeans is especially striking because as the democratic allies of the US, they could expect to get involved in the peace process. Moreover, in contrast to the Soviets during the Cold War, not only are the Europeans not sponsoring radical anti-US forces, but there is not ambiguity in their support of the peace process diplomatically and economically; thus, their demand for inclusion should seem more legitimate in the eyes of Americans. The exclusion of the Europeans despite all this may be best explained by relative power, that is, they are the weaker party, and the US as the superior power tends to pursue an exclusionary leadership even towards its allies.

The supposedly emerging US multilateralism has applied to an even lesser extent toward its partnership with Russia. Rather, it was *vis-à-vis* Russia that the US unilateral approach in the Middle East was most clearly demonstrated. Towards the end of the Gulf War, Gorbachev's attempts to advance compromise proposals, designed to avert the need for a land offensive against Iraq, were dismissed out of hand by President Bush.[103] Although Russia was formally a co-sponsor of the Madrid process for Arab–Israeli peacemaking, in fact the US has continued to lead the Middle East peace process with the Russians fulfilling, on the whole, a secondary role.

As a result, the dominant Russian perception has been one of its continuous exclusion from a co-equal management of major regional conflicts.[104] Accordingly, since winter-spring 1994 Russia has voiced a more assertive demand for a co-equal partnership with the US in leading the Arab–Israeli peace process (and also in the management of the Bosnian and the North Korean crises). In the Middle East, the Russians revived the traditional Soviet position by proposing a reconvening of an international conference (although this time in the format of the Madrid Peace Conference of October 1991) in order to move forward the Israeli-Syrian track of the peace negotiations. And again somewhat similarly to Cold War reactions (even if in a softer manner), both Washington and Jerusalem rejected out of hand the Russian initiative, thereby suggesting, in fact, the US primacy in leading the peace process. Indeed, officials in Jerusalem are reported to say that although Russia is a co-sponsor of the process, 'there are equals and there are greater equals.'[105] During the freeze in the Syrian-Israeli negotiations in 1995, Evgeni Primakov, then chief of the Russian intelligence service, proposed to mediate between the two regional states. Israel, fearful of a negative US reaction to a reinforcement of its intelligence ties with Russia, rejected the idea.[106] Accordingly, the Syrian-Israeli negotiations resumed in late 1995–early 1996 in Maryland under exclusive US auspices.

The Russian demand of a more active role and a recognized equal status with the US in dealing with regional conflicts is not confined to the Middle East. During the Bosnian war, when NATO threatened air strikes against the Serbs in 1994 if they did not remove their weapons from around Sarajevo, the Russians opposed the strikes. The Russian feeling was that the 'West thought it could act in Bosnia without taking much account of Russia.'[107] In order to show that it still mattered, Russia played an important role in brokering a deal which prevented the bombing of its Slavic allies by deploying Russian troops in the Sarajevo area in exchange for the withdrawal of Serbian weapons. As Vitaly Churkin, a deputy foreign minister who brokered Russia's intervention there, pointed out: 'The West should learn a lesson from the current Bosnian crisis. The lesson is that

Russia should be treated as an equal partner, not the way some of them did this time.'[108]

More recently, Russia has demonstrated its persistent adherence to the idea of an international conference for resolving regional conflicts by calling for a summit meeting in which the North Korean nuclear crisis would be discussed – 'and Russia could win some international prestige',[109] but the US insisted that the Security Council was the appropriate forum for such discussions. Yet, Foreign Minister Andrei Kozyrev announced that Russia would not support imposing sanctions on North Korea by the Security Council because the US had not consulted with it beforehand on this issue.

The democratization in Russia since the Gorbachev era has affected the pursuit of a more accommodative approach toward small states, expressed most notably in the new type of relations with the Eastern European states and also in accepting the accommodative nature of the Madrid peace process in the Middle East. Yet there are still considerable limitations to the Russian democratization and this should lead us to expect limits to the application of the accommodative attitude *vis-à-vis* small states. Indeed, recent Russian behaviour in the 'near abroad,' that is, the ex-Soviet republics seems to carry strong elements of coercion.[110] In Brzezinski's view, the Russians might even be interested in a 'cooperative condominium' with the US, which would, in effect, legitimize a Russian sphere of influence in Eastern Europe.[111] To the extent that a less democratic regime emerges in Russia, for example, led by an ultra-nationalist such as Zhirinovsky, one could expect, in accordance with the model presented here, that a much more coercive policy will be exercised *vis-à-vis* Russia's weak neighbors, including those in Eastern Europe. Such a policy could also include elements of an (at least temporary) condominium with other great powers at the expense of Eastern European countries, as was already suggested by Russian politician Vladimir Zhirinovsky with regard to a potential coercive collaboration between Russia and Germany for the division of Poland.

With regard to the US, its accommodative attitude in the post-Cold War era is clearly manifested in the Arab-Israel peace process. The US continues to underline its traditional opposition to the idea of an imposed peace and its support of direct negotiations between Israel and its Arab neighbors without any coercive involvement by the great powers, even under the American hegemony which has emerged in the Middle East following the end of the Cold War, the Soviet disintegration and the Gulf War.

This study alerts us, then, to focus on two major developments in trying to predict patterns of great power peacemaking in regional conflicts in the post-Cold War era. The degree of multilateralism among the great powers will be influenced by the extent of the US retaining or losing its lead in relative (military, diplomatic and economic) capabilities *vis-à-vis* the Europeans, the Japanese, the Chinese and the Russians. To the extent that the US loses its comparative advantage, we may expect that Washington will be much more willing to take part in a multilateral collaborative framework with the other great powers and not to pursue unilatertal initiatives. At the same time, growing US weakness might bring about a turn of the US inward, including disengagement from the Middle East due to the great distance of the US from the region as compared to Russia and the Europeans. Since the intense US leadership brought so much progress in the peace process and since its willingness to provide guarantees to regional settlements has been crucial to the promotion of regional peace, an American disengagement might be very unfortunate for the regional reconciliation process and might even undermine it.

As for the great power attitude to small states, it will be affected mainly by the degree of democratization in Russia and, with regard to certain regional conflicts in East Asia, also by the extent of democratization in China.[112] With regard to the Middle East, so long as the US and, to a lesser extent, the European Union, continue to be the chief external brokers, one may expect the prevalence of an accommodative approach. A nondemocratic Russia or China may entertain less accommodative inclinations toward small states, possibly with an interest in a great power condominium (so long as they are the relatively weaker great powers). However, for the foreseeable future, due to the global power distribution and to geography, this pattern will apply mostly to regions near to Russia and China and much less to the Middle East.

ACKNOWLEDGEMENT

Earlier versions of this analysis were presented in seminars at Princeton (of the Research Program in International Security) and Rutgers Universities. The author is grateful for the useful comments of the participants in these seminars. The author would also like to acknowledge the generous assistance of the Research Program in International Security at the Center of International Studies of Princeton University and especially of its director Aaron Friedberg, and the financial assistance of Israel Foundations Trustees, the United States Institute of Peace, the Davis Institute for International Relations at the Hebrew University and the Truman Institute for the Advancement of Peace at the Hebrew University. The author would also like to acknowledge the advice and comments on earlier drafts of George Downs, Ed Rhodes, William Wohlforth, Arie Kacowicz, Zeev Maoz, Saadia Touval, John Odell, Shmuel Doron, anonymous reviewers of the special issue of the *Journal of Strategic Studies* on Middle East security, and especially the insightful and useful help of Korina Kagan.

NOTES

1. See Andrew Bennett and Joseph Lepgold, 'Reinventing collective security after the Cold War and the Gulf conflict', *Political Science Qtly* 108/2 (Summer 1993) pp.213–37; Charles Kupchan and Clifford Kupchan, 'Concerts, Collective Security, and the Future of Europe', *Int. Security* 16 (Summer 1991) pp.114–61; Neil MacFarlane, 'The impact of superpower collaboration on the Third World', in Thomas Weiss and M.A. Kessler (eds.) *Third World Security in the post-Cold War Era* (Boulder, CO: Lynne Rienner 1991); idem, 'The superpowers and Third World security', in Brian Job (ed.) *The Insecurity Dilemma: National Security of Third World States* (ibid. 1992); Philip Zelikow, 'The new Concert of Europe', *Survival* 34/2 (Summer 1992) pp.12–30; Richard N. Rosecrance, 'A concert of powers', *Foreign Affairs* 71/2 (Spring 1992), pp.64–82; Benjamin Miller, 'Explaining the emergence of great power concerts', *Review of Int. Studies* 20 (Oct. 1994), pp.327–48.
2. See Benjamin Miller, 'Perspectives on Superpower Crisis Management and Conflict Resolution in the Arab–Israeli Conflict', in George Breslauer (ed.) *Soviet Strategy in the Middle East* (Winchester, MA: Unwin Hyman 1990); idem, *When Opponents Cooperate: Great Power Conflict and Collaboration in World Politics* (Ann Arbor: U. of Michigan Press 1995) Ch.6; and Abraham Ben-Zvi, *Between Lausanne and Geneva: International Conferences and the Arab–Israeli Conflict* (Boulder, CO: Westview Press 1990).
3. See Kenneth Waltz, *Theory of International Politics* (Reading, MA: Addison-Wesley, 1979).
4. The following studies have highlighted examples of indeterminacy in neorealist analysis: Thomas Christensen and Jack Snyder, 'Chain gangs and passed bucks: predicting alliance patterns in multipolarity', *Int. Organization* [hereafter *Int. Org.*] 44 (Spring 1990) pp.137–68; Stephen Van Evera, 'Primed for peace: Europe after the Cold War', *Int. Security* 15/3 (Winter 1990–91) pp.7–57; Barry Buzan, *People, States & Fear: An Agenda for International Security Studies in the Post-Cold War Era* (Boulder, CO: Lynne Rienner 1991) Ch.4.
5. For an elaborate discussion, see Miller, 'Explaining the emergence of great power concerts' (note 1).
6. See Joseph Nye, 'Neorealism and neoliberalism', *World Politics* 40/2 (Jan. 1988) pp.235–51; Stephan Haggard, 'Structuralism and its critics: recent progress in international relations theory', in E. Adler and B. Crawford (eds.) *Progress in International Relations* (NY: Columbia UP 1991); Helen Milner, 'International theories of cooperation among nations', *World Politics* 44 (April 1992) pp.466–96; Miller, *When Opponents Cooperate* (note 2).
7. The distinction between crisis management and conflict resolution is elaborated in Benjamin Miller, 'Explaining great power cooperation in conflict management', *World Politics* 45 (Oct. 1992): pp.1–46; and idem, *When Opponents Cooperate* (note 2).
8. For factors affecting great power military interventions, see Benjamin Miller, 'Explaining military intervention: the sources of US engagement in post-Cold War regional crises', Annual Meeting of the Int. Studies Assoc. Chicago, Feb. 1995. For a recent typology of military interventions, see Richard Haas, *Intervention: The Use of American Military Force in the post-Cold War World* (Washington DC: Carnegie Endowment 1994). Thus, Soviet and US military interventions during the Cold War (including in their respective spheres of influence), which were unrelated to regional peacemaking, are not included in the scope of this article. In *Intervention*, Haas classifies peacemaking as one form of military intervention. Yet, he overlooks the non-military aspects of peacemaking, which are frequently the dominant elements in this enterprise. Indeed, peace enforcement might be a more useful term for his purposes. On this point, see Lawrence Freedman, 'The Balkan Tragedy: Why the West Failed', *Foreign Policy* No.97 (Winter 1994–95) p.56.
9. For elaboration of the theoretical logic linking realist factors to times of crises and domestic factors to normal times, see Miller, 'Explaining great power cooperation in conflict management' (note 7); and idem, *When Opponents Cooperate* (note 2).
10. For a recent major work on multilateralism in world politics, see G. Ruggie John (ed.) *Multilateralism Matters: The Theory and Praxis of an Institutional Form* (NY: Columbia UP 1993).
11. See Saadia Touval, 'Superpower peacemaking, 1945–1989', in Linda B. Miller and

Michael J. Smith (eds.) *Ideas & Ideals: Essays on Politics in Honor of Stanley Hoffmann* (Boulder, CO: Westview Press 1993) p.163. I draw especially on Zartman and Touval's conception of mediation. See, for example, I. William Zartman and Saadia Touval, 'Third-Party Diplomacy and Informal Peacemaking', in *Resolving Third World Conflicts* (Washington DC.: US Inst. of Peace 1992).

12. On coercive diplomacy, see Paul G. Lauren, 'Theories of bargaining with threats of force: deterrence and coercive diplomacy', in idem (ed.) *Diplomacy: New Approaches in History, Theory, and Policy* (NY: Free Press 1979) p.193; and Gordon Craig and Alexander George, *Force and Statecraft* (NY: OUP 1983) p.189. This concept corresponds to Schelling's 'compellence'. See Thomas C. Schelling, *Arms and Influence* (New Haven, CT: Yale UP 1966) pp.70–1.

13. Young refers to imposed orders as 'deliberately established by the dominant actors who succeed in getting others to conform to the requirements of these orders through some combination of coercion, cooption, and the manipulation of incentives.' See Oran Young, 'Regime dynamics: the rise and fall of international regimes', in Stephen Krasner (ed.) *International Regimes* (Ithaca, NY: Cornell UP 1983) pp.100–1; and idem, 'International regimes: toward a new theory of intitutions', *World Politics* 34/1 (Oct. 1986) p.110.

14. See George Breslauer, 'Why detente failed: an interpretation', in A. George (ed.) *Managing US-Soviet Rivalry: Problems of Crisis Prevention* (Boulder, CO: Westview Press 1983) p.330; see also Alexander George, 'US-Soviet efforts to cooperate in crisis management and crisis avoidance', in idem, Philip Farley, and Alexander Dallin (eds.) *US-Soviet Security Cooperation: Achievements, Failures, Lessons* (NY: OUP 1988) p.594.

15. See Waltz, *Theory of International Politics* (note 3). Thus, modern systems theory, or neorealism, continues the traditional view of the balance-of-power approach that rough equality among the great powers is the most common situation. See Inis Claude, *Power and International Relations* (NY: Random House 1962) and Richard N. Rosecrance, *The Rise of the Trading State: Commerce and Conquest in the Modern World* (NY: Basic Books 1986) pp.56–8.

16. For recent overviews of these theories, see Joseph Nye, *Bound to Lead* (NY: Basic Books 1990); Jack Levy, 'Long cycles, hegemonic transitions, and the long peace', in C. Kegley, (ed.) *The Long Postwar Peace* (NY: HarperCollins 1991); and Jacek Kugler, 'Political conflict, war and peace', in Ada W. Finifter (ed.) *Political Science: The State of the Discipline* (Washington DC: American Political Science Assoc. 1993) pp.483–510. For a recent brief overview of the balance of power and the hegemonic schools, see Benjamin Miller, 'A "New World Order": From Balancing to Hegemony, Concert or Collective Security?' *Int. Interactions* 18/1 (1992) pp.1–33; and idem, 'Competing Realist Perspectives on Great Power Crisis Behaviour', *Security Studies* 5/3 (Spring 1996) pp.309–57.

17. This refers to the hegemonic stability theory, which focuses on the international political economy. See Stephen D. Krasner, 'State power and the structure of international trade', *World Politics* 28 (1976) pp.317–43; Robert Keohane, 'The theory of hegemonic stability and changes in international economic regimes, 1967–1977', in Ole Holsti *et al.* (eds.) *Change in the International System* (Boulder, CO: Westview Press 1980) pp.131–62; idem, *After Hegemony: Cooperation and Discord in the World Political Economy* (Princeton UP 1984); idem and Joseph Nye, *Power and Interdependence: World Politics in Transition* (Boston: Little Brown 1977).

18. See R. Aron cited in Levy, 'Theories of General War', *World Politics* 37/3 (April 1985) pp.344–74 at pp.348–9, and Robert Gilpin, *War & Change in World Politics* (Cambridge: CUP 1981) p.29. On benevolent vs. coercive hegemony, see Duncan Snidal, 'The limits of hegemonic stability', *Int. Org.* 39/4 (Autumn 1985) pp.579–614.

19. Both variants of hegemonic theory claim the global validity of their arguments (whether in the global international economy or the international political system). Yet, the hegemonies they cite took place, in fact, only on the subsystemic level. See Nye, *Bound to Lead* (note 16). Thus, the US-sponsored international economic regimes did not include the USSR, while theories of international political hegemonies have overlooked continental Europe. See Levy, 'Long cycles, hegemonic transitions, and the long peace.' Accordingly, in the

terms used here, the US was unilateralist-exclusionary in international political economy *vis-à-vis* the USSR – the only other great power of the postwar system. At the same time, depending on the domestic system, certain hegemons behaved accommodatively *vis-à-vis* non-great powers, notably the US *vis-à-vis* West European states (none of which was a great power in the postwar system).

20. These two types of factors (normative and structural) constitute the two main explanations of the democratic peace thesis. See Zeev Maoz and Bruce Russett, 'Structural and normative causes of peace between democracies', *American Political Science Review* [hereafter *APSR*] 87/3 (Sept. 1993) pp.624–38; and Harvey Starr, 'Why don't democracies fight one another? Evaluating the theory-findings feedback loop', *Jerusalem Jnl of Int. Relations* 14 (1992) pp.41–59. See also Michael Doyle, 'Kant, Liberal legacies, and foreign affairs', *Philosophy and Public Affairs* 12 (Summer 1983) pp.205–35; idem, 'Liberalism and world politics', *APSR* 80 (Dec. 1986) pp.1151–69. Doyle draws on Kant. In this study these explanations are examined in a different domain, namely, the orientation of a great power with regard to regional peacemaking. This analysis may thus lend strength to the democratic peace theory while extending its utility.

21. See Ole R. Holsti, Terrence P. Hopmann, and John D. Sullivan, *Unity and Disintegration in International Alliances* (NY: Wiley-Interscience 1973) pp.149–75.

22. In his study of negotiation between strong and weak states, Habeeb suggests that the democratic regime of the strong state serves as a restraint on using coercive measures. He argues that coercion will be used much more by an authoritarian power in its negotiation with small powers. See William Mark Habeeb, *Power and Tactics in International Negotiations: How Weak Nations Bargain with Strong Nations* (Baltimore, MD: Johns Hopkins UP 1988) p.146.

23. On the inclination of democracies to use mediation in settling conflicts between themselves, see William Dixon, 'Democracy and the management of international conflict', *Jnl of Conflict Resolution* 37/1 (1993) pp.42–68.

24. See Bruce Russett, *Grasping the Democratic Peace* (Princeton UP 1993) pp.30–8.

25. See Stephen Walt, *The Origins of Alliances* (Ithaca, NY: Cornell UP 1987) pp.35–6 and the sources he cites. On the congruence between the hierarchical nature of the Soviet domestic system and its hierarchical relations with foreign communist parties, cf. Lowell Dittmer, 'The strategic triangle: an elementry game-theoretical analysis', *World Politics* 33/4 (July 1981) pp.485–515 at pp.496, 501.

26. On this distinction, see Stephen Krasner, *Defending the National Interest* (Princeton UP 1978) Ch.3, and Peter Katzenstein (ed.) *Between Power and Plenty: Foreign Economic Policies of Advanced Industrial States* (Madison: U. of Wisconsin Press 1978). See also Matthew Evangelista, *Innovation and the Arms Race: How the United States and the Soviet Union Develop New Military Technologies* (Ithaca, NY: Cornell UP 1988); John G. Ikenberry, David Lake and Michael Mastanduno (eds.) *The State and American Foreign Economic Policy* (Ithaca, NY: Cornell UP 1988); and Aaron L. Friedberg, 'Why didn't the United States become a garrison state?' *Int. Security* 16/4 (1992) pp.109–42.

27. Krasner, *Defending the National Interest* (note 26) Ch.3; and Evangelista, *Innovation and the Arms Race* (note 26), pp.22–7, 271–2.

28. On 'linkage groups,' see Yaacov Bar-Siman-Tov, *Linkage Politics in the Middle East: Syria between domestic and external conflict* (Boulder, CO: Westview Press 1983) pp.50–1. He draws on the work of Rosenau on linkage politics. See James N. Rosenau, ed., Linkage Politics (NY: Free Press 1969). Transnationalism is analyzed by Robert Keohane and Joseph Nye (eds.) *Transnational Relations and World Politics* (Cambridge, MA: Harvard UP 1972), and Keohane and Nye, *Power and Interdependence* (note 17). On transnational penetration as a cause of alliance formation, see Walt, *Origins of Alliances* ((note 25) pp.46–9. In the area of international trade, Odell found that Latin American states often took advantage of the pluralist system in the US to build domestic allies within the US to help fight for their cause (cited in Habeeb, *Power and Tactics*, note 22, p.7).

29. Other conditions for the effectiveness of such transnational linkage groups are explored by Robert O. Keohane, 'The big influence of small allies', *Foreign Policy*, No.2 (Spring 1971), and elaborated by Benjamin Miller, 'Can Opponents Cooperate: Explaining Great Power

Cooperation in Managing Third Area Conflicts' (PhD dissertation, U. of California, Berkeley, Dec. 1988) pp.355–6.
30. On ethnic lobbies and foreign policy, see Abdul A. Said (ed.) *Ethnicity and US Foreign Policy* (NY: Praeger 1977), and Paul Y. Watanabe, *Ethnic Groups, Congress, and American Foreign Policy* (Westport, CT: Greenwood 1984).
31. See Keohane, 'The big influence of small allies' (note 29).
32. For a partial defense (but also critique) of these actions in a recent comprehensive study which, on the whole, underlines US democratizing effects in the world, see Tony Smith, *America's Mission: The United States and the Worldwide Struggle for Democracy in the Twentieth Century* (Princeton UP 1994).
33. See Saadia Touval, 'The superpowers as mediators', in J. Bercovitch and J. Rubin, *Mediation in International Relations* (NY: St Martin's Press 1992); idem, 'Superpower peacemaking, 1945–1989'.
34. See ibid. p.163.
35. Although in the absence of a countervailing force, democratic powers have also abused their superior power in proximate spheres of influence, including coercive conduct by the US in Central America, relatively speaking, they tend to be somewhat less coercive than authoritarian powers, esp. *vis-à-vis* other democracies. For a comparison of Soviet and American Cold War behaviour in their respective spheres of influence that concludes that Soviet conduct was more coercive, see Jiri Valenta, 'Military interventions: Doctrines, motivations, goals and outcomes', in Jan F. Triska (ed.) *Dominant Powers and Subordinate States: The United States in Latin America and the Soviet Union in Eastern Europe* (Durham, NC: Duke UP 1986). A leading Latin American specialist, Robert Pastor, has argued that 'the Soviet Union long trailed behind the United States in respecting self-determination on its periphery'. See Robert Pastor, *Whirlpool: US Foreign Policy toward Latin America and the Caribbean* (Princeton UP 1992) p.233.
36. For a detailed analysis of the attempts at US-Soviet cooperation in resolving the Arab–Israeli conflict, see Miller, *When Opponents Cooperate* (note 2) Ch.6.
37. On these plans, see William Quandt, *Decade of Decisions: American Policy Toward the Arab–Israeli Conflict, 1967–1976* (Berkeley: U. of California Press 1977) Chs.3 and 5; Nadav Safran, *Israel – the Embattled Ally* (Cambridge, MA: Belknap Press of Harvard UP 1981) pp.431–63; and Steven L. Spiegel, *The Other Arab–Israeli Conflict: Making America's Middle East Policy, from Truman to Reagan* (U. of Chicago Press 1985) Ch.6.
38. Useful analyses of these US accomplishments in peacemaking are: Quandt, *Decade of Decisions*; idem, *Peace Process: American Diplomacy and the Arab–Israeli Conflict since 1967* (Berkeley: U. of California Press 1993); Shlomo Aronson, *Conflict & Bargaining in the Middle East: An Israeli Perspective* (Baltimore, MD: Johns Hopkins UP 1978); Safran, *Israel – the Embattled Ally*; Saadia Touval, *The Peace Brokers: Mediators in the Arab–Israeli Conflict, 1948–1979* (Princeton UP 1982); Spiegel, *The Other Arab–Israeli Conflict* (note 37); Alfred Atherton, 'The Soviet role in the Middle East: an American view', *Middle East Jnl* 39/4 (Autumn 1985) pp.688–715; Abraham Ben-Zvi, *The American Approach to Superpower Collaboration in the Middle East, 1973–1986* (Tel Aviv: Jaffee Center for Strategic Studies 1986); and Harold H. Saunders, 'Regulating Soviet-US Competition and Cooperation in Arab–Israeli Arena, 1967–86', in George, Farley, and Dallin, *US-Soviet Security Cooperation* (note 14) pp.540–80.
39. The most comprehensive treatments of this process are William Quandt, *Camp David: Peacemaking and Politics* (Washington DC: Brookings 1986); and Shibley Telhami, *Power and Leadership in International Bargaining: The Path to the Camp David Accords* (NY: Columbia UP 1990). See also Spiegel (note 37) Ch.8; and Saunders, 'Regulating Soviet-US Competition and Cooperation' (note 38) pp.568–70.
40. William Quandt, 'U.S. Policy toward the Arab–Israeli Conflict', in idem (ed.) *The Middle East: Ten years after Camp David* (Washington DC: Brookings 1988) p.178.
41. But the US has not been the hegemon in the Middle East in the military-strategic sense, at least since the expansion of the Soviet military capabilities *vis-à-vis* the region in the mid- to late-1960s and until the decline of the Soviet Union as a superpower in 1990–91. See Miller, *When Opponents Cooperate* (note 2) Ch.5.

42. For example, in 1988 the figures in millions of dollars were 1,800 and 1,301.5 in military aid to Israel and Egypt respectively and 1,2000 and 873.4 in economic aid to the two countries. For a comparison, a large recipient of US aid such as Turkey received in that year 493.5 millions of dollars in military aid and 32.4 millions in economic aid. Source: Agency for International Development, cited in Congressional Quarterly, *The Middle East*, 7th ed. (Washington DC 1991) p.77.
43. Henry Kissinger, *White House Years* (Boston: Little, Brown 1979) pp.379, 559.
44. See Bruce D. Porter, *The USSR in Third World Conflicts* (Cambridge: CUP 1984) pp.117–18.
45. The analysis here is based on the relevant Middle Eastern chapters in Kissinger's memoirs. See Kissinger, *White House Years*, Chs.10, 14, 15, 28, 30, esp. pp.376, 379, 1247–8, 1279, 1285–90, 1292–6, 1300; and idem, *Years of Upheaval* (Boston: Little, Brown 1982) Chs.6, 11, 12, 13, 17, 18, 21, 23, 24, esp. pp.196, 201–2. See also the interpretations found in Quandt, *Decade of Decisions* (note 37) Chs.3, 5; George, *Managing US-Soviet Rivalry* (note 14) Ch.7; Raymond Garthoff, *Detente and Confrontation: American-Soviet Relations from Nixon to Reagan* (Washington DC: Brookings Inst. 1985); Spiegel (note 37) Chs.6, 7; Atherton, 'The Soviet role in the Middle East' (note 38), and Ben-Zvi, *The American Approach to Superpower Collaboration in the Middle East* (note 38).
46. See Quandt, *Decade of Decisions* (note 37) pp.150–1; and Kissinger, *White House Years* (note 43) pp.1293–4.
47. This was Kissinger's perception of the two-power talks and even of the State Department attempts to accomplish partial agreements between the regional parties unilaterally (1970–71).
48. See Quandt, *Decade of Decisions* (note 37) p. 211. For Kissinger's account of Sadat's preference for American brokerage, see his memoirs, *Years of Upheaval*, Chs.13, 18. Kissinger also refers to Assad's readiness to accept US mediation (Chs.21, 23). On the regional actors' preference for US exclusionary diplomacy, see also O. M. Smolansky, 'The United States and the Soviet Union in the Middle East,' in G. Kirk and N. Wessell (eds.) *The Soviet Threat: Myths and Realities* (NY: Academy of Political Science 1978) pp.99–109 at pp.100–1; Ben-Zvi, *The American Approach to Superpower Collaboration* (note 38) pp.39–41; and Moshe Zak, *Israel and the Superpower Game in the Middle East* (Tel Aviv: Hakibbutz Hameuchad 1986) Ch.5 (Hebrew).
49. For lists of the proponents of this viewpoint, see George Breslauer, 'Soviet Policy in the Middle East, 1967–1972: Unalterable Antagonism or Collaborative Competition?' in George (ed.) *Managing U.S.-Soviet Rivalry* (note 14) p.99, n.1; and Jerome Slater, 'The Superpowers and an Arab–Israeli Political Settlement: The Cold War Years', *Political Science Qtly* 105/4 (1990–91) pp.557–78 at p.560, n.5. See also Richard Nixon, *The Memoirs of Richard Nixon* (NY: Warner Books 1978) pp.482–3.
50. Neil S. MacFarlane, 'Soviet perspectives on Third World security'; Draft MS. U. of California, Berkeley, and Stanford U., *Program on Soviet International Behaviour*, Feb. 1987, p.13. On the Soviet conception of equality during the détente era, see also Coit D. Blacker, 'The Kremlin and detente: Soviet conceptions, hopes, and expectations', in George (ed.) *Managing U.S.-Soviet Rivalry* (note 14) pp.119–37.
51. Christer Jonsson, *Superpower: Comparing American and Soviet Foreign Policy* (NY: St Martin's Press 1984) pp.25–8.
52. The privileges of the permanent members of the UN Security Council are the Cold War formal expression of such great power 'rights' and 'responsibilities' for international peace and security. On the Soviet desire for a formal recognition of its superpower status and preference for formal international agreements, see also G. Breslauer (ed.) *Soviet Strategy in the Middle East* (Winchester, MA: Unwin Hyman 1990); Joanne Gowa and Nils H. Wessell, *Ground Rules: Soviet and American Involvement in Regional Conflicts* (Philadelphia Policy papers, Philadelphia, PA: Foreign Policy Research Inst. 1982) pp.2, 14; George (note 14) Chs.2, 5; and Dimitri K. Simes, 'The domestic environment of Soviet policy making', in Arnold Horelick (ed.) *U.S.-Soviet Relations: the Next Phase* (Ithaca, NY: Cornell UP 1986) pp.154–5.
53. This is the major theme of a book by a veteran Israeli journalist. See Moshe Zak, *Israel and*

the Superpower Game in the Middle East. See also idem, *Israel and the Soviet Union – A Forty Years Dialogue* (Tel Aviv: Ma'ariv 1988) (Hebrew). Zak argues that the common denominator of all Soviet steps in the Middle East since 1945 has been the struggle to reach a recognized partnership with the US in the region. He documents the validity of this assertion in the different stages of Soviet involvement in the Arab–Israeli conflict.

54. See Ya'acov Roi, *From Encroachement to Involvement, A Documentary Study of Soviet Policy in the Middle East 1945–1973* (Jerusalem: Israel Universities Press 1974); idem, *Soviet Decision-Making in Practice, The U.S.S.R., and Israel 1947–1954* (New Brunswick, NJ: Transaction Books 1980). These activities included, mainly, the so-called conciliation committee and the observation of the ceasefire agreements between Israel and its neighbors following the 1948 war. For a brief summary, see Zak, *Israel and the Superpower Game* (note 53) pp.26–8. Because of the US domination of the UN in this period and the subsequent denial of a role for the Soviets in its Middle East activities, Moscow supported in 1948–50 the Israeli position advocating direct bilateral talks with the Arabs. See Saadia Touval, 'Frameworks for Arab–Israeli negotiations – What difference do they make?' *Negotiation Jnl* (Jan. 1987) pp.37–52 at p.45; Zak, *Israel and the Soviet Union* (note 53) pp.369–70.

55. See Smolansky, 'The United States and the Soviet Union in the Middle East', Zak, *Israel and the Superpower Game* (note 53) Ch.2, esp. pp.46–9; and Slater, 'The Superpowers and an Arab–Israeli Political Settlement', pp.564–5. The authors of this statement (issued on 25 May 1950) – the US, Britain and France – called for the maintenance of the status quo and the military balance in the Middle East.

56. Cf. Golan, 'The Soviet Union and the Palestinian issue', in Breslauer, *Soviet Strategy in the Middle East* (note 52).

57. See Breslauer, 'Soviet Policy in the Middle East' (note 49), Lawrence L. Whetten, *The Canal War: Four-Power Conflict in the Middle East* (Cambridge, MA: MIT Press 1974); and idem, 'The Arab–Israeli Dispute: Great Power Behaviour,' in G. Treverton (ed.) *Crisis Management and the Superpowers in the Middle East* (Farnborough: Gower 1981).

58. See Kissinger, *White House Years* (note 43) pp.1285–6, 1288–9, 1293–4; Quandt, *Decade of Decisions* (note 37) pp.150–1.

59. On the evolution of the Soviet position concerning the framework for Arab-Israeli negotiations, see Touval, 'Frameworks for Arab–Israeli negotiations', (note 54) pp.45–6. For a detailed account of the Soviet view of an international conference on the Middle East, see Ben-Zvi, *Between Lausanne and Geneva* (note 2) pp.92–104.

60. Arkady Sovlov (a Soviet diplomat who served as a deputy sec.-gen. of the UN) talked with Moshe Sharett (the man in charge of foreign affairs in the Jewish Agency) about the participation of two squadrons of Soviet bombers in an international force if such a force would be required for the enforcement of the resolution. This is mentioned in David Ben-Gurion, *War Diary* (Tel Aviv: Defense Ministry of Israel 1982; Hebrew) pp.86–7, cited also in Zak, *Israel and the Superpower Game* (note 53) p.21 and p.35, n.10. Whereas the UN secretary general expressed his support for a superpower force (Ben-Gurion, p.239), the US opposed such a force precisely because it required Soviet participation (p.238).

61. On the Soviet proposal to dispatch a joint superpower force in the Suez crisis, see the memoirs of the then US ambassador to Moscow, Charles Bohlen, *Witness to History* (NY: Norton 1973) p.432. On Eisenhower's total rejection, see Dwight Eisenhower, *The White House Years: Waging Peace 1956–1961* (Garden City, NY: Doubleday 1965) pp.89–90; and Donald Neff, *Warriors at Suez: Eisenhower takes America into the Middle East* (NY: Simon & Schuster 1981) p.403. On the 1973 offer, see Miller, *When Opponents Cooperate* (note 2) Ch.5.

62. The Brezhnev Plan, *Pravda*, 24 Feb. 1981 [cited in Soviet and E. European Research Center, Hebrew U.: *The Soviet Union and the Middle East* 6/2 (1981), p.5].

63. See Oded Eran, 'Soviet Policy Between the 1967 and 1973 Wars', in Haim Shaked and Itamar Rabinovich (eds.) *From June to October: The Middle East Between 1967 and 1973* (New Brunswick, NJ: Transaction Books 1978) p.47; MacFarlane, 'Soviet perspectives on Third World security' (note 50) pp.194–5.

64. See Alan Dowty, 'The Role of Great Power Guarantees in International Peace

Agreements', *Jerusalem Papers on Peace Problems*, No.3 (Leonard Davis Inst. for Int. Relations, Hebrew U. of Jerusalem 1975); and Yair Evron, 'The role of arms control in the Middle East', *Adelphi Papers*, No.138 (London: IISS 1977) pp.29–36.
65. Cf. Galia Golan, 'The Middle East,' in Kurt London (ed.) *The Soviet Union in World Politics* (Boulder, CO: Westview Press 1980) pp.105–26 at p.121.
66. Eran, 'Soviet Policy Between the 1967 and 1973 Wars' (note 63) p.47.
67. See the sources cited in Breslauer, which refer esp. to the 1967–72 period: 'Soviet Policy in the Middle East', p.99, n.2; and in Jonsson, *Superpower* (note 51) Ch.5. A similarly qualified conclusion is also reached by other scholars such as Golan, 'The Middle East' (note 65); Garthoff, *Detente and Confrontation* (note 45) esp. p.87; Richard K. Herrmann, 'Soviet policy and the Arab–Israeli conflict: actions, patterns, and interpretations', *Political Science Qtly* 102/3 (Fall 1987) pp.417–40; Peter Mangold, *Superpower Intervention in the Middle East* (NY: St Martin's Press 1978) pp.115–41; and Seth Tillman, *The United States in the Middle East* (Bloomington: Indiana UP 1982) Ch.6, esp. pp.251–3; for corroboration, see esp. the memoirs of Egyptian practitioners (President Sadat and Foreign Ministers Riad and Fahmy and Nasser's confidant, Heikal. See Anwar Sadat, *In Search of Identity* (NY: Harper & Row 1977) esp. pp.228–9; Mahmoud Riad, *The Struggle for Peace in the Middle East* (London: Quartet Books 1981); Ismail Fahmy, *Negotiating for Peace in the Middle East* (Baltimore: Johns Hopkins UP 1983); Mohamed Heikal, *The Road to Ramadan* (NY: Quadrangle 1975); and idem, *The Sphinx and the Commissar* (NY: Harper & Row 1978). Also relevant is the work of a leading State Dept Middle East specialist. See Saunders, 'Regulating Soviet-US Competition and Cooperation' (note 38).
68. See Breslauer, 'Soviet Policy in the Middle East, 1967–1972' (note 49) p.96.
69. Cf. Zak, *Israel and the Superpower Game* (note 53) p.105.
70. Indeed, during the 1980s there was a growing recognition in the Soviet elite that the competitive Soviet conduct of the mid- to late 1970s in parts of the Third World undermined the support for détente among the US public. See Neil S. MacFarlane, 'The Soviet Conception of Regional Security', *World Politics* 37/3 (April 1985) pp.295–316.; and Breslauer, *Soviet Strategy in the Middle East* (note 52).
71. See Smolansky, 'The United States and the Soviet Union in the Middle East (note 48) p.105.
72. For a discussion of the connection between the Soviet desire for a recognized coequal status with the US, and participation in the settlement of international disputes, especially the Middle East peace process during the détente era, see George, 'U.S.-Soviet efforts to cooperate in crisis management and crisis avoidance', in George, Farley, and Dallin, *U.S.-Soviet Security Cooperation* (note 14) pp.588–9.
73. Eran, 'Soviet Policy Between the 1967 and 1973 Wars' (note 63) pp.45–6.
74. George Breslauer, 'Soviet Policy in the Middle East, 1967-1972' and 'Why detente failed', p.334, both in George, *Managing U.S.-Soviet Rivalry* (note 14).
75. See Jonsson, *Superpower* (note 51) Ch.5; Hoffmann, 'Detente', in Joseph Nye (ed.) *The Making of America's Soviet Policy* (New Haven, CT: Yale UP 1984) p.244; Ben-Zvi, *Between Lausanne and Geneva* (note 2) pp.92–104.
76. *Memoirs of Richard Nixon* (note 49) p.430; Kissinger, *Years of Upheaval* (note 45) pp.583–4.
77. Touval, 'Frameworks for Arab–Israeli negotiations' (note 54) p.45.
78. Breslauer, 'Soviet Policy in the Middle East, 1967–1972' (note 49) pp.74–5.
79. For such a testimony, see, e.g., Heikal's report that immediately after the Six Day War, the Soviets started pressuring the Arabs to reach a settlement with Israel even if this required some form of diplomatic acceptance of the Jewish state. See *Sphinx and Commissar* (note 67) pp.186–7. See also Whetten, *Canal War* (note 57) p.46–7. Heikal writes also about Soviet restraining pressures on Nasser in 1968 when he suggested a renewal of the military option against Israel (*Sphinx and Commissar*, p.30). Sadat reports about Soviet pressures and their preference for a diplomatic solution in the months preceding the 1973 war. See the citations in Galia Golan, *Yom Kippur and After: The Soviet Union and the Arab–Israeli Crisis* (Cambridge: CUP 1977) pp.47–55; Dina Rome Spechler, 'The U.S.S.R. and Third-World conflicts: domestic debate and Soviet policy in the Middle East, 1967–1973', *World*

Politics 38/3 (April 1986) pp.435–61 at p.438, n.10. On the differences between the diplomatic positions of the Soviets and the Arabs, cf. Heikal, *Sphinx and Commissar* (note 67) p.195. For example, Sadat was dismayed at the Soviet joint declaration with the US at the May 1972 summit calling for 'military relaxation' in the Middle East, which 'practically' meant 'an implicit acceptance of the status-quo' in the region. See Kissinger, *White House Years* (note 43) p.1247. This declaration, Sadat (*In Search of Identity*, note 67, p.229) recalls, 'was a violent shock to us' because the status quo was seen in Cairo as beneficial to Israel.

80. Cf. Whetten, *Canal War* (note 57) p.154; Jon Glassman, *Arms for the Arabs* (Baltimore: Johns Hopkins UP 1975) pp.87–8; Heikal, *Road to Ramadan* (note 67) pp.112, 117; idem, *Sphinx and Commissar* (note 67) pp.249–50; Golan, *Yom Kippur and After* (note 79) pp.21–2; Porter, *The USSR in Third World Conflicts* (note 44) pp.120–1; Spechler, 'The U.S.S.R. and Third-World conflicts' (note 79) pp.437–8.
81. Sadat, *In Search of Identity* (note 67) pp.185–7, 198, 212, 219, 220–1, 225–31, 286–7.
82. Eran, 'Soviet Policy Between the 1967 and 1973 Wars' (note 63) pp.45–6.
83. Breslauer, 'Soviet Policy in the Middle East, 1967-1972' (note 49) p.96.
84. For comprehensive treatments of US-Israeli relations, see Safran, *Israel* (note 37); Spiegel, *The Other Arab–Israeli Conflict* (note 37); and Abraham Ben-Zvi, *The United States and Israel: The Limits of the Special Relationship* (NY: Columbia UP 1993).
85. See Cyrus Vance, *Hard Choices: Critical Years in America's Foreign Policy* (NY: Simon & Schuster 1983) pp.192–3; Spiegel, *The Other Arab–Israeli Conflict* (note 37) p.338; and Quandt, *Camp David* (note 39) pp.119–20.
86. See Vance, *Hard Choices* |(note 85) p.192; Zbigniew Brzezinski, *Power and Principle: Memoirs of the National Security Adviser, 1977–1981* (NY: Farrar, Strauss, Giroux 1983) pp.73, 108; Martin Indyk, *'To the Ends of the Earth': Sadat's Jerusalem Initiative* (Cambridge, MA: Harvard U., Center for Middle Eastern Studies 1984) p.44; Spiegel, *The Other Arab–Israeli Conflict* (note 37) p.338 and the detailed sources he cites in n.68, p.478.
87. See Raymond Cohen, 'Israel and the Soviet-American statement of October 1, 1977: the limits of patron-client influence', *Orbis* 22 (Fall 1978) pp.613–33; Brzezinski, *Power and Principle* (note 86) pp.107–10, 175; Vance, *Hard Choices* (note 85) pp.192–4; Indyk, *'To the Ends of the Earth'* (note 86) p.44.
88. Quandt, *Camp David* (note 39) p.131.
89. Sadat, *In Search of Identity* (note 67) p.304; Quandt, *Camp David* (note 39) pp.131, 136, 139–42, 145.
90. Although the Soviets backed off from their support of the plan in December 1969, in this case this should be attributed to the Soviet refusal to press their allies – the Egyptians – when they were in a poor military situation. See Whetten, *Canal War* (note 57) p.82 and Breslauer 'Soviet Policy in the Middle East' (note 49) pp.86–7. The Soviet retrogression cannot be explained by domestic opposition, at least not opposition from outside the elite.
91. See Kissinger, *White House Years* (note 43) pp.376–7; Seymour M. Hersh, *The Price of Power: Kissinger in the Nixon White House* (NY: Summit Books 1983) p.220.
92. See Spiegel, *The Other Arab–Israeli Conflict* (note 37) pp.291–305; and Ben-Zvi, *United States and Israel* (note 39) Ch.4.
93. For details, see Ben-Zvi, ibid. pp.97–8.
94. Ibid. p.98.
95. Spiegel, *The Other Arab–Israeli Conflict* (note 37) p.296; Ben-Zvi, *United States and Israel* (note 84) p.99.
96. Ben-Zvi, ibid. p.101.
97. On the theoretical reasons for the greater influence of great powers on their small allies in times of crisis than in noncrisis situations, especially under bipolarity, see Miller, 'Explaining great power cooperation in conflict management' (note 7).
98. For a recent sophisticated analysis of the role of coercive diplomacy in US-Israel relations, see Ben-Zvi, *United States and Israel* (note 84).
99. For treatments of superpower diplomatic cooperation in various regional conflicts in the late 1980s, see the detailed accounts in the following edited volumes dedicated to this subject: R. Kanet and E. Kolodziej (eds.) *The Cold War as Cooperation* (Baltimore, MD:

Johns Hopkins UP 1991); Mark N. Katz (ed.) *Soviet-American Conflict Resolution in the Third World* (Washington DC: US Inst. of Peace Press 1991); and Thomas Weiss and James Blight (eds.) *The Suffering Grass: Superpowers and Regional Conflict in Southern Africa and the Caribbean* (Boulder, CO Lynne Rienner 1992). See also Richard K. Herrmann, 'Soviet behavior in regional conflicts: old questions, new strategies, and important lessons', *World Politics* 44/3 (April 1992) pp.432–66; and Miller, *When Opponents Cooperate* (note 2) Ch.6.

100. See Martin Indyk, 'The postwar balance of power in the Middle East', in Joseph S. Nye Jr and Roger K. Smith (eds.) *After the Storm: Lessons from the Gulf War* (Lanham, MD: Madison 1992); Robert J. Lieber, 'The American role in a regional security regime,' in Efraim Inbar (ed.) *Regional Security Regimes: Israel and its Neighbors* (Albany: SUNY 1995) pp.59–80; and Barry Rubin, *The New Middle East: Opportunities and Risks* (Ramat Gan, Israel: BESA Center for Strategic Studies, Bar-Ilan U., Security and Policy Studies no.19, 1995).

101. See Charles Krauthammer, 'The unipolar moment,' *Foreign Affairs* 70/1 'America and the World' (Winter 1990–91) pp.23–33; Kenneth Waltz, 'America as a model for the world? A foreign policy perspective', *PS*, Vol.24 (1991) pp.667–70; Robert W. Tucker and David C. Hendrickson, *The Imperial Temptation: The New World Order and America's Purpose* (NY: Council on Foreign Relations Press 1992); and Benjamin Miller, 'International Systems and Regional Security: From Competition to Cooperation, Dominance or Disengagement?' *Jnl of Strategic Studies* 18/2 (June 1995) pp.52–100.

102. See Nizan Horowitz, 'Europe: "The Americans take again all the spoils to themselves. We exist only to pay" ', *Haaretz*, 27 Sept. 1995, p.6A.

103. See Miller, 'A New World Order' (note 16) pp.18–19.

104. See former Russian Foreign Minister Kozyrev's article in the *New York Times*, 18 March 1994.

105. See *Haaretz*, 3 Nov. 1994.

106. Aluf Ben, 'Rabin rejected a proposal of the chief of Russian intelligence to go to Damascus as a mediator between the parties,' *Haaretz*, 21 Dec. 1995, p.2A.

107. 'Russia reaches out', *The Economist*, 26 Feb. 1994, p.31.

108. Cited in Ibid.

109. *Time*, June 1994, p.22.

110. For a concise account, see Zbigniew Brzezinski, 'The premature friendship', *Foreign Affairs* 73/2 (March/April 1994) pp.67–82 at 72–5.

111. Ibid. pp.79–80.

112. For a somewhat similar point, see Maynes' notion of 'benign realpolitik'. See Charles Maynes, 'A workable Clinton Doctrine', *Foreign Policy* No.93 (Winter 1993–94).

Confidence and Security Building Measures in the Middle East

ARIEL E. LEVITE and EMILY B. LANDAU

At the outset of the Multilateral Peace Process Negotiations on the Middle East in Moscow (28 January 1992), US Secretary of State James Baker set forth the outline for the Working Group on Arms Control and Regional Security (ACRS). He defined it to be as follows:

> In the first instance, we envision offering the regional parties our thinking about potential approaches to arms control, drawing upon a vast reservoir of experience stemming from attempts to regulate military competition in Europe and other regions.
>
> From this base, the group might move forward to considering a set of confidence building or transparency measures covering notifications of selected military activities and crisis prevention communications. The purpose would be to lessen the prospects for incidents and miscalculation that could lead to heightened competition or even conflict.
>
> In our view, and again, based upon our experience with arms control, we believe such an approach offers the best chance for success.[1]

The approach to the Middle East ACRS process offered by Secretary of State Baker places strong emphasis on Confidence and Security Building Measures (CSBMs) as the principal vehicle for progress at the early stages of the process, drawing heavily on the superpower and European experience. This analysis seeks to explore the basis for such an approach. It begins by addressing the intellectual and academic foundations for a confidence and security building approach to conflict management in general and in the context of the theory of arms control in particular. It briefly describes the origin and evolution of CSBMs in the superpower and European contexts; the defining characteristics of CSBMs; and the role they are designed to play. It then considers the necessary general conditions of ripeness for CSBM application, insights from the cumulative CSBM experience, as well as the relevancy of CSBMs outside the European context in which they originally emerged. Finally, after assessing the role CSBMs could play in the Arab–Israeli context, and the role that CSBMs might play in the Middle East beyond the Arab–Israeli context, this study provides some reflections on the empirical data gained from the multilateral CSBM negotiations that have been carried out in the Middle East thus far.

Theoretical Underpinnings

The advocacy of CSBMs is premised on two basic assumptions. First, that parties to a conflict have a mutual interest to pursue at least some cooperative solutions in order to realize a shared goal. Second, that due to the anarchical nature of the international system (often complicated by the antagonists' shared or individual histories), this cooperation is hindered by psychological and political barriers of mutual distrust and suspicion. The rationale underlying CSBMs is that a gradual process of confidence building is the key to overcoming this obstacle on the way to realizing the mutually beneficial goal.

As facilitators of cooperation, CSBMs belong to the wider category of 'strategies of reassurance' in international relations that have in common the aim of overcoming basic suspicions in order to cooperate in an anarchical international system.[2] All strategies of reassurance help to create norms of cooperation. What sets CSBMs apart from other strategies of reassurance – especially from 'rules of the game'[3] and security regimes[4] – is the fact that they are formal and intentional agreements that are directly negotiated and consensually agreed upon. CSBMs are the product of a clear prior decision to promote confidence and security.

CSBMs focus specifically on the psychological aspect of mutual suspicions and distrust between adversaries,[5] and in this sense they are closer to predispositional, rather than structural, approaches to international relations. Yet, while perceptions lie at the heart of CSBMs, there is nevertheless a strong linkage between suspicions and possible misperceptions, and the basic *interest* to cooperate. Thus states will not be expected to agree on CSBMs (and thus deal with the psychological aspect of lack of trust regarding enforcement of agreements) if there is not a basic interest to cooperate.

The overall shared goal that CSBMs relate to is the achievement of bilateral or regional security and stability. This may be defined as a short-term and specific goal (such as the avoidance of escalation to nuclear war), or as a more ambitious undertaking – primarily, agreement on comprehensive security and arms control accords. In the final analysis, CSBMs may also contribute to the attainment of even more far-reaching political accommodation, although the factor that will ultimately determine the outcome of political negotiations is the resolution of conflicting interests.

The logic underlying CSBMs, as facilitators of cooperation, draws at least in part on scholarly works grounded in the *neoliberalist tradition* in international relations. These studies attempt to explain the existence of incentives for cooperation in an anarchical world, and look at the means of achieving cooperation under anarchy.[6] Neoliberalist studies emphasize the ability of regimes to both promote and enhance mutually beneficial cooperation.[7]

According to the neo-realist approach to international relations, however, 'international anarchy fosters competition and conflict among states and inhibits their willingness to cooperate even when they share common interests.'[8] In fact, Joseph Grieco contends that neoliberalist optimism regarding the possibility of mitigating anarchy's effects and achieving cooperation results from its focus on only one dimension of international anarchy, namely the lack of common government in the sense of absence of any agency that can reliably enforce promises. This view regards *cheating* as the major cause for concern, and leads neoliberals to investigate how institutions can deal with this particular problem. Grieco submits, however, that according to realist theory, anarchy also has another dimension: the lack of an overarching authority that can also 'prevent others from using violence, or the threat of violence, to destroy or enslave them'.[9] Seen in these terms, the key interest of states is first and foremost continued survival.

This understanding of anarchy leads neorealism to focus not only on problems of cheating regarding absolute gains, but also to pay particular attention to the question of *relative capabilities* and *gains*, which states view as bearing directly on their prospects for survival. This concern over relative gains, in turn, poses an additional constraint on cooperation: 'a state will decline to join, will leave, or will sharply limit its commitment to a cooperative arrangement if it believes that partners are achieving, or are likely to achieve relatively greater gains.'[10]

One issue that must be reckoned with is the extent to which this neorealist approach, specifically regarding states' concerns with relative gains, may affect states' willingness to cooperate in the realm of CSBMs.

According to the logic of neoliberalism, once the conditions of ripeness for CSBM negotiations are met, this should constitute both the necessary and sufficient condition for negotiating cooperative measures. According to neorealism, however, ripeness is a necessary, but not necessarily sufficient condition: the concern with relative gains may pose a serious constraint on negotiations, even when there is a basic willingness to pursue mutually-beneficial security arrangements. We will address this issue in our concluding remarks, on the basis of empirical evidence regarding the progress in negotiations on CSBMs in the framework of ACRS thus far.

Our primary focus is on the Middle East, and on the potential contribution of CSBMs to the regional arms control process (ACRS), and more broadly to the Madrid peace process. The academic literature on CSBMs generally tends to view CSBMs as an integral part of the arms control process. It sees them as serving the role of either an important first stage of the process or as a means of complementing or enhancing more traditional modes of arms control.[11] The outline for the ACRS Working Group set forth by Secretary Baker in Moscow (above) epitomizes the first approach.

CSBMs have two clear advantages as precursors for more intense cooperation, especially in the arms control domain. These are their incremental and evolutionary nature and their primary focus on intentions, rather than capabilities.[12] Their incremental nature allows adversaries to accept confidence building measures even when the political basis for fundamental restructuring of the relationship between them is still missing. Their evolutionary nature, and focus on intentions, in turn, mean that their adoption neither diminishes either side's security margins, nor, at least initially, does it require large and painful practical (as distinguished from psychological) adjustments on either side. Implementing them thus is not conditioned on the parties' willingness or ability to introduce profound changes in their security doctrines, force structures, or troop deployment, let alone on making painful reciprocal concessions.

The Origins and Historical Evolution of CSBMs

Confidence Building Measures (CBMs) and thereafter CSBMs (though they were not labeled as such at the time) were initially applied in the superpower and European context to address the mutual fear of unintended escalation. They were motivated by a concern that such escalation, emanating from mutual suspicions and possible misperceptions, could result in an armed conflict, possibly involving nuclear weapons. With time, the wider potential of CSBMs was recognized, especially in terms of their ability to contribute, albeit gradually, to the creation of an atmosphere more conducive to the attainment of more far-reaching goals.

In a sense, CSBMs, as begun in Helsinki and formally defined in the Stockholm accords, should be viewed as an outgrowth of a bilateral confidence-building process that began between the superpowers in the late 1950s/early 1960s. The original teletype 'hot-line' instituted between Moscow and Washington in June 1963, following the Cuban Missile Crisis, is often cited as the first formal CBM between the superpowers. Establishing direct and reliable communication links between the superpowers was above all a testimony to the recognition both sides had reached that notwithstanding their global rivalry, they nonetheless had a common interest in preventing uncontrolled escalation (recall the Harmel report of December 1967), and that this interest could potentially be served by establishing channels for timely clarification of intentions in crisis situations. In the early 1970s the US and the Soviet Union agreed upon three additional bilateral CBMs dealing with the means of preventing nuclear accidents and incidents on and over the high seas.[13] These attested to the widening recognition of a common interest between the superpowers at the time of the detente, although the relationship between the superpowers remained characterized by profound suspicion and intense competition.

On the European side, the 'Helsinki Process' was formally launched in July 1973 with the convening of the Conference for Security and Cooperation in Europe (CSCE). No fewer than 35 countries in Europe and North America elected to participate in the process, thereby vividly demonstrating the 'considerable dissatisfaction [that] had accumulated on all sides concerning the continued division of Europe and the dangerous tensions that had arisen during the course of the Cold War'.[14] The atmosphere of detente as well as the bilateral CBMs agreed upon between the superpowers created a sense that negotiations were possible, although suspicions were still deep. The CSCE turned into an ongoing process that included agreements regarding CBMs and later, CSBMs.

The first set of European CBMs were agreed upon and included in the Helsinki Final Act (1 August 1975). These CBMs required both sides to present data regarding military forces and activities in order to improve channels of communication and clarify military intentions. Two important elements of the CBM regime were notification and observation.[15] The dual objective of advance notification regarding military activities and the use of observers was designed to produce conditions which would enable both sides to differentiate between actual signals of hostile intent and the 'noise' of ongoing military activity. By promoting openness and introducing transparency in the military realm, CBMs would reduce uncertainty and build a measure of confidence regarding the other side's intentions.

The Helsinki CBMs provided more of a general approach to confidence building than significant and binding security measures,[16] and in two follow-up meetings (Belgrade, 1977–78 and Madrid, 1981–83), members of the CSCE agreed to negotiate an expanded CBM regime which would make the CBMs politically binding, militarily significant, and verifiable. They named this new generation of CBMs Confidence and Security-Building Measures (CSBMs) in order to emphasize that they deal not only with mutual confidence, but also with mutual security. The negotiations of CSBMs took place in Stockholm between 1984 and 1986 in the framework of the Conference on Confidence and Security Building Measures and Disarmament in Europe (CDE). The CSBMs that were agreed upon included exchange of information regarding annual calendars, advance notification regarding large military exercises (42 days, one year, or two years – depending on the number of troops involved), obligatory invitation of observers to exercises involving over 17000 troops, and three on-site inspections a year for purposes of verification.[17]

CSBMs were negotiated again in Vienna (1986–89, 1989–92) and in Helsinki (1992), and each stage resulted in agreements that further enhanced the CSBM regime.[18] Each stage of the process has thus resulted in an enhanced confidence and security building context.[19] The (first) Vienna Document 1990 on CSBMs not only broadened the scope of existing CSBMs but also provided measures of communications and consultations between members of the CSCE – the establishment of a network of direct communications for the transmission of messages relating to agreed measures, complementing the existing diplomatic channels. In addition, the Charter of Paris for a New Europe, which was agreed upon by the CSCE states during their 1990 summit, stipulated the creation of a Center for the Prevention of Conflicts, which has been established in Vienna. This Center provides some assistance for the successful application of CSBMs.

Defining CSBMs

Definitions of CBMs (Confidence Building Measures) and CSBMs abound in the professional literature,[20] yet there is some confusion regarding the distinction between the two. This study focuses specifically on CSBMs, of the type that has been recognized and institutionalized in the CSCE process, most explicitly in and after the Stockholm accords.

What are the principal defining characteristics of CSBMs modeled after the European type?

First, CSBMs pertain to the security, principally military, domain. CSBMs are geared to promoting confidence regarding military intentions; they are not designed to prevent nations from carrying out legitimate military activity, nor can they prevent entirely illegitimate military action.

Second, in order to promote mutual confidence, they involve at least a modest degree of cooperative behavior between the concerned parties themselves. As such CSBMs cannot be imposed from the outside, and while they may benefit from a skilled and mutually trusted mediator, they require a measure of understanding and coordination between the concerned parties themselves, facilitated by some direct contacts among them.

Third, CSBMs are exclusively those confidence building measures that are directly negotiated, and consensually agreed upon by all parties to a process. They are premised on prenegotiated reciprocal conduct. Unilateral gestures, even if intended to encourage a response from the other side (such as GRIT – Graduated and Reciprocated Initiatives in Tension Reduction[21]) do not qualify as CSBMs..

Fourth, CSBMs neither jeopardize nor fundamentally affect the key security assets or concerns of any of the parties – they must maintain a sense that they will not be left helpless in the face of a breach. In fact, building confidence implies creating and sustaining the *grounds* for confidence in addition to fostering a sense of trust regarding the other side's benign intentions.[22] Moreover, CSBMs should not harm in any way the national dignity of any of the parties involved..

Fifth, CSBMs do not prejudice any of the parties' positions on the unresolved broader political issues at stake. Finally, CSBMs are designed to have some (however small) direct positive contribution to the situation at hand, in addition to their long term potential for building trust between the parties.

Adopting such a restrictive definition obviously means that we confine our discussion to intentional and explicit cooperative measures that enhance openness and transparency in the security realm in order to reduce uncertainty and build the confidence of each side in their ability to assess the intentions of the other side. We thus consciously exclude from consideration here other types of CBMs, significant as they may be. These may consist of any act or arrangement, in any sphere, that favorably affects mutual expectations beween adversaries, and that serves to reduce uncertainty and promote a measure of confidence between them.

This distinction assumes some significance because CBMs at large have, in recent years, become a *façon de parler* which has taken on the meaning of general good-will gestures or arrangements between adversaries in any realm. Our choice to employ here a much more rigid and restrictive definition should not be understood as suggesting that we deny either the relevance or potential importance of other categories of CBMs, whether in general or in the Middle East context. In fact quite the opposite is true. Much pertinent experience, both bilateral and multilateral in nature, has accumulated outside the European context, most notably between the US and the former USSR as well as between India and its neighbors, Argentina and Brazil, and North and South Korea.

We solely suggest that adopting a narrower definition is warranted by several theoretical as well as normative considerations that lead us to focus on a unique sub-set of CBMs that have special requirements as well as implications.

Having defined CSBMs, let us consider the role they are designed to play. Generally speaking, CSBMs are designed to help the parties overcome psychological and political barriers of mutual distrust and suspicion in order to realize a shared goal. Within this framework, they can be said to have four complementary roles. First, they can serve as a litmus test for intentions over time. Second, they can serve an educational role, familiarizing the parties with each other and improving mutual understanding, both in the immediate area of concern and far beyond it. In addition, they can make a uniquely important contribution in disseminating a cooperative mentality (non-zero sum way of thinking) on security within and among the relevant constituencies in each of the participating states. These include the involved bureaucracies and interest groups, and in the case of democracies, the general public as well. Third, CSBMs can be an ends in themselves, rather than merely a means to a higher end, by institutionalizing dialogue channels and helping in crisis management, conflict prevention, and in some cases provision of humanitarian assistance as well.

Finally, if and when desired, CSBMs can also serve as a symbol of cooperation, sending a broad political message of willingness to move beyond confrontation and competition to cooperation and reconciliation.[23] This last function does not automatically accompany CSBMs. But such arrangements, like other forms of cooperative behavior, do lend themselves to this type of use. They are, in some respects, especially appropriate for such application, given the special public saliency of security cooperation.

Ripeness for CSBM Application

We now turn to a closer examination of the pre-conditions and incentives necessary for concluding CSBM agreements and applying them. Drawing on negotiations theory, we find the concept of 'ripeness' to be a fruitful starting point for discussion of the preconditions necessary for beginning negotiations on CSBMs. William Zartman highlights three basic conditions for initiating negotiations between adversaries in the political realm: (1) the 'hurting stalemate', which implies an uncomfortable and highly unstable situation that both sides feel themselves locked into and from which they cannot escape through accepted means of escalation; (2) the 'way out', which refers to the adversaries' sense that there exists the potential for arriving at some kind of mutually beneficial arrangement; and (3) the 'valid spokesman' which refers to the existence, on both sides, of a representative who is capable (in terms of both personal qualities and the ability to mobilize internal support) of entering into negotiations.[24]

Based on the theory of ripeness as well as the cumulative experience in the East-West context, there appear to be several conditions that must be met for CSBMs to become an acceptable tool of inter-state statecraft.[25] This model of 'ripeness' for CSBM negotiation includes both *incentives* for initiating negotiations as well as certain *preconditions* that must be present in order to be able to adopt this tool. To begin with, in the framework of general conflict there must be a shared interest (between the parties directly concerned) to cooperate, due to a mutually-uncomfortable status quo, and a sense that without cooperative action the causes of discomfort will not be removed. The common interest could be minimal and pertain exclusively to the short term (i.e. not to see the present degree of stability, however imperfect, further undermined) or could be somewhat broader, with an eye to the longer term (e.g. to see relations between the parties transformed to peace and reconciliation).

In addition, there must be mutual recognition of the fact that distrust and suspicion contribute to the mutually-uncomfortable status quo and also present an obstacle to cooperative action and the fulfillment of a shared interest. Then, there must be an actual willingness to enter negotiations. This implies at least some direct contact between the parties, although it may be shallow and narrowly circumscribed. Fourth, there has to be strong leadership on both sides that is capable of winning public support, and does not fear entering into negotiations. Finally, prospects for CSBM agreements are enhanced by favorable objective conditions for the application of most, though not all, CSBMs – these include both technological capabilities (tools of monitoring, inspection and verification), as well as suitable geographic conditions.

CSBMs neither presuppose peace, nor even require a mutual commitment to see peace and reconciliation emerge as the ultimate result of the confidence building process. As stated at the outset, they in fact assume initial relevance and utility only when a considerable degree of conflict and distrust prevails between the parties.

Drawing Insights from the Cumulative CSBM Experience

In general, the cumulative experience with CBMs and especially CSBMs in the European as well as superpower contexts has proven to be highly instructive for CSBM application in other regions. It has served both as a source of inspiration for ideas, and as a useful guide to the necessary tradeoffs associated with them. These facilitate much more focused and less time consuming negotiations for their application elsewhere. In fact, not only the agreements themselves, but also the actual negotiating history have proven to be of great value for interested parties in other regions. Clearly, however, to make them workable, the specific measures must be adapted to the political, military, geographic, and social conditions of each region.

It is worth noting that even when regional conditions make it possible to import largely intact the technical essence of CSBMs from the European or superpower context, it is highly undesirable to do so. Detailed negotiations should precede their application in a different regional context. Such renegotiation is essential in order to intimately familiarize the new regional parties with their letter and spirit, as well as in order to instill in them a sense of both association and pride that they are negotiating their own measures. Otherwise, the technical arrangements, even if accurately copied, could not serve as genuine CSBMs. Moreover, the negotiation process itself is of paramount importance as a CBM in its own right. It familiarizes the parties with each other as well as with their outlook, concerns and sensitivities, and attracts political, bureaucratic, and public attention to the process. All of these are critical for paving the way for agreement in the first place, creating a constituency to implement it, thereby improving the prospects for its success, and increasing its impact well beyond the narrow subject area in which it applies. All of these attributes clearly also pave the way for more ambitious initiatives as well.

Thus, interestingly enough, the cumulative experience suggests that CSBMs can produce some of their intended benefits even during the negotiation stage itself, that is, prior to their formalization and official implementation. At a minimum, a CSBM negotiating process can testify to an improved political climate. In addition to radiating a spirit of cooperation, CSBM negotiations can also contribute significantly to mutual understanding and cooperative education of the participating parties.

Finally, another insight that may be drawn from the cumulative CSBM experience concerns the possibilty and importance of instituting and cultivating bonds between specialized professional constituencies, especially among military professionals. Such bonds are relatively easy to develop between military individuals and services, irrespective of nationality and residue of past adversarial relations, by virtue of common expertise and experience. Furthermore, once in existence, they solidify in important ways the bonds of trust between the participating nations.

Even more importantly, bonds arising from negotiating and implementing CSBMs have proven to be capable of withstanding the deterioration of the overall political relationship between the nations that subscribe to them. A case in point is the Soviet-American MOU on the Prevention of Incidents on or Over the High Seas (INCSEA). Originally negotiated between the respective navies during the detente of the early

1970s, the agreement remained in force and was faithfully implemented during the chill in superpower relations that settled in the mid 1970s. In fact, during this tense period the modest INCSEA CSBM had provided both sides with much-needed professional channels of communications as well as with continuity and predictability in their relationship.

Is the CSBM Experience Transferable to the Middle East?

Both the general formula of ripeness for negotiating CSBMs, as well as the lessons that have been distilled from the European and superpower experience with CSBMs for successful application in other regions are instructive.[26] They seem to provide a firm basis for the analysis of the applicability of CSBMs to the Middle East. Nevertheless, it could still be argued that CSBMs are somehow *uniquely tailored* to the East-West context in which they first emerged. According to this line of reasoning, when considering the transferability of CSBMs (which originated in the context of East-West relations) to the Middle East, one cannot ignore certain fundamental differences that exist between the two arenas.

As many point out, post World War II East-West relations were characterized, at least since the 1960s, by a considerable degree of interstate political stability, a basic balance though not symmetry in military capabilities between the two blocs, diplomatic relations between the parties to dispute, an absence of any major direct wars between them, established (if limited) frameworks of cooperation, and relatively weak territorial claims. Conditions presently existing in the Middle East, however, are inherently different.[27]

Employing the East-West standard in fact leads many to base their conclusions regarding the transferability of CSBMs to the Middle East on the fact that the Middle East conditions are much less hospitable or desirable grounds for establishing CSBMs than those prevailing in Europe in the 1970s or early 1980s, or even the 1960s.[28] This contention rests primarily on the argument that the contemporary Middle East, contrary to Europe of the 1970s, is still beset, as the US special Middle East peace envoy Dennis Ross put it, by a 'complex mosaic of active and recently buried political disputes',[29] complicated and unstable military balances, structural asymmetries between the Arabs and Israel, and active territorial disputes.

The question we must thus initially address ourselves to is whether an element of political stability such as characterized East-West relations indeed constitutes a necessary precondition for negotiating CSBM and must, therefore, be included in our ripeness formula. A related question is whether this caveat fundamentally undermines the basis for applying

CSBMs outside Europe, specifically in the Middle East. A close examination reveals that this argument, while intuitively appealing, does not stand up either empirically or normatively. It misrepresents both the political context in which CSBMs emerged as well as the conditions presently prevailing elsewhere, especially in the Middle East.

To begin with, a thorough review of the cumulative global experience with CSBMs reveals that they are not an inherently European construct. They have been applied elsewhere, not in the least between the superpowers themselves as well as between India and Pakistan or the PRC, Turkey and Bulgaria, Argentina and Brazil, and North and South Korea. The Middle East itself has also had some relevant experience in this area.[30]

Even more importantly, if there is one thing that stands out when we try to analyze the cumulative global experience with CSBMs, it is that they have always emerged in rather similar circumstances to those presently prevailing in the Middle East. For one thing, CSBMs have always been initially implemented in periods and contexts in which profound distrust prevailed between the parties. Usually they evolved in the aftermath of a traumatic or unnerving experience, vividly illustrating some of the risks inherent in the situation existing at the time in the region. They have generally preceded a genuine political transformation of their relationship, thus serving as the forerunners of peace and arms control accords, not their product.

Moreover, relations between the parties to the CSBMs have been typically characterized by critical asymmetries and structural imbalances. These commonly ranged from asymmetries in design and composition of military forces, to vast structural disparities in other security assets, territory, population, and natural resources, to profound societal differences in type of regimes as well as levels of education and technology. These imbalances further underscore the lack of political stability in the relations between the countries involved.

Yet, the relative lack of political stability has proven surmountable whenever and wherever basic conditions of ripeness were present. In fact, this very situation may have actually strengthened the incentive to negotiate CSBMs. Looking to past experience in the Middle East, the Egyptian-Israeli peace process illustrates that much experience with formal CSBMs was gained during the 1974–79 period, when political stability was lacking. The arrangements integrated into the 1974 separation of forces agreement, the 1975 interim agreement, and the 1979 peace agreement,[31] although formal CSBMs only in the sense of explicitness, and not intent (their confidence building role was recognized only after peace had been achieved), were concluded in this period. The other terms of ripeness had been fulfilled, and the lack of political stability in fact increased the perceived necessity to agree on measures directed toward enhancing mutual security.

The cumulative international experience suggests that where CSBMs are concerned, it is appropriate to employ an even narrower definition of ripeness than that employed elsewhere. It is, therefore, easier to meet the requirements of ripeness for CSBMs in the Middle East, and for that matter in other regions as well. Practically speaking, this implies that we need not look at comprehensive stability as a necessary precondition for negotiating CSBMs. To judge the viability of CSBMs in a certain context it should suffice to explore whether a more limited degree of political ripeness prevails. It is for this examination that we now turn to the Middle East.

A basic element of ripeness mentioned above pertains to the awareness of and concern over the costs of war and risks of escalation. When the ACRS process was initiated, both were widely apparent in the Middle East, especially in the aftermath of the Second Gulf War. Exhaustion from war and common interest in arresting the arms race and diverting resources to deal with some of the region's most acute problems (economic development, shortage of water, settlement of refugees, polluted environment) were widespread. Sufficiency in defense capabilities also seemed to exist among all of the prospective key players to a Middle East security regime. Moreover, the relevant extra-regional players (which in the European case have been negligible but in the Middle East are of considerable importance), were, for the first time in more than a generation, committed to a joint effort to foster peace and cooperation in the Middle East.

Even more importantly, in terms of political stability in the Middle East, in the Arab–Israeli context, consider the following. Wars in the Middle East in the past decade have taken place between Arab states, as well as Iran. In fact, Arab–Israeli wars have been significantly scaled back, at least in terms of their objectives, since 1967. Moreover, since 1973 Arab–Israeli military confrontations have been limited in scope, their tragic consequences notwithstanding. This is no mere coincidence, since the establishment of peace between Egypt and Israel in 1979 has removed from the Arab–Israeli powder keg its most explosive element. More recent progress on the Jordanian, and Palestinian tracks has further diffused and stabilized this conflict.

At the outset of ACRS, a broad (though not universal) desire existed in the region to reorient itself toward peace and stability. Furthermore, the guiding principles for doing so (UN Security Council resolutions 242 and 338) had apparently been formally accepted by all the parties to the Arab-Israeli peace process. Even the institutional mechanisms to negotiate and apply CSBMs were in place, in the form of the both the bilateral and multilateral peace processes initiated in Madrid (October 1991) and Moscow (January 1992) respectively.

Admittedly, the Arab-Israeli peace process, and by extension the broader regional effort was not supported by all the states of the region and by some key movements therein. Several major regional powers (notably Iran and Iraq) as well as a few more minor ones (e.g. Libya and Sudan) were (and still are) absent from the process, and to varying degrees they even openly opposed the normalization with Israel inherent in it. But the impact of these forces was largely marginalized by the respective UN sanctions coupled with the US dual containment policy.

In conclusion, therefore, the Middle East at the time of the initiation of ACRS seemed to be in a situation that in some truly important respects was reminiscent of the onset of detente in Europe, and the initiation of the CSCE process. Paradoxically, some of the European CSBMs may be today even more pertinent to the Middle East than to Europe, as the Middle East is still characterized by intense rivalries on the inter-state level, whereas Europe today is more concerned with instabilty generated by intra-state politics.

The analysis of the East-West context in which CSBMs emerged as well as its comparison to the conditions that prevailed in the Middle East when the ACRS negotiations commenced, therefore, support the conclusion that the aforementioned requirements of ripeness necessary for the onset of a confidence building process were fulfilled at that time. Furthermore, even the architecture for negotiations (which was absent in the past) was established and set in motion in the form of the multilateral peace process in general, and the ACRS Working Group in particular.

In sum, it is hardly surprising that the broad applicability to other regions of the European CSBM experience has already been widely acknowledged. Interestingly enough, subscribers to this viewpoint have been not only interested parties and independent researchers but also the United Nations Disarmament Commission (1980) and the United Nations General Assembly.[32]

What Role Could CSBMs Play in the Arab–Israeli Context?

At least three previous studies have focused either on analysis of the role CSBMs have fulfilled in the past in the context of the Arab–Israeli conflict[33] or on attempts to assess the prospects for the future.

Yair Evron was one of the first to consider the role of arms control in the Middle East. In a paper published in 1980 he assessed this role in terms of the linkage between arms control (which according to his definition includes also CSBMs) and politics in the Arab–Israeli region. He concluded that this linkage has three facets: 'first, to be stable and enduring, a political settlement would need concomitant arms-control measures; second, a political settlement would depend, to a large extent, on gradual steps, which would themselves require the support of a considerable number of arms-control agreements and measures; third, settlement would demand some political concessions on both sides.'[34] Overall, Evron views arms control as operating only in the military-security areas, and while measures implemented may have an even considerable impact on political developments, this impact is indirect.[35]

David B. Dewitt also assessed the possible role of CSBMs in the Middle East in an article published in 1987.[36] While Dewitt recognized the *theoretical* potential of CSBMs for reducing both perceived threats and the possibility of surprise attack (thus contributing to conflict management and crisis prevention), he expressed doubt concerning the ability of CSBMs alone to prevent war in the Middle East. He attributed the limited utility of CSBMs in the Middle East mainly to 'the absence of an overarching political-security regime in an environment where limited war is both viable and politically acceptable.'[37] According to him, 'until the cost-benefit calculus changes', CSBMs will remain marginal to the prevention of war, although they may prove critical in conflict management efforts directed toward reducing the frequency and severity of war.[38]

More recent publications have attributed to CSBMs a more and more significant role in the context of Arab-Israeli relations, including greater emphasis on specific measures that may be implemented. While many still express caution in terms of expecting too much from CSBMs until the political environment has improved, there is recognition of the role CSBMs may play in the framework of the peace negotiations already underway. They could serve as a means of enhancing the negotiations process, reducing the frequency and severity of war, and, in the longer term, contributing to the development of a Middle East security regime.[39]

In view of our own early discussion, it should be clear that CSBMs are modest steps and flexible arrangements. They are relatively easy to negotiate and entail few, if any, risks in implementation. Yet, they have considerable utility and potential in several complementary areas. At the present state of Arab-Israeli relations, we believe CSBMs to have an especially important role to play in virtually all of the areas that we set forth above, namely, as a test of intentions over time, as a means of familiarizing the parties with each other, as a tool of crisis management and prevention, and as a symbol of cooperation. They could help defuse some of the present tensions and risks. They could lay the ground, psychologically and physically, for more ambitious undertakings in the area of regional security cooperation and arms control in the future. Just as importantly, they may serve as one building block toward overall peace and historical reconciliation between the Arabs and Israel.

The last point does warrant some elaboration here. Virtually all of the

Arab parties to the peace process demand from Israel far-reaching territorial concessions. In addition, Israel is simultaneously being called upon by its Arab rapporteurs to make additional concessions in the areas of arms, doctrine, military posture, and defense-industrial base. Yet, the Arab demands are made at a time in which Israel's acceptance into the region is still being challenged, and even openly rejected by some forces in the Arab and Muslim world. Worse still, some of these forces are actively engaged in a brutal, often indiscriminate, struggle against Israel and Israelis wherever they may be.

The peace process coupled with the day-to-day security realities with which Israel lives thus confront Israel with rather painful choices. Making the necessary choices on how to deal with them obviously is an internal Israeli affair. Yet, the Arabs clearly have a vested interest in these choices systematically going in one direction rather than the other. It follows, therefore, that they must assist Israel to reach the 'right' conclusions and make the desired fateful choices. To do so, it is in the Arab self-interest to engage Israel in a variety of CSBMs directed at all of the above functions. Cooperation of Arab states with Israel in the area of CSBMs would surely serve as a litmus test for Israel regarding Arab intentions.

Over time CSBMs could help Israel alter its traditional security calculus. Furthermore, they would solidify the Israeli public's confidence in and active support for its government's choices in favor of peace. The latter is of utmost importance since Israel is a vibrant democracy and the required choices would inevitably involve sacrifices of tangible of security assets. These do not come lightly to a nation whose very existence has been repeatedly threatened, and to a state that is locked into a structurally inferior, highly vulnerable, geo-strategic position. Arab cooperation with Israel in the area of CSBMs and beyond, therefore, logically seems to be a *sine qua non* for Israel for it to be able to take such painful decisions responsibly. The peace process with Egypt in the post-Yom Kippur War period bears witness to both sides of the equation. The 'political price' of CSBMs to the Arabs thus seems well worth paying.

Here it must be emphasized that the Arab (irrespective of public statements on this issue) and Israeli vested interest in establishing CSBMs actually goes even further. It clearly extends to the need to avoid, to the extent possible, misunderstandings and miscalculations, and to economize, wherever possible, on defense expenditures. CSBMs are of critical importance precisely during the precarious transition time from a state of war to relations of peace. In this period, CSBMs are instrumental in initiating contacts between the security establishments of all relevant parties, and securing the continuity of these contacts over time.

Even more importantly, since such periods of transition are typically characterized by real, graver than before, threats, but initially few, if any, dividends of peace, CSBMs are essential for ensuring that these risks are jointly dealt with swiftly and effectively, lest they set back the entire peace process. Furthermore, the gravest contemporary challenges to the security of the region do not discriminate well between Arabs and Israelis. Confronting them necessitates joint or at the very least coordinated Arab-Israeli responses, and CSBMs can go a long way toward facilitating them.

Middle East CSBMs Beyond the Arab-Israeli Context

CSBMs have an important role to play in the Middle East also beyond the Arab-Israeli context, and for several complementary reasons. First and foremost among them is the scope of the region. Unlike Latin America, Oceania, or even Europe, the region does not easily lend itself to a straightforward geographical delineation. But in security terms it stretches all the way from the Horn of Africa and the Persian Gulf (and perhaps even beyond it), to the Maghreb, to southern Europe, and to some of the Asian republics of the former Soviet Union. This vast area is afflicted by numerous cross-cutting rivalries, some within the Arab or Islamic worlds, others that involve extra-regional parties as well. Furthermore, many extra-regional powers have a vested interest in the security situation in the region. At times they also have a significant presence in, and/or influence on developments in the region. Finally, some Arab countries which might on the surface appear closer together, do have bitter rivalries separating them, some that have profound security, even military implications. Yet, they lack many of the cooperative security institutions and arrangements of the nature that is envisaged for the region (see below). Consequently, a multilateral, region-wide cooperative security architecture might thus prove useful in devising arrangements that will introduce a measure of stability into these intra-Arab contexts as well. Moreover, the states of the Middle East could surely benefit from the experience, the good services, and the resources of some of the extra-regional states in dealing with the region's diverse problems.

Reflecting on the Empirical Data: Some Early Observations on the CSBM Negotiations in the Middle East

The Middle East ACRS process was practically launched in Washington in May 1992. One year later, in May 1993, it evolved into a two track (named 'baskets') process. The agenda for one of them, the so called 'operational basket', consists primarily of CSBMs, in the maritime, communications, pre-notification, and information exchange areas. Since May 1993, several rounds of expert meetings (lasting several days at a time) to discuss concrete ideas for CSBMs in each of these areas have taken place. It is obviously premature to reach any definitive conclusions on the viability and impact of this process. But some preliminary observations on this issue are nonetheless presently possible.

The onset of CSBM negotiations was preceded by necessary conditions of ripeness, yet, as was to be expected, the actual initiation of the process has in fact brought to the fore at least four factors which diminished the hope for rapid progress in establishing comprehensive CSBMs in the Middle East.

One factor impeding progress on the negotiation of Arab–Israeli CSBMs was a combination of a real and perceived asymmetries in weapons systems and force structures, geo-strategic conditions (population size, territory), and vulnerabilities between Israel and the Arab countries. These created a situation in which both sides still diverged in the way they defined their primary threats. Israel fears Arab conventional strength, and Arab countries fear Israel's technological superiority in general, and its assumed nuclear capability in particular. The asymmetries in force structures are manifest in other areas as well, including air force versus missile forces, and militia (reserve system) versus standing forces.

An additional factor that further diminished the prospects for rapid advancement in the negotiation of CSBMs was the opposition to CSBMs in certain Arab circles. For reasons of political expediency, Arab sources have explained this opposition as resulting from a shortcoming of the nature of CSBMs themselves, namely that 'they may help consolidate peace, but they cannot make peace'. Advocates of this position have claimed that this conclusion was substantiated by their reading of the East-West experience, which has led them to argue that advancement on the bilateral track is the necessary first stage. Such arguments have served the Syrians in particular in justifying their nonparticipation in the multilateral negotiations. In late October 1991, Syrian President Asad related specifically to confidence building measures:

> Many people say that confidence-building measures can be adopted among different countries and achieve results like what took place between the East and West. But, there were no wars between the East and West, neither was there occupation of other countries...in such cases confidence-building measures might be useful for proceeding toward a better understanding. In our case . . . one party occupies the land of the other parties . . . what measure can build confidence among us here in the region other than straightening out matters.[40]

Taken at face value, President Asad discounts mutual suspicions and distrust as an obstacle to attaining the shared goal of bilateral peace. Asad, however, actually reflects a broader sentiment in certain Arab circles, namely that normalization of relations with Israel is fraught with risk for individual Arab parties as well as the Arab world as a whole. Premature normalization may weaken the pressure on Israel to make territorial concessions and may thus be contemplated only as a dividend (or bonus to Israel from the attainment of peace) rather than as a prelude to it. But, even further down the road, such normalization may not be cost free for the Arabs, undermining other core national and Pan-Arab interests. It may diminish national or Arab influence over Middle East events, and result in a loss of control at both the inter-state and intra-state levels. Furthermore, anxiety over their potential impact on civil-military relations in non-democratic Arab societies in which the regime is heavily dependent on the military's backing has also been especially pronounced. All of these fears obviously constitute a further obstacle to early agreement on any arms limitation accords and to a lesser extent also on their CSBM precursors.

Matters are further complicated by the political, security, and bureaucratic overload of the bilateral peace negotiations on some of the key players that are taking part in it. This holds true especially for Israel (who is involved simultaneously in all of these negotiating tracks), but is also relevant for other regional parties that may have had smaller and/or fewer specialized institutions and experienced individuals for handling external dialogues on political-military affairs. However, while the impact of this factor may be considerable at the outset of the process, it is inherently a transient phenomenon. Gradual progress in the bilateral tracks, and buildup of specialized institutions and accumulation of expertise is steadily diminishing its adverse influence.

Last but not least are the difficulties stemming from the absence from the ACRS process of Syria and Lebanon. Even more serious is the non-participation in and even outright opposition to the entire peace process by several key regional parties: Iran, Iraq, and to a lesser extent additional Arab League states as well (e.g. Libya, Sudan and Djibouti). The impact of Iran's position is of particular concern, given its proven potential for undermining not only Gulf security, but also projecting instability into other parts of the region.

A radical, internally unstable, and externally isolated Iran is hardly a recipe for long term stability and security in the Gulf, or for that matter the entire region. Yet, the prospect of integrating Iran into the peace process does not presently appear a viable option either, for reasons having to do both with its own policy and the concerns of others. Still, the ACRS CSBMs have offered a unique opportunity to partially reconcile these realities. They have provided an agenda for a regional dialogue on cooperative security which can be undertaken without the support, let alone the active participation of Iran. The same clearly could not be said to hold true for more ambitious *region-wide* arms control initiatives, which could not be contemplated without these partners.

CSBM negotiations may have also made it possible to project enough progress to encourage Iran to scale back its ideological opposition to the process, without threatening it to the point that it would feel an acute need to directly interfere with the process. Evidence to support this contention can be found both in the active participation in the ACRS process of virtually all the Gulf states, (both friendly and hostile to Iran), as well as in some recent statements made by senior Iranian officials regarding their willingness to respect Arab-Israeli peace accords.[41] Looking into the future, there is even greater potential in institutionalization of a Middle East security dialogue initially tied to the CSBM agenda. This would create a structure into which Iran, Iraq, and Libya could be ultimately integrated, without derailing the process, much as was the case with the dramatic expansion of the CSCE process in Europe.

Some of the above mentioned obstacles are clearly not without precedent. They complicated the early stages of the negotiating process between the superpowers and in Europe, and were successfully, if gradually, overcome. Others, however, are particular to the Middle East. Both types of obstacles are likely to compound and slow down the confidence building process.

What is, nonetheless, remarkable is the extent to which progress in working out Middle East CSBMs was attained in just a few meetings of the 'operational basket' of the ACRS process between May 1993 and the fall of 1995. In this period, not only did the diverse difficulties and obstacles not stifle the process, but quite to the contrary, they may also have even invigorated it. This assessment holds true if one measures progress not only in terms of the bonding, mutual education and familiarization effects of the process, but also in terms of the ability to draft, finalize, and even approve formal agreements.

A formal agreement on the setting up of an ACRS Communication Network modeled after the OSCE one, and the use of part of its hub infrastructure, was attained and partially implemented. The system began in the spring of 1995. Additional progress was made in finalizing texts of agreements on maritime confidence building measures (in the areas of Search and Rescue at Sea, Prevention of Incidents on or Over the High Seas – INCSEA – and information exchange) as well as pre-notification of large scale land-based exercises and troop movements. Certain categories of military information exchanges were also agreed upon, and the formats for carrying them out were also worked out. Numerous other areas for confidence-building cooperative security activity were identified and preliminarily discussed. Finally, approval was also given for setting up several regional security institutions, the first of which, in Amman, was due to commence initial operation before the end of 1995.[42]

The list of accomplishments is indeed impressive. Yet, one must hasten to add that not all of the 15 national delegations from the region presently participating in the ACRS process[43] have been equally keen on the progress made to date. While most, but not all, have at least passively participated in some of the CSBM negotiations, the number of truly active participants has rarely exceeded a third of the regional parties. The implementation of approved activities and agreements was slow and at times partial and erratic. While a solid group of at least half the participants has been active, and all of the others have given the process and its products at least a formal blessing, Egypt stands out as the regional participant most resistant to cooperative regional security arrangements, CSBMs included. The combination of its political clout coupled with the consensus decision-making rule has put Egypt in a position to bring the group activities to a standstill at will, an option that it has elected to exercise since November 1995.

Conclusions

How best to explain the degree of progress achieved to date on CSBM negotiations in the ACRS process? How does it square with our original expectations? In terms of the initial conditions of ripeness necessary for the onset of a confidence building process, our discussion of the transferability of the CSBM experience to the Middle East suggests that these conditions were fulfilled when the ACRS CSBM process began. The more interesting question at this point is how to account for the fact that the obstacles to rapid progress in the negotiation of CSBMs have not precluded progress altogether, and that in fact some impressive gains have been made. We submit that to answer this question we must assess the empirical evidence in reference to three factors: the nature of CSBMs, the regional political context, and calculations of relative gains, as identified in neorealist literature. Let us touch briefly on each of these factors and tentatively assess the role it plays in this context. This assessment, however is necessarily provisional and must be continuously revisited and reassessed in light of further developments.

One key element in our explanation indeed has to do with the nature of CSBMs. The empirical evidence clearly suggests that CSBMs have considerable appeal at times in which strained political relations stand in the way of more ambitious undertakings in the cooperative security domain. Their appeal apparently has to do less with their prospects for breeding trust as such, and more with their modest and non-threatening character. They usually appear acceptable, at times attractive, to political as well as military elites precisely because they do not inherently represent any fundamental reorientation of inter-state relations, while leaving open or at least creating the possibility of such developments down the line, not in the least by supporting the evolution of the process, and creating competent professional constituencies to sustain it.

The appeal of CSBMs appears to be further enhanced by a related feature, namely that they do not depict a fundamental political change or profound restructuring of intra-state relations. Nor do they require reassignment of bureaucratic responsibilities or reallocation of significant resources. By virtue of their small scope, incremental evolution, and non-legally binding (at times even voluntary) character, they seem less demanding or threatening internally as well as externally and may even seem a rather attractive substitute for more demanding arms control steps that some parties advocate. Furthermore, by virtue of being solely politically (as opposed to legally) binding, they do not require parliamentary ratification, making them psychologically and practically more palatable. In fact, they are amenable to political reversal at any time, although in practice this option is rarely exercised. There appears to be no fundamental difference in compliance between legally binding and politically binding commitments.

Our review of developments in the ACRS process since its inception, and especially since mid-1993, suggests that the logic underlying CSBMs has indeed made inroads into the strategic thinking of quite a few of the regional parties. They are all better informed about the benefits potentially inherent in CSBMs as well as the marginality of the risks inherent in them. This, however, does not hold true for Egypt, a issue that we will return to below.

A second factor that helps explain the relative (though in retrospect, short-lived) success of the CSBM agenda in the Middle East is grounded in regional political conditions. Since the inception of the process in early 1992 much has happened in the region. If basic conditions of ripeness existed before the process began, the impressive progress made to date in the bilateral tracks of the Arab–Israeli process has made progress in CSBM negotiations more easily attainable today. It should suffice to recall in this context the Oslo and Cairo accords and the interim agreement now nearing conclusion between Israel and the Palestinians, the conclusion of a Treaty of Peace between Israel and Jordan, and the progress achieved toward bilateral settlement between Syria and Israel.

While progress in CSBM negotiations actually had preceded the breakthroughs on the bilateral peace tracks, the latter undoubtedly helped it along and expedited progress. These breakthroughs have served to further weaken, if not altogether to diffuse, many of the obstacles standing in the way of a genuine security dialogue in the region, first and foremost by diminishing the saliency of the Arab–Israeli conflict.

In addition, several features of the architecture of the CSBM process may actually have been conducive to progress in this area. These include the role of the co-sponsors, especially the US, and the direct contribution of some extra-regional parties such as Canada, the Netherlands, and Turkey. The latter, who are well versed in CSBMs, agreed to 'mentor' specific CSBM activities in the context of ACRS and brought to the table established practices that served as a useful point of departure for ACRS CSBM discussions. A multilateral (as opposed to bilateral) framework has also paradoxically made it easier to discuss CSBMs effectively, although this factor may well also hinder progress in the future, especially if and when more problematic parties such as Syria, Iraq, Iran, Libya agree to join the process.

A similar impact may be attributed to the unique combination of two decision-making ground rules agreed upon by the ACRS Working Group, namely decisions by consensus on every single issue by the parties directly concerned, coupled with voluntarism in application. This combination is likely to prove counter-productive when agreements on arms limitation and reduction are negotiated, but it is ideally suited for facilitating a modest CSBM beginning.

Finally, we return to the theoretical concern we discussed at the outset regarding the question of the impact of states' preoccupation with relative gains on the prospects for CSBM negotiations. According to the neoliberalist approach, CSBMs are designed to facilitate cooperation when such cooperation is deemed desireable, and the initial conditions of ripeness for negotiation of CSBMs are in place. The question remains whether states' concerns with relative gains nevertheless pose a serious obstacle to the negotiation and implementation of cooperative security arrangements.

Our examination of the ACRS CSBM negotiations reveals that in fact most parties presently associated with the ACRS process did not seem overly concerned with relative gains. Moreover, some of the states that *were* concerned with relative gains (e.g. Qatar, Jordan, Tunisia) seemed to feel that it actually works in favor of cooperation with Israel in negotiating CSBMs – for example, as a means of countering Egypt's hegemonic aspirations in the region. In addition, there are other concerns that each regional participant has *vis-à-vis* states outside the Middle East that affect their calculation of relative gains within the ACRS process. Finally, the US is capable of influencing participants' calculations of relative gains, and mitigating the potentially adverse effect of these considerations on negotiations.

In theory, multilateral settings have an advantage over bilateral settings for negotiations in the sense that whereas when only two sides are involved, calculations easily become zero-sum, a multilateral setting opens up a broader range of options. Empirical evidence from ACRS negotiations reveals that the number of participants, and the salience of extra-regional parties, have served to alter perceptions of relative gains, and in a real sense actually facilitated arriving at, and sustaining, an agreed-upon agenda for security dialogue. It would have been harder to produce such a result between two tightly-controlled opposing blocs.

This positive side of the relative gains question does not, however, hold true for Syria, as the above mentioned statement by President Asad suggests. But Syria is presently outside the process and consequently its immediate impact on its course has been limited. This leaves Egypt as the sole party to the process fundamentally opposing its preoccupation with CSBMs.

Egypt, historically enjoying natural pre-eminence in the Arab world, seems especially concerned with the consequences of the Arab–Israeli normalization process inherent in the entire multilateral track of the peace process of which ACRS is only a part. It is apparently particularly alarmed by the potential harm to Egypt of Arab–Israeli, or for that matter regional, CSBMs. It is believed that CSBMs truly multilateralize the relations in the region, while benefiting first and foremost Egypt's foremost rival for regional hegemony in the post peace era, namely Israel. CSBMs are perceived of as freeing Israel from its traditional handicap of regional isolation and preoccupation with existential security while unleashing its superior economic and technical might, and connections with the West, to dominate the region.[44]

Worse still, CSBMs have also been seen by the Egyptians as directly undermining the traditional role Egypt has played, and wishes to continue playing in the region as the leader and primary guarantor of security of the Arab world, as well as the principal mediator between Arabs and Israel (a role for which it has been generously renumerated by the US since the mid-1970s). Consequently, the Egyptians not only oppose the heavy emphasis on CSBMs that is presently evident in the ACRS process, but also wish to harness the process to serve their similarly motivated aim of weakening Israel's military superiority and qualitative edge in both the conventional as well as non-conventional domains.

Yet, Egypt for nearly four years had consistently failed to dominate the ACRS agenda and to slow down progress on CSBMs. This was the case because Egypt's concerns had, at minimum, not been shared by most other parties, which has meant that Egypt found itself relatively isolated in its rejectionist position. Moreover, as mentioned above, the key role played by the US co-sponsor in navigating the process had also proven extremely important in encouraging the different players to get the process started and to keep it alive until it assumes a life of its own. Thus, while calculations of relative gains have harmed Egypt's own position, they have not necessarily had an adverse effect on overall cooperation on regional security, especially regarding CSBMs.

But, it is exactly this state of affairs that has come around to haunt ACRS. The progress made in the realm of CSBMs, in which all other Arab particpants have taken part, thereby marginalizing Egypt's regional role, have pushed Egypt to the point that it senses its core strategic (regional) interests (as delineated above) are undermined. The dangers inherent in continued cooperation in ACRS at this point look as if they outweigh potential benefits as far as Egypt is concerned. This highlights the limitations of CSBMs when a state feels that a core strategic interest is threatened by cooperation.

In reflecting on the question why CSBMs met with success in the framework of ACRS, we find that it has to do primarily with the multilateral setting within which negotiations took place, and with certain inherent features of CSBMs, particularly the fact that they are modest in scope (see discussion above), and that they focus specifically on the establishment of means for assessing future intentions.[45] Thus, both the negotiations framework and the fact that CSBMs are a relatively appealing form of cooperative behavior have contributed to states' ability to negotiate cooperative measures.

In the final analysis, the analytic conclusions do seem to be borne out by the empirical experience. CSBMs in the Middle East no longer look like an oxymoron. As we look ahead, the prospects for devising and implementing CSBMs in the region both in the Arab–Israeli context and beyond it appear better than ever. Some of these could be region wide, others sub-regional, and others could include extra-regional participation as well, whether by additional Mediterranean states or others. Some of these arrangements may also start more modestly and expand or undergo transformation thereafter.

As tools of diplomacy and arms control CSBMs do have certain unique functional as well as structural qualities (such as modularity and flexibility) that make them ideally suited and valuable for regions and contexts in which the transition from adversarial inter-state relations to a more benign mix of cooperation and competition is underway, however hesitantly. The Security Basket of the CSCE process, in which the most elaborate CSBM inventory has emerged, provides the best presently-available reservoir of ideas for pursuing CSBMs. And the experience accumulated to date in the context of the ACRS process presently seems to reinforce, however tentatively, the deductive reasoning regarding the transferability of this model to other regions.

Finally, we should also be very aware of the limitations of CSBMs. CSBMs are, by no means, a panacea to the security problems plaguing a region. As is becoming once again painfully apparent, the ability to realize their significant potential for improving the security climate depends heavily on the broader political context in the region. Moreover, by their very nature, CSBMs are modest steps that cannot by themselves transform the Middle East security scene. Yet, within the constraints imposed by these stark realities, CSBMs have made and are likely to continue making a largely positive contribution to the arms control and regional security process in the Middle East.

NOTES

1. US Dept of State Office of the Assistant Secretary/Spokesman 'Remarks by Secretary of State James A. Baker III before the Organizational Meeting for the Multilateral Negotiations on the Middle East', House of Unions, Moscow, 28 Jan. 1992.
2. Richard Ned Lebow and Janice Gross Stein, 'Beyond Deterrence', *Jnl of Social Issues* 43/4 (1987) pp.41–61.
3. See Raymond Cohen, *International Politics: The Rules of the Game* (London: Longman 1981).
4. See for example Stephen D. Krasner, 'Structural Causes and Regime Consequences: Regimes as Intervening Variables', *International Organization* [hereafter *Int. Org.*] 36/2 (Spring 1982).
5. One of the major obstacles to cooperation in international relations is the problem of distrust. John Herz first coined the term 'security dilemma' in his analysis of international relations in the nuclear age; the term is premised on the notion that a lack of central authority in international relations leaves actors with a constant sense of distrust regarding the intentions and actions of other actors: John Herz, *International Politics in the Atomic Age* (NY: Columbia UP 1959) p.231. In this context see also Robert Jervis, *Cooperation Under the Security Dilemma*, ACIS Working Paper, No.4 (Los Angeles: Center for Arms Control and Int. Security 1977).
6. Regarding the basic incentive to cooperate, Joseph S. Nye Jr, in an article on realism and liberalism, cites Hayward Alker's support for Hedley Bull's concept of an 'anarchic society,' 'which admits the absence of any formal government above states, but does not define anarchy as the absence of communication, cooperation, and governance.' [Joseph S. Nye Jr, 'Neorealism and Neoliberalism', *World Politics* 40/2 (Jan. 1988) p.249]. See also Hedley Bull, *The Anarchical Society: A Study of Order in World Politics* (NY: Columbia UP 1977) pp.24–41; and Robert Lieber, *No Common Power: Understanding International Relations* (NY: HarperCollins 1991) pp.10–15, 345–7. For theoretical background material regarding the conditions under which cooperation may emerge in an anarchical international system see: Robert Axelrod, *The Evolution of Cooperation* (NY: Basic Books 1984); Kenneth A. Oye, 'Explaining Cooperation Under Anarchy: Hypotheses and Strategies', *World Politics* 38/1 (Oct. 1985) pp.1–24; and Kenneth Oye (ed.) *Cooperation Under Anarchy* (Princeton UP 1986).
7. See Joseph S. Nye, 'Neorealism and Neoliberalism'; Robert O. Keohane, 'Realism, Neorealism and the Study of World Politics', in idem (ed.) *Neorealism and Its Critics* (NY: Columbia UP 1986); and David A. Baldwin (ed.) *Neorealism and Neoliberalism: The Contemporary Debate* (NY: Columbia UP 1993).
8. Joseph M. Grieco, 'Anarchy and the Limits of Cooperation: A Realist Critique of the Newest Liberal Institutionalism', *Int. Org.* 42/3 (Summer 1988) p.485. Grieco notes that his essay does not distinguish between realism and neorealism because on crucial issues (the meaning

of anarchy, and the problem of cooperation) modern realists are very much in accord with the classic realists.
9. Grieco, 'Anarchy and the Limits of Cooperation' (note 8) pp.497–8. Many of Grieco's arguments (esp. pp.495–503) appear also in a later article that includes his response to some neoliberalist responses to his original critique of neoliberal institutionalism: Joseph M. Grieco, 'Understanding the Problem of International Cooperation: The Limits of Neoliberal Institutionalism and the Future of Realist Theory', in David A. Baldwin (ed.) *Neorealism and Neoliberalism: The Contemporary Debate* (NY: Columbia UP 1993) pp.301–38.
10. Grieco (note 8) p.499.
11. See Yair Evron, 'Arms Control in the Middle East: Some Proposals and Their Confidence-Building Roles', in J. Alford (ed.) *The Future of Arms Control: Part III: Confidence-Building Measures*, Adelphi Paper No.149 (London: IISS 1979); Jonathan Alford, 'CBMs and Verification', in K. Kaiser (ed.) *Confidence-Building Measures* (Bonn: Res. Inst. of the German Soc. for Foreign Affairs 1983) p.61; and Hans Gunter Brauch, 'Confidence-Building and Disarmament Supporting Measures', in W. Epstein and B. Feld (eds.) *New Directions in Disarmament* (NY: Praeger 1981) p.147.
12. Regarding the distinction between intentions (CSBMs) and capabilities (arms control) see: Jonathan Alford, 'Confidence-Building Measures in Europe: The Military Aspects', in Alford, *Future of Arms Control* (note 11) p.3.
13. See *Arms Control and National Security: An Introduction* (Washington DC: Arms Control Assoc. 1989) pp.98–9; and *A Chronology of United States Arms Control and Security Initiatives, 1946–1990* (US Information Agency 1990) pp.24–33.
14. Gordon A. Craig and Alexander L. George, *Force and Statecraft: Diplomatic Problems of Our Time*, 2nd ed. (NY: OUP 1990) p.172.
15. See, for example, Victor-Yves Ghebali and Fred Tanner, 'Confidence-Building Measures in Arms Control: The Mouse That Roared?', *International Defense Review* 10 (Oct. 1988) pp.1269–72.
16. See Johan J. Holst, 'Confidence Building Measures: A Conceptual Framework', *Survival* 25/1 (Jan.-Feb. 1983) p.10.
17. See for example John Grin and Henry van der Graaf (eds.) *Unconventional Approaches to Conventional Arms Control Verification* (Amsterdam: VU UP 1990) p.4.
18. Heinz Vetschera, 'Regional Security Arrangements in Europe: The CSCE Experience with Confidence-Building Measures, Crisis Mechanisms and Conflict Prevention', (paper in preparation).
19. For an overview and summary of the various stages in the process see: Richard E. Darilek, 'East-West Confidence-building: Defusing the Cold War in Europe', pp.17–25, and Cathleen S. Fisher, 'The Preconditions of Confidence-building: Lessons from the European Experience', pp.42–5: both articles appear in Michael Krepon (ed.) *A Handbook of Confidence-Building Measures for Regional Security*, Handbook No.1 (Washington DC: Henry L. Stimson Center 1993).
20. For some of the more salient studies of confidence building, see Johan Jorgen Holst and Karen Alette Melander, 'European Security and Confidence-building Measures', *Survival* 19/4 (July/Aug. 1977) pp.146–54; Jonathan Alford, 'Confidence Building Measures in Europe: The Military Aspects' in idem, *Future of Arms Control* (note 11) pp.4–13; Holst, 'Confidence-building Measures (note 16) pp.2–15; Stephen Larrabee and Dietrich Stobbe (eds.) *Confidence-Building Measures in Europe* (ibid. 1983); Rolf Berg and Adam-Daniel Rotfeld, *Building Security in Europe: Confidence Building Measures and the CSCE* (NY: Ins. for East-West Security Studies 1986); R.B. Byers, F. Stephen Larrabee, and Allen Lynch, *Confidence-building Measures and International Security*, Institute for East-West Security Studies, East-West monograph series No.4 (ibid. 1987); Igor Scherbak, *Confidence-building Measures and International Security-The Political and Military Aspects: A Soviet Approach*, UNIDIR/91/36 (NY: UN 1991).
21. See Charles E. Osgood, 'Disarmament Demands GRIT', in Burns H. Weston (ed.) *Toward Nuclear Disarmament and Global Security* (Boulder, CO: Westview 1984) pp.337–44.
22. See Thomas Schelling, 'Confidence in Crisis', in K. Kaiser (ed.) *Confidence-Building Measures* (Bonn: Res. Inst. of the German Soc. for Foreign Affairs 1983) p.90.

23. According to Kenneth Oye, there are strategies that can be adopted by states to foster the emergence of cooperation between them: Kenneth Oye, 'Explaining Cooperation Under Anarchy', pp.16–17.
24. I. William Zartman, 'The Middle East – The Ripe Moment?', in G. Ben-Dor and D. Dewitt (eds.) *Conflict Management in the Middle East* (Lexington, MA: Lexington Books 1987) pp.284–5. See also Richard N. Haass, 'Ripeness and the Settlement of International Disputes', *Survival* 30/3 (May–June 1988) pp.245–6; and Richard N. Haass, *Conflicts Unending: The United States and Regional Disputes* (New Haven, CT: Yale UP 1990) Ch.1.
25. See: Emily Landau, 'Confidence Building Measures and Their Application in the Arab–Israeli Conflict' (MA Thesis: Tel Aviv Univ.1992) (Hebrew). An additional researcher subsequently reached similar conclusions regarding the importance of ripeness for negotiating CSBMs. Cathleen Fisher, 'The Preconditions of Confidence-building: Lessons from the European Experience', pp.34–7 suggests three types of factors that contributed to successful negotiation and implementation of the European CSBMs: contextual factors, processual factors, and political developments in East-West relations.
26. For an excellent collection of essays on the issue of the European CSBM experience and its potential adaptability to other regions, see UN Dept for Disarmament Affairs, *Confidence and Security Building Measures: From Europe to Other Regions*, Disarmament : Topical Papers No.7 (NY: UN 1991).
27. On the differences between the two arenas see: Geoffrey Kemp, *The Control of the Middle East Arms Race* (Washington DC: Carnegie Endowment for Int. Peace 1991) pp.124–8. See also Richard E. Darilek and Geoffrey Kemp, 'Prospects for Confidence- and Security-Building Measures in the Middle East', in Alan Platt (ed.) *Confidence Building in the Middle East* (Washington DC: US Inst. of Peace Press 1992) pp.25–9.
28. See e.g. Darilek and Kemp, 'Prospects for CSBMs' (*supra*); and David B. Dewitt and Gabriel Ben-Dor (eds.) *Confidence Building in the Middle East* (Boulder, CO: Westview 1994).
29. Dennis B. Ross used this phrase when echoing Arab resistance to CBMs in a speech he delivered at Tel Aviv University on 24 July 1992 (unpub. transcript).
30. See Michael Krepon (ed.) *A Handbook of Confidence-building Measures for Regional Security*, 2nd ed. (Washington DC: Henry L. Stimson Center 1995) esp. pp.41–69.
31. For detailed descriptions of these agreements see Itshak Lederman, *The Arab–Israeli Experience in Verification and Its Relevance to Conventional Arms Control in Europe*, Occasional Paper 2 (Center for Int. Security Studies at Maryland 1989); and Brian S. Mandell, 'Anatomy of a Confidence-Building Regime: Egyptian-Israeli Security Cooperation, 1973-1979', *Int. Jnl* 45 (Spring 1990) pp.202–23. See also Janice Gross Stein, 'A Common Aversion to War: Regime Creation by Egypt and Israel as a Strategy of Conflict Management', in Ben-Dor and Dewitt (eds.) *Conflict Management in the Middle East* (note 24) pp.59–77.
32. United Nations Disarmament Commission, 'Guidelines for Confidence Building Measures at the Global and Regional Levels', 1980. This logic has found its way into the UN General Assembly resolution 47/52G which explicitly endorsed CBMs on the regional level.
33. See note 31; these studies have focused primarily on Israeli-Egyptian relations.
34. Yair Evron, 'The Role of Arms Control in the Middle East', Adelphi Paper No.138, in Christoph Bertram (ed.) *Arms Control and Military Force*, Adelphi Library 3 (Hampshire: Gower 1980) p.102.
35. Ibid. p.67.
36. David B. Dewitt, 'Confidence- and Security-Building Measures in the Middle East: Is There a Role?', in Ben-Dor and Dewitt, *Conflict Management in the Middle East* (note 24) pp.241–59.
37. Ibid. p.253.
38. Ibid. pp.247, 254.
39. See: Darilek and Kemp, 'Prospects for CSBMs in the Middle East' (note 27) pp.29–31; and Gerald M. Steinberg, 'Middle East Arms Control and Regional Security', *Survival* 36/1 (Spring 1994) pp.126–7. For specific suggestions regarding CSBMs that may be applied, see: Shai Feldman, *Arms Control: An Agenda for Israel*, JCSS Memorandum No.35, Nov.

1991 (Hebrew); articles by Richard E. Darilek and Geoffrey Kemp, Michael Krepon and Peter D. Constable, W. Seth Carus and Janne E. Nolan, and Charles Flowerree and Brad Roberts in Platt, *Arms Control and Confidence Building in the Middle East* (note 27); and Steinberg (*supra*).
40. SANA in Arabic, 1530 GMT, 27 Oct.1991 in *SWB*, ME/1215, A/2, 29 Oct. 1991. For evidence of the continuation of the approach whereby territorial agreements must precede security arrangements see for example a commentary by Syrian radio: Syrian Arab Republic Radio, 1137 GMT, 13 July 1995 in *SWB*, ME/2356, MED/3-4, 15 July 1995.
41. In this context, see a 1995 statement made by Iranian president Rafsanjani in an interview with *Middle East Insight*. In answer to a question whether Iran could see itself at the point where it can declare its impartiality toward the Arab-Israeli peace process, Rafsanjani answered: 'Practically speaking, we do not take any action against the peace plan. When we see this whole process is unjust, we state our opposition as a matter of principle. But if the content of the peace plan is just, the substance is just, we shall go along with it.' George A. Nader, 'Interview with President Ali Akbar Hashemi Rafsanjani', *Middle East Insight* 11/5 (July–Aug. 1995) p.11.
42. See Alan Makovsky, Bruce Jentleson, et al. *Building a Middle East Community: The Future of the Multilateral Middle East Peace Process* (Washington Inst., forthcoming).
43. The 15 participating regional parties are Mauritania, Morocco, Algeria, and Tunisia, Egypt, Israel, Jordan, and the Palestinians, Oman, Qatar, Kuwait, Bahrain, UAE, Saudi Arabia, and Yemen.
44. For a discussion of these and related themes, especially regarding Egyptian fears of Israel's attempts to utilize the peace process in order to dominate the Middle East, see Fawaz A. Gerges, 'Egyptian-Israeli Relations Turn Sour', *Foreign Affairs* 74/3 (May–June 1995) pp.69–78.
45. Grieco (note 8) notes that the concern with future intentions is a major factor that bears upon states' preoccupation with relative gains: ibid. p.500. In fact, CSBMs deal directly with intentions, and the importance of building confidence with a clear eye to sustaining the grounds for confidence over time.

The Middle East Peace Process and Regional Security

BEN D. MOR

In the aftermath of the 1991 Gulf War, the Middle East was poised on the verge of a diplomatic breakthrough. After nearly five decades of sustained conflict, an unprecedented opportunity was created to achieve peace between Arabs and Israelis in this war-torn region. Indeed, despite some false starts and several crises, initial hopes were vindicated: in September 1993, upon the signing of the Oslo Agreement, Israel and the PLO launched their long-awaited reconciliation; a year later, in October 1994, Israel and Jordan concluded a peace treaty. However, within two years, what promised to be an auspicious beginning gave way to a dangerous impasse: as 1996 comes to a close, negotiations are stalled, threats of violence are proliferating, and the 'spirit of Oslo' seems to be dissipating.

This contribution seeks to review the current status of the peace process and to evaluate its impact on regional security: How likely are the Israeli-Syrian and Israeli-Palestinian negotiations to produce a settlement? How is the May 1996 election of Likud in Israel going to affect the peace process? What are the current and long-term prospects for regional stability? These questions will be explored from a social-choice perspective, which is developed in the first part of the analysis. This perspective implies a focus on the parties' preferences for mechanisms of conflict management, the structures educed by such mechanisms, and the strategies by which the actors seek to promote their objectives within the structure that constrains them. The key argument is that the parties perceive negotiations as occurring within a coercive structure, which affects their bargaining positions in ways that are detrimental to the peace process and endanger regional stability.

It is equally important to note what this study does not attempt to do. First, it does not seek to provide a comprehensive analysis of regional security in the Middle East.[1] Rather, its scope is limited to the effects of the peace process on regional stability. Second, the account does not try to assess the likelihood or desirability of different forms of negotiated settlements (such as security regimes) or their implications for the future of the region. Instead, it looks at peacemaking as a *process* by which conflicting preferences are aggregated into collective outcomes. The process itself – and the parties' perceptions of its meaning and purpose – can affect regional security in several ways, which are examined here. Third, the analysis is not intended as a comprehensive survey of the peace process to date. Rather, it concentrates on recent developments that occurred after the May 1996 electoral victory of the Likud Party in Israel.

The following section develops the social-choice framework and explains its applicability to the study of regional security. This is followed, in the third section, by a few examples of social-choice processes that are designed to illustrate the theoretical ideas. The fourth section undertakes a bilateral analysis of the Israeli–Syrian and Israeli–Palestinian negotiations and their expected impact on regional stability. Finally, the fifth section briefly reviews the perspectives of other regional and international actors and discusses their current and future role in the peace process.

Regional Security as a Social-Choice Process

One way of thinking about the relationship between peacemaking and regional security is in terms of a *social-choice process*. Young suggests that 'social choice can be conceptualized as a form of dispute settlement or conflict resolution ... [which] involves the achievement of collective outcomes in situations where the preferences of the relevant actors are initially incompatible or in conflict.'[2] In domestic politics, the process by which divergent preferences are aggregated into social outcomes is codified or reflected in the formal and informal rules and procedures of various government institutions. Indeed, once such rules, procedures, and norms define the parameters of the 'game', they constitute the *structure* within which individuals pursue their preferences. The nature of the structure presents actors with certain constraints and opportunities, which in turn affect the strategies that actors select in order to promote their preferences. In the international arena, where formal rules are absent in most cases (and where sovereign states may not accept their legitimacy when they do exist), it is more difficult to define the mechanisms of preference aggregation. However, the logic of social-choice analysis is the same – to trace the process by which the differing preferences of states are aggregated into collective outcomes. The questions raised by such an analysis are 'how collective outcomes occur, to what extent those outcomes reflect the will of the system's units, and how social processes could be reordered to the benefit of all.'[3]

One advantage of the social-choice perspective is that it helps to maintain the distinction among the components that comprise regional security and locates them at the appropriate level of analysis. As the above description indicates, four components should be taken into account: state preferences, structure, strategies, and outcomes. These components are closely intertwined, as will become evident from the discussion below. For analytic purposes, however, each element will be presented separately and introduced in turn.

A regional sub-system can be characterized as a geographically bound system of interdependent actors. These actors, or states,[4] are characterized by their *preferences*, which are defined over alternative outcomes produced by the social-choice process. Each outcome can be seen as a possible resolution of disputed issues. A preference order over alternative resolutions reflects the values or goals of the state. An important aspect of any analysis of preferences is the process by which they are formed. Where state preferences are concerned, the issue involves the by-now familiar debate over the merits and shortcomings of the unitary-actor assumption. Bueno de Mesquita and Lalman suggest two general formulations of this assumption: according to the first (realist) conception, 'the leader is the person who decides what goals to choose and what strategy to implement in pursuit of those goals'; according to the second (domestic/constrained) conception, the leader plays a role in formulating goals but is essentially an agent entrusted with selecting the means to achieve whatever objectives are selected by the domestic political process.[5]

The first and more parsimonious conception, which is usually justified when a strong and centralized leadership can be said to exist, obviates the need to consider intra-state preference aggregation. Because the following analysis looks at processes of social choice at the interstate level, it treats the relevant states as unitary actors (equating their preferences with those of the national leader). This perspective is not meant to imply that domestic influences are unimportant, and references to internal constraints are made at various points in the discussion. Rather, space limitations preclude a more detailed analysis of their role, whose integration with the interstate bargaining level would require a comprehensive, 'two-level game' framework.[6]

When (state) preferences for outcomes are incompatible – giving rise to conflict – and when actors are interdependent, there must be some process by which collective outcomes are ultimately produced. The social choice approach refers to *preference aggregation* as the process by which an outcome is formed from the diverging preferences of the actors. This, then, is the second component that should be brought into the picture. Young suggests that three central mechanisms of social choice operate at the international level: bargaining, coercive diplomacy, and organized warfare. Of particular importance to the analysis of the peace process is the first mechanism, which is defined as 'efforts to reach collective or group choices through negotiations in which the participants make offers and counteroffers, and in which outcomes occur only when all relevant participants agree to a specified settlement'.[7] The latter part of this definition is characteristic of social-choice processes in which all participants have veto power.

The three mechanisms constitute *structures* within which states in an anarchic setting pursue their foreign policy objectives. Morrow describes their operation as follows:

> In the absence of a central authority, implicit social choice procedures have arisen in the international system. These procedures regulate how the actors' preferences are aggregated into outcomes... International structure resides in those elements of the international system that resolve conflicts in preferences ... Like preferences and structure in domestic politics, international structure constrains the actors' pursuit of their preferences; compared to those preferences, it is quite durable.[8]

Different mechanisms of preference aggregation confer different structural advantages to states. Thus, when the process of social choice is organized warfare, national capabilities – or rather their distribution – become the structural derivative that distinguishes some system actors (the more powerful) from others (the weaker).[9] On the other hand, when negotiation is the prevalent, accepted mechanism, military power is much less relevant to the process by which outcomes are produced. Thus, one dimension of conflict that we shall address more fully below concerns the preferences that states have for different mechanisms of preference aggregation: because the structure that a given mechanism educes favors some states over others, they develop different preference orders over alternative processes of social choice.

From the perspective of the single regional actor or state, structure presents a 'menu' for choice: it restricts differentially the range of possibilities upon which states can act, thus affecting 'opportunity' conditions. But 'the motivations that lead people to avail themselves of opportunities' – or 'willingness'[10] – is not solely a function of structure. Preferences also play a role in shaping behavior, and at times they can compensate for lack of structural advantages that capabilities confer.[11] One advantage of game-theoretic models (to be reviewed later) is that they explicate the relationship between structure (i.e. rules of play) and preferences by showing how these two components interact to yield *strategy*, the third component of the framework.

Actors consider the effects of structural mechanisms when they estimate the consequences of strategy choice. However, neither the distribution of structural advantages over different actors, nor their preferences for outcomes, are known with certainty. Therefore, incomplete information and misperception imply that outcomes – the fourth component – often deviate from expectations. But even under complete information, certain configurations of preferences and structure induce strategic choices that yield paradoxical outcomes. In other words, when structure mediates preferences, outcomes are not necessarily related to preferences in a monotonic manner.[12] Indeed, strategies intended to achieve one outcome may end up producing its opposite, as illustrated, for example, by the dynamics of the 'security dilemma'.[13] The investigation of the relationship between preferences, strategic choices, and collective outcomes – the subject of the next section – provide important insights into the second question posed above, namely whether systemic outcomes represent the preferences of the system's units.

This latter question also allows us to conceptualize regional security in terms of a social-choice process. In order to do so, the distinction between the state and system levels needs to be maintained. One may assume that a primary goal of all states is to reduce and eliminate threats to core values (such as sovereignty, territorial integrity, safety of population, and so on). At this basic level, preference formation involves the evaluation of alternative outcomes with respect to the core values of the state. To the extent that the outcomes produced by the system provide for these values, the state considers itself to be secure. At the system (or collective) level, then, security is a social-choice outcome that is associated with: (1) a prevailing mechanism of preference aggregation, and (2) a *distribution* of the security-related preferences of all regional state-actors.

Thus, at any given time, disputed issues are resolved by means of negotiation, coercive diplomacy, or war (see next section). The prevailing mechanism educes a structure in which states are differentially advantaged. Realizing the nature of the structure and the constraints and opportunities it presents, states select strategies designed to achieve their security-related preferences. The resulting outcome is a collective one, for which different states have different valuations, depending on whether the outcome realizes basic security concerns. Hence, each possible regional outcome can be associated with a distribution of preferences over the individual states that comprise the region. We can say that regional security is *high* when, at the collective level, (1) the prevailing mechanism of preference aggregation is non-violent, and (2) the distribution of security-related preferences is such that no actor, following rational calculation, has an incentive to employ a violent strategy.

This conception has the advantage that is allows us to assess regional security by means of game-theoretic criteria, such as Nash equilibrium and Pareto efficiency.[14] (These criteria pertain to the third question mentioned above, namely 'how social choice processes can be reordered to the benefit of all'.) Because the realization of one criterion does not necessarily entail the other, it is possible to make more refined distinctions among regional (sub)systems in terms of the security they provide their members. For example, two regional systems can be stable in the sense that none of their respective members finds it strategically rational to resort to violence. However, because equilibrium does not necessarily imply efficiency (as is evident from the noncooperative outcome in Prisoners' Dilemma), one region may provide stability with efficiency – say, joint cooperation that all actors prefer – whereas the other region may provide stability without efficiency, say through a system of nuclear deterrence.

The definition of regional security also enables us to conceive of *security regimes* in social-choice terms. Because different mechanisms of preference aggregation educe structures that confer advantages asymmetrically, it is only natural that states prefer structures in which they are more likely to realize their quest for security. A structure of coercion, whether coercive diplomacy or war, favors risk-prone actors with superior military capabilities. A bargaining (negotiation) structure, on the other hand, favors issue-specific capabilities and diplomatic skills. Thus, for example, the prevailing mechanism of preference aggregation in the European Union encourages strategies that capitalize on economic strength (or asymmetrical interdependency) and the building of political coalitions. Within this structure, military power is devalued as a means of conflict management.[15] Hence, for negotiations to become an *institutionalized* mechanism of preference aggregation in a region – and not just an occasional mode of interaction within a structure of coercion – states must believe that the outcomes it produces serve their security goals better than alternative mechanisms. Moreover, for a bargaining structure to persist, outcomes must be stable in the sense that the costs of defection exceed the constraints on action.[16] A security regime, therefore, is a bargaining structure within which all actors consistently prefer the peaceful resolution of disputed issues over the threat or use of force.[17] Note that this definition comprises the two dimensions of regional security as defined above (i.e. a mechanism of preference aggregation and a distribution of preferences), implying that security regimes are one form of regional security.

Because actors may have different preferences for mechanisms of social choice, different mechanisms can coexist within a given region, characterizing different sub-sets of actors. Thus, some actors may form a security regime; others may evolve a stable system of deterrence (coercive diplomacy); and still others may settle disputes by war. From a systemic perspective, then, regional security becomes a *set* of outcomes over which actors form their security-related preferences. It is possible, therefore, that outcomes produced by the interaction of one set of actors create a security threat (real or perceived) for another actor or set of actors. The question then concerns the mechanism by which the conflict is resolved and, once again, preferences for mechanisms of social choice become relevant. Ultimately, therefore, especially in a region with a very high degree of interdependence, one region-wide mechanism becomes institutionalized, whether among individual states or blocs of states. Thus, although Egypt and Israel have managed their relationship by negotiation for more than two decades now, the Middle East as a region is characterized by a structure of coercion.

The current Middle East peace process can also be interpreted as a conflict over mechanisms of preference aggregation. The decision of the involved parties to settle disputed issues through negotiation was at one level – the global one – an outcome induced by the structure of the post-Cold War international system and the preferences of the only remaining superpower. At a regional level, the decision was induced by the failure of the parties to realize their security concerns by means of coercive strategies within a coercive structure. However, the current attempt at negotiation does not reflect the institutionalization of bargaining as a social-choice mechanism. Rather, negotiations continue to take place within a structure of coercion, where a shift to violent strategies is a continuous threat and a real possibility. Therefore, the challenge and test of the peace process lies in the ability to produce outcomes that consistently meet the security interests of all involved parties to a greater extent than would be possible by other means. At the same time, such outcomes, if achieved, could be perceived as threatening to excluded actors, who are part of the overall coercive structure. A second challenge, then, is to shield the peace process from outside attempts to unsettle it.

These issues are examined in the next section, which provides a few illustrations of the dynamics involved in preference aggregation. The examples are highly stylized: they are designed as heuristic means of conveying a theoretical idea, not as full-fledged explanations. Still, they are useful in that they help identify the types of micro-macro relationships that can be analyzed from a social-choice perspective. As such, they also frame the questions that direct the empirical analysis in the remainder of this contribution.

Some Examples of Preference Aggregation

Let us assume, initially, that there are two players, or blocs of players, in a regional sub-system. These actors have different preferences with respect to the mechanism of preference aggregation – negotiation, coercive diplomacy, or war – by which disputed issues are to be resolved. Since preferences for mechanisms of preference aggregation have to be aggregated as well, suppose the following rules apply: (1) Because negotiation requires the consent of *both* parties, this mechanism is selected only if both actors 'vote' for it; (2) if the actors' votes diverge, then the most extreme mechanism becomes the social choice: thus, if one actor votes for negotiation (N) and the other for coercive diplomacy (CD), the latter becomes the mechanism of preference aggregation; likewise, if one actor votes for coercive diplomacy and the other for war (W), the latter prevails. Assume further that both players are aware of these rules and of their consequences.

Two clarifications are in order before we proceed. First, it is important to stress that, from the perspective of the actors, preferences for social-choice mechanisms are not preferences for strategies but rather for *outcomes*. Each such outcome pertains to a different 'structure', as defined above (i.e. a structure of negotiation, coercive diplomacy, or war), within which actors have to pursue their security goals. Because structures confer advantages differentially, actors develop preferences over them; and because structures arise, as collective outcomes, from the interaction of actors' strategies, the strategy selection of each actor is designed to promote the structure it prefers most. Hence the *strategy* of 'voting' for a certain mechanism should be distinguished from that mechanism as a collective *outcome*. (In the models to be presented next, strategies are denoted by regular letters whereas outcomes are *italicized*.)

The emphasis on basic structures at the system level also explains the dichotomous view of negotiation and coercive diplomacy that underlie the models in this section. It is true, of course, that coercive tactics can be integrated into accommodative strategies, and vice versa. Indeed, once a certain structure evolves, actors may rationally consider which specific mix of accommodative and coercive tactics would best promote their objectives within that structure. But the analysis in this section (and in the empirical one) is not concerned with the structure-specific design of strategies but rather with the more fundamental question of which structures actors would like to effect in the first place. Having distinguished three such mutually-exclusive structures, the strategies of the actors are defined accordingly.

Table 1 provides the preferences of the players for the different mechanisms and the outcomes of different combinations of players' votes.

Thus, player **A** prefers coercive diplomacy to negotiation, and negotiation to war (hence, $CD > N > W$). Player **B**, on the other hand, has this preference ordering: $N > W > CD$. Now, in order for a player to decide which vote to cast, it compares those combinations of votes (given in the columns) in which its own choice varies and the other player's choice is fixed.[18] For example, **A** compares columns 1 and 3 (where **B**'s choice is N) and 2 and 4 (where **B**'s choice is W). In the first case, columns 1 and 3 yield outcomes *CD* and *N*, respectively, and because **A** prefers *CD* to *N*, its best choice when **B** selects N is CD (in column 1). In the second case, **A** is indifferent, because both columns yield the same outcome (*W*). Thus, **A** is better off choosing CD (which is a weakly dominant strategy). Knowing this, player **B**'s choice is reduced to columns 1 and 2, of which it prefers the latter, given its preference for *W* over *CD*.

TABLE 1

Preference order ↓	1	2	3	4
Player **A**: $CD > N > W$	CD	CD	N	N
Player **B**: $N > W > CD$	N	W	N	W
Outcome	*CD*	*W*	*N*	*W*

The result (*W*) we obtain from Table 1 is paradoxical: although it is the product of rational choice, it is inferior to another outcome that the players could have obtained – the choices in column 3 yield outcome *N*, which is better for both players than outcome *W* (and hence Pareto superior). This 'paradox of dominance'[19] is even more perplexing if we consider that **A** obtained its worst outcome because it chose its dominant strategy – had **A** instead selected its *dominated* N-strategy, it would have done better.[20] Of course, when the players choose their strategies simultaneously, there is no reason for **B** to expect that **A** would choose a dominated strategy. Moreover, even if **A** is allowed to choose first, **B** has no guarantee that, once it reciprocates, **A** will not switch back to CD in order to get its best outcome (in column 1).

Table 1 provides a dramatic illustration of the theoretical point raised earlier in the discussion, namely that outcomes are not necessarily related to preferences in a monotonic manner: although **A** 'votes' for its best outcome, it obtains its worst. In fact, the result is even stronger, given that players are fully aware of the rules of the game and of each other's preferences (i.e. there is no misperception or miscalculation): thus, *because* **A** votes for its best outcome, it obtains its worst. It is important to stress that **A**'s experience in this example is not a result of non-strategic thinking on its part; on the contrary, the system is 'wired' in such a way that strategic choice – or the rational pursuit of national security policy – is transformed into an outcome that is most injurious to national interests.

Still, awareness of the trap – made possible by complete information – may allow the players to escape their predicament. Specifically, **A** can offer **B** a unilateral credible commitment that it would indeed choose, and adhere to, its dominated strategy. In other words, A has to make a 'self-binding commitment'.[21] But what happens when the players lack complete information? Suppose **A** and **B** are fully aware of the rules of preference aggregation, but do not know each other's preferences. Consider Table 2, where successive rounds of play divulge new information about players' preferences, leading to adjustments in strategy choice.[22]

TABLE 2

Preference order ↓	Stage 1	Stage 2	Stage 3	Stage 4
Player **A**: $CD > N > W$	CD, revealing: $CD > N, W$	CD	N, revealing: $CD > N > W$	N
Player **B**: $N > W > CD$	N, revealing: $N > W, CD$	W, revealing: $N > W > CD$	W	N
Outcome	CD	W	W	N

In Stage 1, each player votes for its most preferred outcome (which is rational if no additional information about preferences is available), thus revealing something about its own preference order. The rules of aggregation produce outcome *CD*, which is best for **A** and worst for **B**. As a result, the latter player switches its strategy and votes for its next-best outcome, inducing *W* in Stage 2. Now **A** obtains its worst outcome, realizing, at the same time, that **B**'s preference order – and the rules of aggregation – preclude a repetition of outcome *CD*. Consequently, **A** shifts to N in Stage 3, revealing a preference for *N* over *W*, which allows **B** to switch back to N in Stage 4. Outcome *N* is stabilized because, having played the game and discovered **B**'s preferences, **A** is deterred from attempts to achieve *CD*. The implication of this game at the dyadic (regional) level is that *war* must occur in order for the players to learn about each other's preferences. Only after preferences are clarified in this way can the players settle at the negotiation outcome.

Let us now introduce into this system a third actor, player **C**, whose preferences are $W > CD > N$.[23] How does the incorporation of such a player affect the interaction of the other two? Preserving the *same* rules of preference aggregation as in the previous example, we obtain Table 3. Note that the first game is 'embedded' in this new one: each column in Table 1 is represented by two columns in Table 3, the latter differing only in terms of player **C**'s strategy. For example, in the first column of Table 1, **A** chooses CD and **B** chooses N; this choice is replicated in the first two columns of Table 3, which vary only in terms of **C**'s choice. The introduction of this latter player, though, induces **A** and **B** to choose N, rather than CD and W, respectively.[24] As a result, negotiation is now selected as the mechanism of preference aggregation between **A** and **B**. Because the system comprises three actors, it is possible for negotiation (between **A** and **B**) and war (between **C** and one or both of the former) to coexist in the system.[25]

TABLE 3

Preference order ↓	1	2	3	4	5	6	7	8
Player **A**: $CD > N > W$	CD	CD	CD	CD	N	N	N	N
Player **B**: $N > W > CD$	N	N	W	W	N	N	W	W
Player **C**: $W > CD > N$	W	CD	W	CD	W	CD	W	CD
Outcome	W	CD	W	W	N	N	W	W

The addition of the third player to the system seems to remove one paradoxical outcome and introduce another. On the one hand, the monotonic relationship between preferences and outcomes is restored in the case of **A** and **B**. (Indeed, the systemic outcome is now Pareto efficient, meaning that a shift to any other outcome would hurt at least one of the players.) On the other hand, there is now a new aspect in which the outcome is paradoxical: whereas in the previous example the system 'selected' war as the mechanism of preference aggregation between **A** and **B**, the introduction of a new radical player (**C**) – who prefers this outcome most – results in the selection of a more *peaceful* process between **A** and **B**.

This paradox is easily explained: once **C** is introduced with its dominant W-strategy, CD can no longer be the outcome of the game; left with a choice between N and W, there is now a preference convergence between **A** and **B**, both of whom prefer the former outcome.[26] In other words, the introduction of **C** 'eliminates' the conflict that previously existed in the preferences of **A** and **B** with respect to the process of preference aggregation.[27] The threat that **C** poses to both of them (outcome *W*) leads them to the kind of cooperation (mutual selection of N) that evaded them previously. Indeed, if we replace **C** with a *less* radical player – say **C2**, whose preferences are $CD > W > N$ – the social outcome becomes, paradoxically, *W*, rather than N.[28]

Clearly, the results we obtain from the models depend on the rules of preference aggregation that underlie them. Thus, if we eliminate the first rule – assuming instead that the social choice always accords with the most violent strategy – then no cooperation is possible between **A** and **B** in Table 3. What the new rule implies, in contrast to the previous two rules, is that the most radical element in the set of actors determines the rules of preference aggregation for the entire system. Substantively, though, this need not be the case: the Egyptian-Israeli peace, for example, withstood some serious challenges, such as the war in Lebanon and the Palestinian uprising (*Intifada*). Hence, it is possible for a dyad to shield its mode of interaction from the effects of more violent relationships in the system (as **A** and **B** do in the third model, under the first set of rules). The conditions that enable two actors to do so involve not only the process of selecting negotiation as a mechanism of preference aggregation, but also the ability of this mechanism to produce an agreement that promotes the issue-specific preferences of the parties. When the latter occurs, the actors develop a vested interest in maintaining the agreement, which in turn reinforces the structure of negotiation.

The Middle East Peace Process

NEGOTIATIONS IN A COERCIVE STRUCTURE

The current round of Middle East peace negotiations began in late 1991, against the background of changing international and regional realities shaped by the collapse of the Soviet Union in 1989–90 and the Gulf War of early 1991. The latter two events had a major impact on the international politics of the Middle East. The Soviet withdrawal from the region (a process that had begun before its collapse) removed a long-time superpower patron from the scene, producing a realignment of Middle East coalitions. The implications of this structural transformation became clearly evident during the 1990 Gulf crisis, when the US assumed a leading role in organizing an unlikely coalition, composed of Western powers alongside conservative and radical Arab regimes, to thwart Saddam Hussein's attempt at a *fait accompli* in Kuwait. The success of the military campaign, as well as the ability of the Bush administration to secure Israeli restraint during the Iraqi Scud-missile attacks, provided further evidence of America's newly acquired and uncontested position of influence in the region. Thus, following the war, the US capitalized on its hegemonic status and convened the Madrid Peace Conference in October–November 1991.

However, the first diplomatic breakthrough was achieved only after Yitzhak Rabin had won the June 1992 elections in Israel, and only after the deadlock in the Washington talks persuaded him to seriously pursue the secret Oslo negotiations between Israel and the PLO. The resulting Oslo Agreement and Washington Declaration of Principles (DOP) of September 1993, which formally terminated the Israeli-Palestinian rivalry, appeared to remove the major source of lingering and festering hostility in the Arab–Israeli conflict. It provided a new impetus to the peace process, leading to the Jordanian–Israeli Peace Treaty of October 1994. Thereafter, however, the process began to lose momentum under the terrorist blows of Palestinian and Israeli extremists, culminating in the assassination of Prime Minister Rabin in November 1995. The approaching 1996 elections in Israel and the US further diminished the prospects for diplomatic progress, whose future became even more uncertain following the electoral victory of Likud leader Benjamin Netanyahu. Indeed, at this writing (December 1996), the Middle East seems to be settling once again into the all-too-familiar patterns of conflict: the Israeli-Palestinian talks over the Hebron redeployment are stalled, with the more demanding challenges still ahead; the Israeli–Syrian border is tense and on the verge of heating up dangerously; Israel's relations with Egypt and Jordan are at their lowest in a long time; and southern Lebanon continues to be the site of occasional clashes between Israel and the Hizballah. In all respects, the peace process appears to be disintegrating.

Given this background, a basic question concerns the degree to which the experience of the past five years has set in motion a process that will lead in the long run to the institutionalization of negotiations as a mechanism of conflict management. Prior to Rabin's assassination, during 1993–94, the pace of diplomatic breakthroughs and the collapse of barriers that previously appeared insurmountable, created the impression that the peace process was robust and perhaps even irreversible. However, once progress was arrested, the strategies employed by the involved actors increasingly assumed patterns consistent with what we defined earlier as a structure of coercion. The latter structure, of course, has conditioned strategies and interactions in the Arab–Israeli conflict over the past five decades (even during the height of the peace process, the regional arms race continued unabated). Theoretically, though, the recent increase in threats of violence, implicit or explicit, may reflect either a deep-seated belief that disputed issues in the Arab–Israeli conflict will continue, as before, to be settled by force, or they may reflect tactical calculations designed to induce opponents to renew negotiations and to offer concessions.

These two possibilities suggest different interpretations of the peace process (and the crisis it is undergoing at present). Under the first interpretation, current negotiations derive from the realization that five decades of coercive diplomacy and war have failed to achieve outcomes favorable to the warring sides in the Arab–Israeli conflict. Therefore, employing the terms suggested above, preferences for mechanisms of social choice have shifted, and the peace process reflects a genuine interest in effecting a bargaining structure. Within such a structure, the Arabs may reason that they stand to be advantaged: non-violent demands to change the status quo are consistent with American and West European norms of conflict management, thus bringing pressure to bear on the Israelis; military power is devalued as a means of perpetuating the status quo; and Israel is weakened due to internal divisions, which are enhanced by the prospect of relinquishing control over the occupied territories. Likewise, Israel may reason that within a structure of bargaining, it is more likely to obtain outcomes consistent with its security concerns, namely reducing the five-decade long threat to its existence by means of a political settlement and a security regime. Given this scenario, the current crisis in the peace process and the proliferation of threats of violence by the disputants are only calculated tactics in a diplomatic strategy, or reflexes conditioned by the long experience of conducting foreign policy in a coercive environment.

On the other hand, the peace process can be interpreted not as reflecting a fundamental change in preferences for mechanisms of conflict management, but as a shift of strategy – the product of constraints imposed by a hegemonic power – within a structure of coercion. In this structure, outcomes are strongly influenced by the balance of military capabilities. Thus, the Arabs may reason that the balance is tilting in their favor, due to the acquisition of large quantities of missiles capable of wreaking havoc on Israel's population centers. And because the intensity of preferences affects outcomes as well, the Arabs may also reason that their willingness to suffer costs exceeds that of the Israelis. The effects of the Iraqi Scud attacks on Israel during the Second Gulf War can lend credence to such estimates. Israel, on its part, can rely on deep-penetration bombing and nuclear weapons to provide the kind of deterrence that will allow it to freeze the territorial status quo. Given this scenario, the crisis in the peace process is not the result of tactics designed to support negotiation positions, but a phase in an ongoing, coercive conflict that may still escalate.

Clearly, the two scenarios represent the extremes of a continuum, which defines a range of possibilities that are more complex and nuanced: the Arab states do not constitute a monolithic bloc; the disputants do not necessarily have the same preference for modes of conflict management; perceptions play a major role in any scenario; and so on. However, the two scenarios have a familiar ring to them: the first has dominated the self-presentation rhetoric of the two sides, whereas the second has underlain their deepest concerns and suspicions. Thus, at the perceptual level, the peace process has not progressed enough to reduce uncertainty about preferences, intentions, and goals, which induces the actors to adopt strategies that combine cooperation (negotiation) and confrontation (arms races, troop movements, and threats). In a system in which preferences for mechanisms of conflict management are unclear, worst-case analyses and mixed signals increase instability and enhance the risk of escalation. This point is conveyed by the second model (Table 2) analyzed above: even if the two sides share a preference for negotiation over war, incomplete information can lead to the latter outcome.

Let us be more specific about the implications of negotiations that are conducted within a coercive structure, as opposed to negotiations in a bargaining structure. Rational-choice models of bargaining point to the existence of a 'zone of agreement' as a necessary condition for a final settlement. This interval lies between the negotiators' 'reservation prices', which are the values they attach to the absence of agreement, or to what they can obtain unilaterally. A rational negotiator will reject an offer that is worse than its reservation price.[29] But how do negotiators establish their reservation prices? Morrow suggests that '[t]he structure determines what is likely to happen in the absence of an agreement, and those possible futures are evaluated by each side's preferences.'[30] In a coercive structure, the 'possible futures' imply the threat or use of force as the final arbiter of disputed issues related to national security, especially in the context of an enduring rivalry. Because the distribution of capabilities has a decisive influence on outcomes in a coercive structure – favoring stronger states in relation to weaker ones – the former tend to have higher reservation prices,[31] and all states are encouraged to increase capabilities so as to improve their bargaining positions, reduce the reservation prices of opponents, and secure themselves if negotiations fail. The latter is particularly likely to happen when the balance of power is uncertain but roughly symmetric, and when preferences are intense, because the parties are induced to adopt intransigent positions. Hence in a coercive structure, military power and security negotiations are closely linked and the potential for instability is high. In contrast, a bargaining structure, when institutionalized, dramatically reduces or eliminates violence from the 'possible futures' entailed by the failure of negotiations. The effect on reservation prices is to enlarge the zone of agreement and make a final settlement much more likely (thus reinforcing the bargaining structure over time). Bargaining tactics are used, but when sanctions are threatened, they do not involve violence (again, negotiations in the European Union or North America are prime examples).

The question with respect to the current peace process in the Middle East is not whether it is taking place in a coercive or bargaining structure – quite clearly, the former applies. Rather, the question is whether the parties involved in the process have (and believe others to have) a common preference for a system in which negotiations will become the institutionalized mechanism of conflict management.[32] This preference defines the extent of concessions that have to be made in the peace process: an agreement that reduces conflict in the short run to allow actors to improve their capabilities for waging conflict in the long run is different from an agreement that resolves basic issues and renders force irrelevant to the conduct of interstate relations. The former is consistent with the belief that a coercive structure will continue to apply in the Middle East once the peace process is concluded; the latter is consistent with the belief that a bargaining structure can be effected. How negotiations are conducted, and with what results, depends on whether the opponents view diplomacy as the continuation of war by other means (to turn the Clausewitzian dictum around), or whether they regard diplomacy as a means of banishing violence from their relationship. (Which assumption applies also affects relations with actors that are excluded from the process.)

THE ISRAELI-SYRIAN PEACE PROCESS

From this perspective, an assessment of the peace process is not very encouraging. In Israel, the current prime minister, Benjamin Netanyahu, views the spirit of Oslo and the vision of a 'new Middle East' – cultivated by former Foreign Minister (in Rabin's government) and Prime Minister Shimon Peres[33] – as 'particularly amusing.' In an interview in November 1996,[34] Netanyahu conveyed his understanding of the political and strategic environment confronting Israel:

> ... the basic hostility to Israel is still widespread. Therefore, our ability to reach peace with our neighbors exists first and foremost due to our deterrent power, following the estimate in wide circles in the Arab world that Israel possesses great power. Once this estimate breaks down, all the political progress we have achieved to date will break down as well.

Furthermore, 'if Israel is perceived as weak in the very difficult negotiations on the final settlement, there will always be a reason to attack it'. Even if an agreement is achieved, it is likely to be fragile: the instability deriving from developments in the 'new' Middle East – the phenomenon of Islamic fundamentalism, the unprecedented increase in Arab military power, and the potential threat of Iranian nuclear capability – all imply that 'the conflicts in the Middle East will not cease and history of course will not reach its end.' Thus, 'until further notice, we are in the Middle East in an age of iron walls. What these iron walls do is buy us time', pending 'positive internal changes' in the Arab world.

It is instructive to compare Netanyahu's analysis of Israel's strategic environment with the kind of system in which a security regime can arise and flourish. Jervis associates the following characteristics (among others) with the post-1815 Concert of Europe: (1) '... "self-interest" was broader than usual, in that statesmen believed that they would be more secure if the other major powers were also more secure'; (2) 'For this system to work, each state had to believe that its current sacrifices would in fact yield a long-run return, that others would not renege on their implicit commitments when they found themselves in tempting positions'; and (3) 'Because reciprocity was expected to guide actors' behavior, statesmen did not fear that if they made concessions in one case, others would see them as weak and expect further concessions.'[35] The third point, which is particularly relevant to the peace process, conveys the kind of attitude that Netanyahu and the Israeli right blame Rabin and Peres for having adopted. A repeatedly voiced concern of the former is that ceding any part of the occupied territories will give rise to a series of demands and concessions that will not stop at the 'Green Line' boundary (Israel's pre-1967 borders). This domino-theory approach to the peace process rejects the possibility of maintaining a hierarchy of interests:[36] all interests are equally vital, and if Israeli resolve to keep a foothold in Hebron is weakened, so will its determination to defend Tel Aviv.

Netanyahu's perception of the current and future threats facing Israel in the Middle East – in particular, the proliferation of conventional and nonconventional missiles – has led him to reconsider Israel's security policy. According to reports in the press, he endorses the development of an Israeli missile force (whether based on large quantities of Scud-equivalent missiles or on Tomahawk-like cruise missiles), in addition to the anti-missile defense system (the 'Wall', based on the *Hetz* [arrow] interceptor missile) whose development is already underway. These plans, which also include a massive investment in the ability of the air force to conduct long-range operations against missile sites, call for significant increases in Israel's defense expenditures. Thus, Netanyahu has recently suggested that the defense budget be made a fixed percentage of GNP. These proposals reflect his understanding that peace agreements cannot be considered a substitute for military power, a conception he blames Rabin and Peres for cultivating.[37]

It is clear, then, that Israel's current leadership operates within a framework that views force as the mechanism of preference aggregation in the Middle East in both the short and long runs. The relationship of military power to reservation prices is immediate and explicit, thus embedding the peace process within a coercive structure. From Netanyahu's perspective, the international politics of the Middle East approximates to a zero-sum game, in which Israel as a status quo power confronts a largely undifferentiated, revisionist, and unremittingly hostile Arab world. This view obviates the need to consider self-fulfilling dynamics and the security-dilemma implications of rising defense expenditures and the procurement of offensive capabilities.[38]

This is not to say that Netanyahu, seeking to preserve the status quo, is not interested in a stable system of deterrence, supported by some kind of agreement on security arrangements that will reduce the threat of surprise attack and the risks of unwanted escalation. However, given his skepticism about the security provided by negotiated agreements, it is not at all clear that he would be willing to pay the full territorial price involved in establishing an Israeli-Syrian security regime. The Prime Minister attaches critical importance to what he calls the 'strategic-height' problem that Israel would face if it withdrew from the Golan Heights – the ability to stop the descent of Syrian tanks. He also rejects the view according to which territorial control of the Golan Heights is less critical to Israeli security in an age of missile proliferation.[39] On the contrary, Netanyahu believes that ground defense becomes even more important when the opponent possesses missile capabilities. Thus, in the late 1996 *Haaretz* interview cited above, he suggested that '... when we enter this negotiation we will enter it with a demand identical to that of the Syrians. If they demand all of the Golan Heights, so will we. I don't see any reason why we should diminish our demands ... '[40] The alternative (short of war) to a withdrawal from the Heights – a balance of power resting on enhanced Israeli deterrent capabilities – appears to be more consistent with Netanyahu's overall approach.[41] This approach suggests a preference for coercive diplomacy as a mechanism of conflict management, because it is most likely to produce outcomes commensurate with what the Prime Minister perceives to be Israel's political and security interests.

The Syrian side of the equation is more difficult to decipher. For two decades, the Assad regime adhered to a confrontational strategy *vis-à-vis* Israel, based first on pan-Arab military strength and subsequently (after the 1979 Egyptian-Israeli peace treaty) on achieving Soviet-supported 'strategic parity' with Israel. However, the domestic economic crisis of the 1985–87 period (a product of the drive to strategic parity), Syria's isolation in the international and Arab arenas, and – most importantly – the collapse of the Soviet patron, forced Assad in the past few years to reassess his policy toward Israel. The Gulf crisis and war only reinforced this process by demonstrating America's hegemonic status and the superiority of Western military technology. Thus, following heavy pressure by the Bush administration, the Syrians agreed in July 1991 to join the peace process launched in Madrid.[42]

Direct talks with Israel signified an important change in Syrian policy. Moreover, despite the agonizing pace of the negotiations, the two sides eventually came close to a declaration of principles, based on a territory-for-peace exchange and mutual (but not necessarily symmetrical) security arrangements. The Syrians were led to understand that Rabin and Peres would agree to cede control of the Golan Heights up to the international border (but not the 1967 lines), provided Syria conceded on the nature of peace and security arrangements.[43] Still, the Syrians refused to clarify their position on the substance of peace they were willing to offer, insisted on a shorter schedule for Israeli withdrawal, and objected to the idea of reducing Syria's regular forces. Moreover, if an agreement was indeed reached on basic principles for negotiation, the Syrians refused to put it in writing. Thus, after Likud won the elections of May 1996, the new prime minister announced that he was not obligated to these understandings (in contrast to the Oslo agreement with the PLO) – in effect turning the clock backwards to the pre-Madrid period – and offered instead a 'Lebanon first' deal, a non-starter that was flatly rejected by the Syrians.

Syrian intransigence in the negotiations with two of Israel's most dovish governments (under Rabin and Peres) raises questions about Assad's attitude toward the peace process in general. A Syrian strategic analyst has argued that 'Syria has reconciled itself incrementally to the reality of Israel and has shown its readiness to establish peaceful and normal relations.'[44] Although Assad does not view the latter as obligated by UN Resolution 242, he does not rule out normalization as a product (rather than a condition) of full Israeli withdrawal from the Golan Heights, within a comprehensive settlement that includes a just solution of the Palestinian problem. As the militarily weaker party of the two, Syria prefers to achieve its goals by diplomatic means. However, full withdrawal from the Golan is a *sine qua non* for any agreement.[45]

Israeli analysts are somewhat less confident that Assad is genuinely committed to peace (as opposed to nonbelligerency). Heller has defined the problem from the Israeli perspective as follows:

> ... Assad's rigidity extends to every aspect of the negotiations and seems to reflect an attitude that peace, rather than being an objective in itself, is simply a better way than war to get back lost territory. Unlike Sadat, who communicated his conviction that peace was a benefit for both sides and a value to which Egypt was also committed, Assad seems to interpret 'land for peace' to mean that land is what Syria gets and peace is what Israel gets.[46]

Other observers have pointed to the 'inner struggles' that the prospect of peace with Israel generates for Assad, who 'does not want to abandon ideological principles and finds it difficult to cross psychological barriers'.[47]

Still others argue that for Assad, the conflict with Israel extends beyond territory and 'involves the destiny of the Arab nation and its very existence'. Thus, 'peace with Israel is only one option in Assad's strategic menu'.[48]

These arguments echo our earlier discussion of the difference between negotiations within a coercive structure and negotiations designed to effect a bargaining structure. Mandell claims that Assad is not prepared to end Syria's rivalry with Israel: 'A committed rival, he sees no contradiction in sustaining both the peace process and military competition ... ' Rather, an agreement that leads to full Israeli withdrawal from the Golan opens for him the opportunity to pursue the rivalry by other means, namely 'it allows Syria to fulfill its quest for regional hegemony within the Arab world.'[49] Indeed, Assad has done little to commit himself to the peace process, both externally and internally. Still, in contrast to Netanyahu, who prefers to freeze the status quo in the Golan, Assad is interested in restoring the pre-1967 situation, something he has failed to accomplish by coercive diplomacy or war. Hence, although it is not clear what concessions on security arrangements, normalization, Lebanon, and the control of water resources the Syrian leader will be required – and will agree – to make in exchange for land, in the short run negotiations appear to be his best strategy.

This latter proposition does not imply, however, that Assad views the peace process as a means of effecting a bargaining structure. As was noted above for Netanyahu, it is doubtful that such a structure would produce outcomes favorable to Syria's long-term interests, such as maximizing its role in the region while minimizing Israel's, maintaining close ties with Iran, preserving Syrian control over Lebanon, and securing the regime at home.[50] A preference for negotiations within a coercive structure raises questions about reservation prices which, in the case of Syria, depend on what the Assad regime thinks it can achieve unilaterally, namely by means of force.

Prior to addressing this question, the relevance of the first model (Table 1) discussed in the previous section should be noted. To recall, in this model player **A**'s strategy of 'voting' for coercive diplomacy – its best outcome – results instead in its worst outcome, because **B**, who prefers coercive diplomacy least, shifts to its second preference – war – in order to obtain its next-best outcome. In this way, both players arrive at a collective outcome that is Pareto inferior. The analogy to the Israeli–Syrian case is clear: Even if the two parties return to the negotiating table, an intransigent position by Netanyahu could be interpreted by Assad as a preference for freezing the status quo through reliance on Israeli deterrence (i.e. a mechanism of coercive diplomacy); in that case, if Assad's preferences resembled those of player **B**, he would shift to a war strategy.

Although the inferior joint outcome in the first model can be avoided if A resorts to a self-binding commitment, no such relief is possible in the second model (Table 2), where information is incomplete. This situation, unfortunately, may be even more applicable to current Israeli–Syrian relations. As noted, reservation prices in negotiations within a coercive structure are strongly influenced by the balance of military capabilities, which indicates what each party can hope to achieve unilaterally. In the Israeli-Syrian case, that balance, or rather its expected consequences, are presently unclear. Since 1973, the two sides have not fought a full-scale war (although a limited clash did occur, with dire consequences for the Syrians, during the 1982 Israeli invasion of Lebanon[51]). Since then, the proliferation of missiles in the region has introduced a significant element of uncertainty as to the likely outcome of a war that would involve their use. Under the best scenario, these weapons are viewed by their owners – Syria included – as augmenting deterrence by providing a matching response to the uncontested power of Israel's air force.[52] Under the worst scenario, the missiles are valued for their compellent power, or as a deterrent against Israeli escalation following a limited Syrian offensive on the Golan Heights. In either case, this new component in Syria's military power could lead Assad to consider the capabilities ratio as roughly equivalent.[53]

In the second model (Table 2) presented earlier, incomplete information about preferences results in war, although both players prefer negotiations. Only after war *reveals* the preferences of the players, can the negotiation outcome be stabilized. To the extent that a preference for war derives from actors' estimates of the military balance, symmetric capabilities, whose consequences are difficult to evaluate, generate incomplete information. Moreover, because preferences are also related to motivation, which can compensate for structural (i.e. power-related) weakness, uncertainty is further enhanced.

The missile component in the Syrian arsenal – and the response favored by Netanyahu – are likely to affect the peace process in two ways. First, if the Syrians consider their missile force (and vast stocks of chemical weapons[54]) to create rough military equivalence, their reservation price in the negotiations will be higher. Moreover, they may conclude that Israel's reservation price has declined for the same reasons, which will lead them to interpret Israeli toughness as mere tactics. The result will be to make the Syrian position all-the-more intransigent. Second, Israel's plans for an anti-missile defense system injects a critical element of time into the equation. If the Syrians conclude that the window of opportunity is closing, lack of progress at the negotiating table will put pressure on them to capitalize on their temporary advantage while they can.

In summary, the preferences of Israel and Syria for mechanisms of conflict management, their perception of negotiations as embedded within a coercive structure, and their issue-specific preferences – all of which are interrelated – are likely to yield Pareto-inferior outcomes that involve violence. In this sense, the peace process as a mechanism of preference aggregation does not necessarily promote regional security; on the contrary – it stands to reveal that there is no zone of agreement, or, if a very narrow one exists, the parties may fail to discover it. However, as long as the process continues (and it is stalled at present), the two countries have some commitment to its pursuit and third parties can try to affect it. This latter point (to be addressed below) implies that the larger regional and international structure of which Israel and Syria are a part can impose constraints and provide opportunities that will favorably affect these actors' strategies.

THE ISRAELI-PALESTINIAN PEACE PROCESS

An impressionistic indication of the current status of the Israeli–Palestinian peace process is provided by the following facts: according to the Oslo agreement, negotiations over the final settlement of the conflict were scheduled to begin in May 1996; at this writing – six months later – the Israeli-Palestinian talks over the Israeli Defence Forces (IDF) redeployment in Hebron (mandated by the Interim Agreement of September 1995, dubbed Oslo II) are deadlocked due to a disagreement over the type of light weapons that the Palestinian police will be allowed to carry. More than a comment on the feasibility of the deadlines that had been set in the Oslo I and Oslo II agreements, these facts convey the extent of the difficulties that still lie ahead, beyond the implementation of the Interim Agreement: Jerusalem, the Jewish settlements, the Palestinian refugees, security arrangements, final borders, and the issue of a Palestinian state.[55]

The momentum initiated by the 1993 Oslo agreement was arrested as a result of terrorist acts inflicted by Palestinian and Israeli extremists who oppose the peace process. Particularly destructive were the bombing attacks carried out by Hamas inside Israel, which eroded the confidence of Israelis in the ability of the Palestinian Authority to control the activities of the Islamic organization. The attacks also increased the appeal of Likud's call for security prior to peace, thus contributing to the May 1996 electoral victory of Benjamin Netanyahu. Because the latter envisons a far more restricted form of Israeli–Palestinian settlement, his preferences have added another set of obstacles to those that had already plagued the peace process. Indeed, in late September the territories exploded in a bout of violence reminiscent of the *Intifada*, following the Prime Minister's decision to inaugurate a much-disputed tunnel in Jerusalem. When Palestinian policemen opened fire on Israeli troops, many Israelis became even more skeptical about the value of agreements signed with Palestinian Chairman Yasser Arafat.

Since the tunnel incident, little has happened in the negotiations to restore the parties' confidence in the ability of the peace process to produce a mutually satisfactory agreement. In fact, recent statements by Netanyahu on the Israeli–Palestinian conflict reflect beliefs that are consistent with his zero-sum interpretation of Middle East politics, as reviewed above: 'We confront a Palestinian nationalism that branches out of the big tree of Arab nationalism in general, which contains a very deep irredentist aspiration to apply the Palestinian Covenant – which has not been nullified yet – to the remainder of the territory of the State of Israel. To all of "Palestine".' Therefore, '... if we accept automatically ... what I call the Palestinian principle, the principle that the Palestinian national minority in Judea and Samaria is entitled to self-determination, this principle will necessarily extend to the national [Arab] minority in Israel itself. This thing will have no end.' Hence, Netanyahu perceives Palestinian objectives as unlimited, as aimed at the incorporation (if not destruction) of Israel itself, from which he deduces the risks involved in the kind of concessions that the Israeli left supports: 'The premise of the Meretz people [the liberal-dovish party which was Labor's chief coalition partner under Rabin and Peres] is that if we give this [the Palestinian] movement what it demands in the first stage – a state in the territories of Judea and Samaria and half of Jerusalem – its national aspirations would be contained and arrested at the 'Green Line' [pre-1967] boundary. I think this premise is simply unrealistic.'[56] Thus, Netanyahu strongly opposes a Palestinian state, which he sees as posing a real threat to Israel, and offers autonomy instead, notably excluding East Jerusalem. Ultimate authority over the territory will remain in Israeli hands, especially in matters pertaining to security.

Because a Palestinian state with East Jerusalem as its capital is the ultimate objective of the Palestinians, it is not clear how negotiations can produce an outcome that is satisfactory to both sides. Although Netanyahu has often voiced his firm belief in the principle that 'the path to peace is through negotiations and not through violence',[57] the preferences he has expressed for the final form of settlement – when juxtaposed with the Palestinians' – cast doubt on the existence of a zone of agreement between the parties. Clearly, declaratory policy does not necessarily reflect the red lines that define reservation prices, which negotiators have an interest in concealing. However, a few indicators suggest that in the Israeli (Likud)-Palestinian case, initial offers may not be far removed from the parties' true reservation prices: the agonizing pace of negotiations over the less controversial issues (such as the implementation of the Interim Agreement); the tight link between declaratory policy and fundamental ideological tenets; the specificity (as opposed to fuzziness) of publicized positions; and the high domestic costs involved in a retreat from self-binding commitments. If these are valid indicators, then negotiations will expose the absence of a zone of agreement.

As in the Syrian case (and in the first model presented earlier), an Israeli attempt to freeze the status quo is very likely to produce a violent outcome. Even if the Netanyahu government continues to negotiate, the mere fact that talks are taking place will not prevent this outcome from occurring. As noted, preferences for mechanisms of conflict management derive from their (relative) ability to produce outcomes that meet the values and goals of the parties. If negotiations fail in this respect, Israel's strategy will be interpreted as reflecting a preference for 'coercive diplomacy', namely supporting the status quo by means of deterrent threats. As the party seeking to change the status quo, the Palestinians cannot hope to achieve their issue-specific objectives under this mechanism, which could lead them to impose violence as a means of conflict management. In contrast to the Syrian case, however, the shift to violence may be spontaneous rather than controlled (and hence more difficult to reverse), because Arafat's authority is fragile and contested.

The prospect of renewed violence constitutes the critical element in the parties' reservation prices for negotiation. In contrast to the Syrian situation, there is less uncertainty about the nature and consequences of the ensuing violence: the *Intifada*, the bombing attacks of Hamas, and the upheaval following the tunnel affair, provide a recent indication of the cost that the Palestinians can impose on Israel (although the scope of the violence is expected to be greater); likewise, there is little doubt that the IDF have the capability to reoccupy the major cities in Gaza and the West Bank. This outcome would be the lesser of two evils for Arafat, who would not survive a diplomatic capitulation to Israel but could conceivably restore his position as the leader of all-out Palestinian resistance. In contrast to Arafat, whose leadership is challenged by opponents of accommodation with Israel, the major opposition to Netanyahu comes from the left, which supports the peace process. This difference in the structures of public opinion should raise Arafat's reservation price and lower Netanyahu's (although the latter is also pressured by extremists in his own party and in the Israeli right). However, even if a narrow zone of agreement exists in the objective sense, it may not be discovered due to the perceptions of the parties: thus, Arafat may exaggerate Netanyahu's reservation price and Netanyahu may underestimate Arafat's. Indeed, the Israeli Prime Minister has interpreted recent Palestinian (and Arab) warnings of impending violence as manifestations of an adjustment period that naturally occurs when 'you move from a policy of give and give [under Labor] to a policy of give and take [under Likud].'[58] If Netanyahu adheres to this interpretation, the conflict could escalate to violence even before negotiations are given a chance to reveal whether or not a zone of agreement exists.

Some Final Considerations: The Larger Context of the Peace Process

The grim prognosis offered above was based on an analysis of bilateral relations. However, the Israeli-Syrian and Israeli-Palestinian conflicts are embedded within the larger regional and international contexts, where other actors have a close interest in the process and outcome of negotiations. Under certain conditions, some of these actors could prevent the conflict from escalating, revive the peace process, and restore confidence in its ability to produce outcomes favorable to the parties. Others could attempt to unsettle the peace process, with varying degrees of success. In lieu of a summary, then, this article concludes with a brief review of the relevant actors and their potential effect on the future of the peace process.[59]

Closest to the interaction are Egypt and Jordan, both of which have formal peace treaties with Israel. Egypt, as the dominant Arab power in the region, has since 1979 conducted peaceful yet competitive relations with Israel, which it sees as its contender for regional hegemony. In a variety of ways, Egypt has expressed its preference for a less pronounced Israeli role in the region,[60] rejecting both the grand designs for a 'new Middle East' put forward by Peres and the confrontational foreign policy of Netanyahu. Since the latter's election, however, relations between Egypt and Israel have become extremely strained, and Egyptian statements have assumed an ominous tone, long absent from the two countries' relationship. Following the escalation of tensions along the Israeli-Syrian border and the deadlock in the talks over Hebron, Egyptian President Hosni Mubarak warned that the peace treaties between Israel and Egypt and Jordan were being endangered and that 'Israel would commit the gravest error if it initiated an additional war – because we will not remain idle.' Israeli officials estimate that in case of a war between Israel and Syria, Mubarak and the Arab League would provide Syria with a 'political safety net'.[61]

Part of the Egyptian campaign (in which Jordan is a less vocal participant) is designed to affect Israeli public opinion and thereby bring domestic pressure to bear on Netanyahu. However, this strategy could be counter-productive, escalating overall tensions and reinforcing the Israeli right's perception of an hostile Arab encirclement of Israel. The vociferous attacks on Netanyahu and Israel in the Egyptian press may help Mubarak score some points in the domestic debate on the peace process, but they also bind the Egyptian President to a policy of rhetorical escalation. Egypt and Jordan could play a more constructive role by combining quiet behind-the scenes diplomacy with public assurances of their commitment to preserve the momentum of the peace process. Mubarak is currently under pressure by Assad and Arafat to take a firm public stance against the Netanyahu government; yet if Egypt joined a tight diplomatic coalition against Israel, it would undermine its capacity to serve as facilitator and mediator between the disputing parties. This latter function could be Egypt's most important contribution to the peace process.

Two other regional actors that should be considered are Iraq and Iran. The 1991 Gulf War significantly reduced the threat emanating from the former, and the regime of Saddam Hussein is likely to remain emasculated in the short run. Of greater concern is fundamentalist Iran, which combines aspirations for primacy in the Gulf with messianic ambitions to spread the Islamic revolution throughout the region. Although Iran currently lacks the military capability to achieve its grand design, its drive to acquire or develop a nuclear device could pose a grave threat to regional security. The broader implications cannot be examined here.[62] As concerns the peace process, however, such a development, like the Iraqi invasion of Kuwait in 1990, could have a paradoxical effect: 'A more aggressive Iran would only push together Israel, the Arabs, and the United States into a defensive coalition.'[63] Whether Iran becomes the next Iraq or not, its regional ascendancy would impart a much greater sense of urgency to the peace process and exert pressure on the parties to settle their differences. This point is conveyed by the third model (Table 3) presented earlier: the introduction into the system of a third, radical player pushes the other two to adopt cooperative strategies in their relationship.[64]

Finally, it goes without saying that the United States is in a unique position to support the peace process and induce greater flexibility in the negotiations. Thus far, President Bill Clinton has been reluctant to exert strong pressure on the parties, and American foreign policy under Secretary of State Warren Christopher lacked the vigor necessary for effecting a diplomatic breakthrough. However, with the re-election of the President and the nomination of UN Ambassador Madeleine Albright to replace Christopher, the US can play a much more active role in the peace process. Syria and the Palestinians would like to see a far greater American involvement in the negotiations, in the hope that the administration would coerce Netanyahu into concessions. Having won a second term in office, President Clinton enjoys greater freedom to do precisely that. Yet, however instrumental the US can be in softening the positions of the parties – whether by imposing sanctions or offering assurances and guarantees – the greater challenge lies in providing leadership and a stable framework within which the pursuit of peace can unfold. A policy of crisis intervention can perhaps prevent the current deadlock from escalating into violence, but it is unlikely to generate expectations for a steady progress that will restore confidence in the ability of the peace process to produce a mutually beneficial outcome.

In summary, the analysis conducted here suggests that the Middle East peace process, in its present form, is unlikely to yield a settlement and most probably will end in violence. In fact, a review of the parties' preferences and perceptions indicates that negotiations will only help establish the absence of a zone of agreement, thus inducing a shift to coercive mechanisms of conflict resolution. In this sense, the peace process could become a threat to regional security: as long as intransigence is interpreted as a negotiation tactic, the parties can maintain some hope that positions will be modified with time, as the process unfolds; but once intransigence is perceived to be indicative of real reservation prices, the parties are reduced to a choice between acquiescence and violence. Given the intensity of preferences and the perception of closing windows of opportunity, the latter alternative is likely to be chosen. At this point in time, only decisive American intervention – supported by constructive Egyptian and Jordanian mediation – can resuscitate the peace process and prevent the region from plunging into another round of violence.

NOTES

The author would like to thank Uri Bar-Joseph, Steven J. Brams, and two anonymous referees for useful comments and suggestions on an earlier draft.

1. For such an analysis, see the essay by Zeev Maoz in this issue.
2. Oran R. Young, 'Anarchy and Social Choice: Reflections on the International Polity', *World Politics* 30/2 (Jan. 1978) p.245.
3. James D. Morrow, 'Social Choice and System Structure in World Politics', *World Politics* 41/1 (Oct. 1988) p.75.
4. The set of regional actors need not consist exclusively of states (it certainly does not in the Middle East); indeed, non-state actors may have a strong impact on regional security, even exceeding that of relatively-minor state actors. However, because the politics of a region are governed first and foremost by its most powerful actors (as is the case in the global system), and because these actors are almost always states, the discussion will focus on them, though much of what will be said below may apply to non-state actors as well.
5. Bruce Bueno de Mesquita and David Lalman, *War and Reason* (New Haven, CT: Yale UP 1992) pp.16–17 (quote on p.17).
6. For a theoretical discussion of the impact of public opinion on peacemaking (and a case study of the Oslo agreement), see Ben D. Mor, 'Peace Initiatives and Public Opinion: The Domestic Context of Conflict Resolution', *Jnl of Peace Research* (forthcoming 1997). The two-level game framework is developed in Robert Putnam, 'Diplomacy and Domestic Politics: The Logic of Two-Level Games', *International Organization* 42/3 (Summer 1988) pp.427–60.
7. Young, 'Anarchy and Social Choice' (note 2) p.250. The mechanism of 'coercive diplomacy' is defined as 'the use of belligerent (but largely nonviolent) moves together with persistent threats of violence to induce others to acquiesce in one's preferred outcome in situations of social choice' (ibid. p.254); the mechanism of 'organized warfare' is defined as 'the use of

large-scale violence or physical compulsion to force others to accept one's preferred outcome in situations where preference orderings diverge substantially' (ibid. pp.252–3).
8. Morrow, 'Social Choice and System Structure' (note 3) p.79.
9. Morrow (ibid.) argues that the distribution of capabilities is a reflection of structure, not the structure itself, which is 'the implicit social choice process of coercion in international politics'. This is analogous to domestic politics, where institutional rules and procedures are the structure, and the positions that individuals occupy within it 'reflect how institutions favor these actors' preferences'.
10. For the 'menu' analogy, see Bruce M. Russett, 'A Macroscopic View of International Politics', in James N. Rosenau, Vincent Davis, and M. A. East (eds.) *The Analysis of International Politics* (NY: Free Press 1972) pp.109–24. The concepts of 'willingness' and 'opportunity' are presented by Benjamin A. Most and Harvey Starr, *Inquiry, Logic and International Politics* (Columbia: U. of S. Carolina Press 1989). The quote is in Bruce Russett and Harvey Starr, *World Politics: The Menu for Choice*, 3rd ed. (NY: W. H. Freeman 1989) p.25.
11. Morrow makes this point in connection with the Vietnam War, in which the large structural advantage possessed by the US was outweighed by the intense preference of the North Vietnamese for achieving unification. See Morrow, 'Social Choice and System Structure' (note 3) pp.82–3.
12. This idea is illustrated by the paradox of voting, which created interest in processes of social choice. For a discussion, see, *inter alia*, William H. Riker, *Liberalism Against Populism* (San Francisco, CA: W.H. Freeman 1982), and Steven J. Brams, *Rational Politics* (Washington DC: Congressional Quarterly Press 1985). Paradoxes of power, such as the Paradox of the Chair's Position, exhibit in a similar fashion how outcomes can be disjoined from individual-level characteristics, such as the possession of resources. In addition to Brams, *Rational Politics*, see Zeev Maoz and Dan S. Felsenthal, 'Self-Binding Commitments, the Inducement of Trust, Social Choice, and the Theory of International Cooperation', *Int. Studies Qtly* 31/2 (June 1987), pp.177-200; and Zeev Maoz, *Paradoxes of War* (Boston: Unwin Hyman 1990) Ch.8. The important point to note with respect to these paradoxes is that the interdependent actors are subject to and operate within a certain 'structure' – whether institutional rules or the configuration of preferences – over which they have no control (at least for the duration of the interaction).
13. See John N. Hertz, 'Idealist Internationalism and the Security Dilemma', *World Politics* 2/2 (Jan. 1950) pp.157–80; Kenneth N. Waltz, *Man, the State and War* (NY: Columbia UP 1954); and Robert Jervis, 'Cooperation Under the Security Dilemma', *World Politics* 30/2 (Jan. 1978) pp.167–214.
14. Informally, an outcome is a Nash equilibrium if no player can gain by unilaterally departing from it. An outcome is Pareto efficient (or Pareto optimal) if no other feasible outcome is better for at least one player without being worse for at least one other.
15. It is possible, of course, for military force to be irrelevant to the relationships of governments within a region but applicable to their relationship with actors outside it. On this point, see Robert O. Keohane and Joseph S. Nye, *Power and Interdependence* (Boston: Little, Brown 1977) p.25.
16. See Morrow, 'Social Choice and System Structure' (note 3) p.80.
17. Similarly, Stein defines a 'stable security environment' as 'one which makes military force unattractive as the principal instrument of conflict management.' See Janice Gross Stein, 'The Security Dilemma in the Middle East: A Prognosis for the Decade Ahead' in Baghat Korany, Paul Noble, and Rex Brynen (eds.) *The Many Faces of National Security in the Arab World* (NY: St Martin's Press 1993) p.57.
18. For the general solution concept of sophisticated voting, see Robin Farquharson, *Theory of Voting* (New Haven, CT: Yale UP 1971). Note that Table 1 does not include combinations that contain the players' worst outcomes. This is because voting for such an outcome is a strategy that is dominated by at least one other strategy. Hence the table contains admissible strategies only.
19. For further discussion and applications of this paradox, see Felsenthal and Maoz, 'Self-Binding Commitments' (note 12).

20. Prisoners' Dilemma (PD) illustrates the same principle. There are important differences, however: in PD, both players have dominant strategies (whereas in our example only **A** does) and both suffer symmetrically by obtaining their next-worst, rather than next-best outcome. The current example is a more pointed illustration because it shows how trying to obtain one's best outcome can result in one's worst.
21. Felsenthal and Maoz, 'Self-Binding Commitments' (note 12) p.187. Practically, such a commitment can be accomplished by means of public diplomacy that raises the cost of defection, or by means of a third party (the US would be the natural candidate for this role in the Middle East) which can subsequently extract a penalty for defection and/or compensate the harmed player. For further discussion of this idea, see Felsenthal and Maoz (note 12).
22. This model draws on the 'sequential negotiation model' developed in Steven J. Brams, *Theory of Moves* (Cambridge: Cambridge UP 1994) pp.187–95.
23. We assume that the preference ordering of the other two players is unaffected by the introduction of the third player, and that all players' preferences apply to the entire system. That is, if **A** prefers *CD* to *N*, this implies that coercive diplomacy is **A**'s preferred mechanism of preference aggregation *vis-à-vis* all actors in the system.
24. In this table, **A** compares column 1 to 4, 2 to 5, 3 to 6, and 4 to 8; **B** compares column 1 to 3, 2 to 4, 5 to 7, and 6 to 8; and **C** compares column 1 to 2, 3 to 4, 5 to 6, and 7 to 8. This comparison yields a weakly dominant W-strategy for **C**. Removing the latter's dominated CD-strategy reduces the game to columns 1, 3, 5, and 7. In the reduced game, both **A** and **B** acquire a weakly dominated N-strategy, making column 5 the dominant-strategy Nash equilibrium.
25. In that case it would be more accurate to designate the outcome in column 5 as, say, *N-W*. However, if this outcome is better for **C** than *N* (when this player compares cols 5 and 6), it maintains its dominant W-strategy. In the reduced matrix, if *N-W* is better for **A** than *W* (when it compares surviving columns 1 and 3), then it maintains its dominant N-strategy. Finally, if *N-W* is better for **B** than *W* (when it compares surviving cols 5 and 7), the game reduces to column 5. More will be said below about the assumption that different rules of preference aggregation can coexist within a single system.
26. In the reduced matrix, following the elimination of **C**'s dominated strategy, the only outcomes that survive are *N* and *W*.
27. Note that the preferences of the three players generate a paradox of voting, which means that although individual preferences are transitive, the social ordering is not. Assuming the rules of aggregation specified above are substituted for majority voting, there is no social choice that is a Condorcet candidate, namely an outcome that can defeat any other in pairwise contests: *CD* defeats *N*, *W* defeats *CD*, but *N* defeats *W*. However, once player **A** votes strategically for its next-best outcome (*N*), it thwarts the selection of *W*, its worst outcome. This result resembles the Paradox of the Chair's Position: in the reduced matrix of Table 2, **C** can be seen to have a tie-breaking vote, inducing *W* whenever **A** and **B** disagree; this causes the latter two to gang up on the Chair, who obtains its worst outcome (*N*) as a result. For details on the two paradoxes, see Brams, *Rational Politics* (note 12).
28. The reason is this: **C2** has a dominant CD-strategy; once its W-strategy is removed from the matrix, **A** acquires a dominant CD-strategy, to which **B** responds with W in order to prevent its worst outcome from occurring. (Again, **A** can thwart this outcome – and restore cooperation with **B** – if it resorts to a self-binding commitment.)
29. See Howard Raiffa, *The Art and Science of Negotiation* (Cambridge, MA: Harvard UP 1982).
30. Morrow, 'Social Choice and System Structure' (note 3) pp.81–2.
31. Henceforth, references to 'high' or 'rising' reservation prices indicate *greater* minimal demands (consistent with a seller's perspective in a single-issue buyer-seller interaction).
32. Specific requirements associated with this possibility are addressed by Gabriel Ben-Dor, 'Stabilizing Peace in the Middle East: Beyond the Egyptian-Israeli Peace Treaty' idem and David B. Dewitt (eds.) *Conflict Management in the Middle East* (Lexington, MA: D.C. Heath 1987) pp.45–55.
33. See Shimon Peres with Arye Naor, *The New Middle East* (NY: Henry Holt 1993); and

Shimon Peres, *Battling for Peace: A Memoir* (NY: Random House 1995).
34. 'A new Middle East? What an amusing idea', interview with Ari Shavit, weekend supplement of *Haaretz*, 22 Nov. 1996.
35. Robert Jervis, 'Security Regimes', in Stephen D. Krasner (ed.) *International Regimes* (Ithaca, NY: Cornell UP 1983) pp.180–3, *passim*.
36. See Hans J. Morgenthau and Kenneth W. Thompson, *Politics Among Nations*, 6th ed. (NY: McGraw-Hill 1985) Ch.32.
37. Aluf Ben, 'Netanyahu's terrorist', *Haaretz*, 26 Nov. 1996, p.B2.
38. As Jervis notes, '[s]ome decision makers seem oblivious to the fact that increasing their arms can have undesired and unintended consequences. If such leaders are in power, the chances for developing a security regime will be decreased, not by the structure of the situation but by the ignorance of the actors.' See Robert Jervis, 'Security Regimes' (note 35) p.176. See also Barry Buzan, *People, States and Fear*, 2nd ed. (Boulder, CO: Lynne Rienner 1991) p.192.
39. For this argument, see Zeev Maoz, 'The strategic depth and other legends', *Haaretz*, 30 June 1995.
40. Interview with Ari Shavit (note 34). The Prime Minister was not asked, however, whether he would refuse to withdraw from the Golan under any circumstance, and he did not volunteer a statement to that effect.
41. Jervis notes that a security regime and a balance of power and can be distinguished by whether 'the restraints on state action ... are norms internalized by the actors', or whether these restraints 'arise from the blocking actions of others and the anticipation of such counteractions.' Robert Jervis, 'Security Regimes' (note 35) p.185.
42. Eyal Zisser, 'Syria and Israel: Toward a Change?', in Efraim Inbar (ed.) *Regional Security Regimes* (Albany: State U. of NY Press 1995) pp.151–74.
43. In Dec. 1995, the Syrian foreign minister confirmed that Syria had agreed to nine of ten points in a proposal made by Prime Minister Peres. This statement, however, was strongly rejected by the Prime Minister's Office. See *Maariv*, 12 Dec. 1995.
44. M. Zuhair Diab, 'The Prospects for Peace between Israel and Syria: A Syrian View', in Efraim Karsh and Gregory Mahler (eds.) *Israel at the Crossroads: The Challenge of Peace* (London: British Academic Press 1994) p.85.
45. Ibid.
46. Mark A. Heller, 'Assad's rigidity', *Jerusalem Post*, 31 July 1995.
47. Zisser, 'Syria and Israel' (note 42) p.169.
48. Efraim Inbar, 'Israeli Negotiations with Syria', *Israel Affairs* 1/4 (Summer 1995) p.96.
49. Brian S. Mandell, 'Getting to Peacekeeping in Principal Rivalries: Anticipating an Israel-Syria Peace Treaty', *Jnl of Conflict Resolution* 40/2 (June 1996) pp.242, 245.
50. Rubin notes that '[s]ince any diplomatic solution would increase US influence; favor Egypt, Israel, and Jordan over Syria; reduce Syrian influence on the PLO; and make Israel a stronger rival, Syria would be even more of a second-rate power.' See Barry Rubin, 'The New Middle East: Opportunities and Risks', BESA Center for Strategic Studies, Security and Policy Studies No.19, Bar-Ilan University, Feb. 1995, p.20.
51. Diab argues that Syria lost in that encounter 'partly because the leadership misread Israel's intentions, whereby Syrian forces were not redeployed and augmented for defence'. See Diab, 'The Prospects for Peace' (note 44) p.77. If that is also the lesson drawn by the Syrian leadership, then it does not view the Lebanon clash, which in any event occurred more than a decade ago, as indicative of Syrian capabilities at present.
52. This is suggested in a study by Yiftah Shafir of the Jaffee Center for Strategic Studies at Tel Aviv University. See review in *Haaretz*, 1 Dec. 1996, p.A6.
53. For an argument that an expectation of victory is not a necessary condition for Syrian war initiation, see Zeev Maoz, 'The probability that Syria will go to war – on a significant increase', *Haaretz*, 18 Aug. 1996.
54. For a detailed analysis of Syria's nonconventional capabilities, see Dany Shoham, 'Chemical Weapons in Egypt and Syria: Evolution, Capabilities, Control' [Hebrew], BESA Center for Strategic Studies, Security and Policy Studies No.21, Bar-Ilan University, June 1995.
55. For an overview of these and related issues, see Hussein Sirriyeh, 'Is a Palestinian State

Politically Feasible?', *Israel Affairs* 2/1 (Autumn 1995) pp.46–58; and Bernard Reich, 'The Art of the Impossible: Making Peace in the Middle East', *Mediterranean Qtly* (Spring 1996) pp.60–86.
56. Interview with Ari Shavit (note 34). Some elements of Likud and other right-wing parties interpret current Palestinian (as well as Arab) interest in compromise as a tactical move within a broad multi-staged strategy designed ultimately to bring about the destruction of Israel. In contrast to the anarchy-derived argument of realists that states tend to infer intentions from capabilities, in the Israeli–Palestinian conflict great importance and significance are attributed to political rhetoric, whose analysis if often entirely divorced from power realities. Palestinian statements conveying maximalist long-term goals are perceived as existential threats, which explains why Palestinian Council Chairman Abu Ala (one of the architects of the Oslo agreement) sought recently to pressure the Netanyahu government by stating that 'if Israel does not respect the [Oslo] agreements, the Palestinians will also demand Haifa, Jaffa, and Safed' (*Haaretz*, 6 Dec. 1996).
57. Press conference with Prime Minister Benjamin Netanyahu, the Mayflower Hotel, Washington DC, 3 Oct. 1996. Excerpts provided by the Information Division, Israel Foreign Ministry, Jerusalem.
58. Interview with Ari Shavit (note 34).
59. For an in-depth survey and analysis, see Rubin, 'The New Middle East' (note 50).
60. *Jerusalem Post*, 11 June 1996.
61. *Haaretz*, 18 Nov. 1996.
62. For detailed analyses, see Patrick Clawson (ed.) *Iran's Strategic Intentions and Capabilities*, McNair Paper 29 (Washington, DC: National Defense U. April 1994).
63. Rubin, 'The New Middle East' (note 50) p.16.
64. Although Syria has maintained close ties with Iran as a counter-balance to Iraq, the Assad regime is vulnerable to the fundamentalist threat and, like Egypt, Jordan, Saudi Arabia, and the Gulf states, the Syrian president would not like to see a new bid for supremacy in the Gulf. (It is notable that Syria opposed the destruction of Iraq in the 1991 Gulf War, fearing that the regional balance would be upset.)

About the Contributors

Zeev Maoz is Professor of Political Science and the Head of the Jaffee Center for Strategic Studies. He has published widely in the area of international relations and strategic studies. His articles have appeared in the *American Political Science Review, World Politics, International Studies Quarterly, Journal of Conflict Resolution*, among others. His most recent book is *Domestic Sources of Global Change* (University of Michigan Press, 1996)

Gerald L. Sorokin is Assistant Professor of Political Science at the University of Iowa. During the spring of 1996, he was a visiting fellow at the Jaffee Center for Strategic Studies at Tel Aviv University. His publications include articles in the *Journal of Conflict Resolution* and *International Studies Quarterly*. His current research looks at the role of peacekeeping operations in regional conflict management.

Martin Sherman currently teaches in the Political Science Department at Tel Aviv University. His main areas of research interest are decision making, rational actor models of political systems, and the influence of regime structure on strategic policy. He filled various positions in the Israeli government, both in operational and advisory capacities.

Gideon Doron is Associate Professor of Political Science at Tel Aviv University and the Chairman of the Israeli Political Science Association. He is also the Chairman of the Board of the Second Authority for Television and Radio in Israel. He has published extensively on a wide range of subjects in political science and public policy, and was formerly head of the Department of Political Science at Tel Aviv University, where he is currently teaching.

Benjamin Miller is Senior Lecturer of International Relations at the Hebrew University of Jerusalem. He is the author of *When Opponents Cooperate: Great Power Conflict and Collaboration in World Politics* (Ann Arbor: University of Michigan Press, 1995). He has published numerous articles on international relations theory and international security in journals such as *World Politics, International Studies Quarterly, Review of International Studies, Security Studies, Journal of Strategic Studies*, and *International Interactions*.

Ariel E. Levite took his PhD in Government at Cornell University. He specializes in international security issues, and his latest books include *Intelligence and Strategic Surprise* (New York: Columbia University Press 1987), *Offense and Defense in Israeli Military Doctrine* (Westview Press 1988), and *Israel's Nuclear Image: Arab Perceptions of Israel's Nuclear Posture* (Hebrew) (Tel Aviv: Papyrus, 1994). He is a part-time Senior Research Associate at the Jaffee Center for Strategic Studies, since assuming the post of appointed Deputy Director and Head of Arms Control, Directorate for Foreign Affairs, Arms Control and Regional Security, Israel Ministry of Defense.

Emily B. Landau took her BA in Political Science and English Literature and her MA in Political Science (International Relations) at Tel Aviv University. She is a Research Associate and member of the Project on Israel's National Security at the Jaffee Center for Strategic Studies, and currently a PhD candidate in the Department of International Relations, Hebrew University, Jerusalem. She is co-author of *Israel's Nuclear Image: Arab Perceptions of Israel's Nuclear Posture* (Hebrew) (Tel Aviv: Papyrus 1994).

Ben D. Mor is Lecturer in International Relations at the University of Haifa, Israel, where he also teaches in the MA Program on National Security for the Israeli Defense Forces. He is the author of *Decision and Interaction in Crisis* (Praeger, 1993) and editor (with Frank P. Harvey) of *Conflict in World Politics* (Macmillan, 1997). His current research examines the evolution of enduring international rivalries.

Index

Albright, Madeleine, 197
Algeria, 15; civil war, 9, 31
alliances, 5–6, 7, 19, 20, 24, 25, 46, 47–9,
  50, 51, 52, 53, 66–7, 99, 110
  in Middle East, 20–3, 25, 47, 48, 55, 59,
  66–8, 99
  see also Syria, Egypt
Arab–Israeli conflict, 12, 13, 47, 72, 104,
  153, 155, 157–8, 160, 184–9, 195–6
  Confidence and Security Building
  Measures, 143–4, 153–68
  Egypt-Israel peace, 20, 53, 55, 56, 58,
  116, 117, 127, 154, 155, 158, 178, 183,
  196–7
  implications for regional security, 31–2
  Jordan-Israel peace, 184
  Lebanon War, 62, 183, 192
  normalization, 161, 166
  peace process, 20, 22, 23, 31, 32, 98–9,
  114, 117, 119–20, 130, 155, 164–5, 172,
  173, 178 *see also* Madrid peace process
  Six Day War, 53, 60, 64, 86–7, 92, 95
  Syrian–Israel relationship, 59–66, 184,
  189–93
  terrorism, 184, 187, 193, 195
  War of Attrition, 60
  Yom Kippur War, 60, 61, 65, 86, 98, 192
Arab League, 19–20, 196
Arafat, Yasser, 194, 195, 197
arms control, 143, 154, 156–7, 161, 162,
  164, 165, 167 *see also* Confidence and
  Security Building Measures
  theory of, 143, 146
Arms Control and Regional Security
  (ACRS), Working Group, 32, 143, 146,
  155, 156, 159–68
Asad (Assad), Hafez, 60–3, 120, 160–1,
  189–91, 197

Baghdad Pact, 19, 54
Baker, James, 143, 146
Bosnian War, 130, 131–2
Brezhnev, Leonid, 122
Bush, George, 131
Bush administration, 117, 128, 183, 189

Canada, 165
Carter, Jimmy, 125
chemical weapons, 18, 26, 192
Chernenko, Konstantin, 122
China, 133
Christopher, Warren, 197
civil conflicts, in Middle East, 14, 18, 22, 30,
  31, 72
Clinton administration, 128, 197
Cold War, 2, 49, 62, 64, 72, 103–5, 114–33
Concert of Europe, 2, 188
Conference on Confidence and Security
  Building Measures and Disarmament in
  Europe (CDE), 148
Conference for Security and Cooperation in
  Europe (CSCE), 147, 148, 156, 162, 167
Confidence Building Measures (CBMs), 146,
  147, 148, 149–50
Confidence and Security Building Measures
  (CSBMs), 143, 148, 152
  between Argentina and Brazil, 149, 154
  between India and Pakistan or PRC, 149,
  154
  between North and South Korea, 149, 154

between Turkey and Bulgaria, 154
defining characteristics of, 148–50, 157, 163–4, 167
European experience with, 143, 144, 146–8, 151–2, 153, 154, 160, 162, 167
in Arab–Israeli conflict, 144, 154, 155, 156–68
in Middle East, 144, 153, 154, 155, 156, 159, 167
relation to arms control, 145, 146, 154, 156
relation to bilateral peace, 164–5
ripeness for application, 146, 150–1, 153–6, 160, 163
role of, 150, 157
superpower experience with, 143, 144, 146–7, 151–3, 154, 162
theoretical foundation of, 144–6
crisis management, 106, 147, 150, 157
Cuban Missile Crisis, 147

Dayan, Moshe, 125
Djibouti, 161
domestic regimes, as explanation of great power diplomacy regarding regional conflict, 104, 105, 107, 108, 109–14, 124–7, 128–9
as explanation of international conflict, 25, 30–1, 73–4, 75–6, 83–98
Dulles, John Foster, 54

economic development, impact on regional security, 24, 25, 29–30
Egypt, 15, 22, 29, 84, 165, 184, 196–7, 198
alliance with Syria, 55, 56, 57, 59–61
attitude toward CSBM negotiations in ACRS, 163, 164, 166–7
economic growth, 30
Islamic movement, 31
patron-client relationship, Soviet Union, 52, 62, 119–20, 124, 128
Europe, 153, 156
East Europe, 132
West Europe, 114, 129, 130, 133, 185
West Europe, involvement in mediation of Arab–Israeli conflict, 130, 133
European Union, 130, 133, 177, 186

Ford administration, 126
France, 72, 114
patron-client relationship, Israel, 63–5

Geneva peace conference, 116, 121, 126
Germany, 132
Golan Heights, 62, 129, 189, 190, 191, 192
Gorbachev, Mikhail, 53, 55, 57, 122, 129, 131

Graduated and Reciprocated Initiatives in Tension Reduction (GRIT), 149
Great Britain, 73, 114
Gulf War (1990–91), 9, 15, 18, 19, 23, 26, 50–1, 67, 72, 86, 92, 95, 99, 129, 131, 132, 155, 172, 183, 185, 189, 197

Hamas, 193, 195
Harmel Report, 147
Hebron, 188, 193, 196
hegemonic theory, 108
Helsinki Process *see* Confidence and Security Building Measures, European experience with
Hizballah, 184
Hussein, Saddam, 95, 197

international conference for peace in the Middle East, 121–2, 124
international conflict, domestic constraints approach, 74, 75–6, 83–98
domestic constraints approach, expected utility maximizing (EUM) rational decision-maker, 74, 76–83, 92–6, 97
realpolitik paradigm, 74, 75–6, 83, 85, 96
social choice approach to, 176–8, 179–83, 186
sources of, 23–4, 73–85
Intifada, 183, 193, 195
Iran, 15, 29, 30, 31, 84, 128, 129, 155, 156, 191, 197
missile race, 18
multilateral talks, 32, 33, 161, 162, 165
nuclear power, 187, 197
regional aspirations, 197
Iran–Iraq War (1980–88), 9, 12, 15, 18, 19, 22, 26, 72, 73, 85–6
Iraq, 15, 19, 29, 31, 84, 128, 129, 156, 197
massacre of Kurds, 9
missile and nuclear technology, 18, 87
multilateral talks, 32, 33, 161, 162, 165
Israel, 15, 18, 22, 29, 54, 84, 86, 91, 131, 161
legitimacy, 54, 63, 158
Likud government, 172, 173, 184, 187–9, 190, 194, 195–6, 197
military expenditures, 57–8, 60, 63, 188–9
military service, 63
military superiority, 118, 119, 160, 166, 187
missile attacks, response to, 129, 183, 185
missile race, 18, 188
patron-client relationship, US, 52, 55, 56, 58, 63–8, 114, 118, 119, 125, 126–7, 129
patron-client relationship, France, 63–5
peace negotiations, Palestinians, 172, 173, 184, 193–6 *see also* Arab–Israeli conflict, peace process

peace negotiations, Syria, 131, 164, 172, 173, 189, 190–193 *see also* Arab–Israeli conflict, peace process
security concerns, 6, 55, 158, 166, 185, 187–9, 194, 195
security policy, 47, 52, 63–6, 98, 158, 185, 188, 191

Japan, 129, 133
Jordan, 15, 19, 22, 84, 163, 165, 184, 196, 198
civil war, 30
Islamic movement, 31

Khartoum summit, 20
Kissinger, Henry, 116, 118, 124
shuttle diplomacy, 116, 126
US Middle East strategy, 119–20
Kuwait, 129

Lebanon, 72, 83, 84, 86, 128, 129, 161, 184, 191
civil war, 31
liberalism/neoliberalism, 104, 145–6, 165 *see also* international conflict
Libya, 29, 72, 156, 161, 162, 165

Madrid peace process, 117, 130–2, 146, 155, 156, 183–98
multilateral talks, 32–4, 143, 156, 166 *see also* Arms Control and Regional Security (ACRS)
mediation, 107, 110 *see also* United States, Soviet Union
Middle East, alliances *see* alliances, Middle East
regional boundaries, 8, 34, 159
Middle East conflict, 12–15, 22–3, 153, 155
domestic sources of, 25, 30–1, 73–4, 75, 83–98
Egyptian–Libyan border dispute, 72
explanations of, 25, 72–4 *see also* Arab–Israeli conflict
military allocations, 25, 55
Israel, 57–8
Middle East, 15–18, 26, 30, 52–3
Syria, 56–7
military expenditures *see* military allocations
military intervention, 106
US, in Africa, 112
US, in Central America, 112
US, in Guatemala, 112
US, in Iran, 112
US, in Southeast Asia, 112
USSR, 112
missiles, 18, 23, 124, 160, 185, 188, 189, 192
anti-missile defense system, 188, 192

Mubarak, Hosni, 196–7

Nasser, Gamal Abdel, 59–60, 95
NATO, 52, 131
negotiations theory, 150, 166 *see also* social choice theory
Netanyahu, Benjamin, 184, 187–9, 191, 192, 193, 194, 195–6, 197
Netherlands, 165
Nixon, Richard M., 124, 126
North Korean nuclear crisis, 103, 131, 132
nuclear war, 145
accidents, 147
deterrence, 177, 185
nuclear weapons, 146, 160, 185, 187

Osiraq, Israeli strike on, 87
Oslo agreements *see* Israel, Palestinians

Palestinians; Palestinian Authority, 31, 193
peace negotiations with Israel, 172, 173, 184, 193–6 *see also* Arab–Israeli conflict, peace process
patron-client relationships, 47, 49, 50, 51, 52, 53
in Middle East, 47, 52 *see also* US, USSR, Israel, Egypt, Syria
Peres, Shimon, 187, 188, 190, 194, 196
Poland, 132
population growth, impact on regional security, 29
Primakov, Evgeni, 131

Qatar, 165

Rabat summit, 20
Rabin, Yitzhak, 30, 184, 188, 190, 194
Reagan, Ronald, 116
peace initiative, 1982, 116
realism/neorealism, 104, 105, 112, 145–6, 163, 165–6, 174 *see also* international conflict
regional peacemaking, great power approach to, 104
explanation of, 104–14, 129, 132–3
regional security, conceptualization of, 2–8, 174, 176–8
factors affecting, 25–6, 91–2
Middle East, 26–31, 32–4, 72–4, 92, 98–9, 155, 159, 161–2, 165, 167, 178
Middle East, impact of CSBMs on, 145, 163
Middle East, impact of peace process on, 172, 173, 183–98
non-military factors, 26–31
Western Europe, 92, 99, 186

regional sub-system, 174, 179
Rogers initiatives, 116, 126
Ross, Dennis, 153
Russia, 103
  diplomacy *vis-à-vis* the Middle East, 103, 129, 130, 131, 132, 133
  diplomacy *vis-à-vis* regional conflicts, 103, 131–3

Sadat, Anwar, 30, 119, 120, 124, 190
  visit to Jerusalem, 126
Saudi Arabia, 15, 22, 84
  missile race, 18
'security complex', 8
Security Council, 123, 132
security dilemma, 176
security policy, factors affecting, 50–2, 53
security regimes, 3, 155, 157, 159, 173, 177, 178, 185, 188
Shultz, George, Shultz plan, 117
social choice theory, 172, 173–8, 179–83, 186, 191, 192
  in Arab–Israeli conflict, 184–98
Soviet Union, 73, 83, 103, 183
  arms supplies, 124
  diplomacy *vis-à-vis* Eastern Europe, 114
  diplomacy *vis-à-vis* Middle East conflict, 104, 114, 115, 116–29, 183
  diplomacy *vis-à-vis* Middle East conflict, offer of military presence, 122, 124–5
  economic resources, 123
  patron-client relationship, 183
  patron-client relationship, Egypt, 52, 62, 119–20, 124, 128
  patron-client relationship, Syria, 55, 56, 61–3, 128
  relations with Israel, 117–18
Stockholm accords *see* Confidence and Security Building Measures, European experience with
'strategies of reassurance', 144
Sudan, 30, 156, 161
  civil war, 9, 31
Syria, 15, 84, 129
  activity in Lebanon, 72, 184, 191
  alliance, with Egypt, 55, 56, 57, 59–61, 62
  chemical weapons, 192
  internal legitimacy, 54, 59, 60, 61, 62, 63, 191
  military expenditures, 56–7, 59, 60, 61, 62, 63, 189
  missile race, 18, 192
  multilateral talks, 32, 33, 160–1, 165, 166
  patron-client relationship, Soviet Union, 55, 56, 61–3, 128, 189
  peace negotiations with Israel, 131, 164, 172, 173, 190–3 *see also* Arab–Israeli conflict, peace process
  security concerns, 55, 59, 60, 61, 62, 191
  security policy, 47, 52, 59–63, 189–93
systems theory, 105, 108

terrorism *see* Arab–Israeli conflict
Third World, regional security, 3, 9
Tripartite statement, 121
Tunisia, 165
Turkey, 19, 29, 165
  Islamic movement, 31
  security concerns, 6

UN Disarmament Commission, 156
UN General Assembly, 156
UN partition resolution, 122
United States, 73, 103, 165, 185
  financial assistance, 117, 118, 126–7, 129
  mediation in Arab–Israeli conflict/peace process, 65–6, 103, 104, 114, 115, 116–33, 165, 166, 167, 184, 197–8
  patron-client relationship, Israel, 52, 55, 56, 58, 63–8, 114, 118, 119, 125, 126–7, 129
  strategic activity with regional actors, 22, 183–4
US Arms Control and Disarmament Agency (ACDA), 53

Vienna Documents *see* Confidence and Security Building Measures, European experience with

Yeltsin, Boris, 103
Yemen, 84
  civil war, 9, 19, 26, 30, 31, 72
  Egyptian involvement in, 72

Titles in Strategic Studies

Military Power
Land Warfare in Theory and Practice
Brian Holden Reid (Ed)
Senior Lecturer in War Studies, King's College London and Resident Historian, Joint Services Command and Staff College, Bracknell

The contributors to this volume consider the multifarious aspects of the Anglo-American approach to war. The essays range from study of volunteer soldiering in the Mexican War of 1846–48, analyses of operations in the Two World Wars, to a reconsideration of the nature of future warfare.

265 pages 7 maps, fig., table 1997
0 7146 4768 3 cloth £29.50/$39.50   0 7146 4325 4 paper £15.00/$19.50

Airpower
Theory and Practice
John Gooch
University of Leeds

'Overall, this is an interesting and eminently readable book of contemporary essays in Air Power. The quality of the research and analysis are high and a number of little-known aspects of Air Power's gestation are articulated.'
Group Captain Andrew Lambert, RUSI Journal

284 pages 10 illus. 5 maps 1997
0 7146 4657 1 cloth £30.00/$39.50 0 7146 4186 3 paper £16.00/$22.50

Seapower
Theory and Practice
Geoffrey Till (Ed)
Royal Naval College, Greenwich

'Geoffrey Till has edited a collection of eight articles written with the dual aim of exploring the relationship between landpower and seapower and the connections between naval theory and practice ... These are worthwhile, well written and thoughtful articles.'
Paul Halpern, Mariner's Mirror, 1995

210 pages table, fig 1994
0 7146 4604 0 cloth £27.50/$35.00 0 7146 4122 7 paper £14.50/$17.50

Israeli Strategy After Desert Storm
Lessons of the Second Gulf War
Aharon Levran
Brigadier General, Israeli Defence Forces (Retired)

Iraq's invasion of Kuwait and the subsequent Gulf War had a traumatic effect on the Middle East, and its implications were particularly serious for Israel, which felt obliged to reassess its strategic and military perspectives. This book examines the lessons that the Gulf War holds for Israel.

192 pages   1997
0 7146 4755 1 cloth £35.00/$47.50   0 7146 4316 5 paper £17.50/$25.00
A BESA study in Middle East security

American War Plans 1941–1945
Steven Ross
US Naval War College, Newport, Rhode Island

This important new book examines major American and Anglo-American war plans. Rather than discuss the history of planning which has been done by many scholars, Ross considers the execution of the plans, compares the execution with the expectations of the planners and attempts to explain the differences.

210 pages   1997
0 7146 4634 2 cloth £27.50/$39.50   0 7146 4194 4 paper £16.00/$19.50

Masters of War
Classical Strategic Thought
Revised Edition
Michael I Handel
US Naval War College, Newport, Rhode Island

'Michael Handel's selection of side-by-side quotations from their principle works is both apposite and enlightening. Masters of War *is therefore a handy addition to the library of anyone seriously interested in military affairs and strategic thought'*
Dr Zakheim, US Deputy Under Secretary of Defence 1981-1987

320 pages colour maps 1996   Second Revised Edition
0 7146 4674 1 cloth £35.00/$47.50   0 7146 4205 3 paper £17.50/$24.95